Refiguring
ENGLISH
STUDIES

Refiguring English Studies provides a forum for scholarship on English Studies as a discipline, a profession, and a vocation. To that end, the series publishes historical work that considers the ways in which English Studies has constructed itself and its objects of study; investigations of the relationships among its constituent parts as conceived in both disciplinary and institutional terms; and examinations of the role the discipline has played or should play in the larger society and public policy. In addition, the series seeks to feature studies which, by their own form or focus, challenge our notions about how the written "work" of English can or should be done; and to feature writings which represent the professional lives of the discipline's members in both traditional and nontraditional settings. The series also includes scholarship that considers the discipline's possible futures or that draws upon work in other disciplines to shed light on developments in English Studies.

Theodore Baird about 1950.

Fencing with Words

A History of Writing Instruction at Amherst College during the Era of Theodore Baird, 1938–1966

ROBIN VARNUM

American International College

Refiguring English Studies

Stephen M. North, Series Editor

SUNY at Albany

National Council of Teachers of English
1111 W. Kenyon Road, Urbana, Illinois 61801-1096

Manuscript Editor: *Sheila A. Ryan*
Production Editor: *Michael Greer*
Interior and Cover Design: *Jenny Jensen Greenleaf*

NCTE Stock Number 16779-3050

Library of Congress Cataloging-in-Publication Data

Varnum, Robin. 1950–
    Fencing with words : a history of writing instruction at Amherst
College during the era of Theodore Baird, 1938–1966 / Robin Varnum.
        p.   cm. — (Refiguring English studies)
    Includes bibliographical references (p.   ) and index.
    ISBN 0-8141-1677-9
    1. English language—Rhetoric—Study and teaching (Higher)–
–Massachusetts—Amherst—History 20th century.   2. Baird, Theodore,
1901–   .   3. Amherst College.   I. Title.   II. Series.
PE1405.U6V37   1996
808' .042'071174423—dc20   95-52765
                                                                  CIP

For my mother
Rosemary Purdy Varnum Vaughan

CONTENTS

ACKNOWLEDGMENTS

I have had a great deal of support in putting this book together. I would like first to thank my editor, Stephen North, and the several reviewers to whom he sent my manuscript for their helpful criticism and advice. I would like also to thank the members of my doctoral guidance committee, Charles Adams, David Bloome, Peter Elbow, and Anne Herrington, for helping me with the book in its earlier incarnation as a dissertation. Third, I would like to thank the members past and present of the Damned Good Group, especially Robin Dizard, Helen Fox, Christina Gibbons, Sherrill Harbison, Sara Jonsberg, Ruth Owen Jones, Sarah Kilborne, Tom Leamon, Lion Miles, and Anne Mullin, for listening to drafts of my chapters and for giving me feedback and friendship.

I am also grateful to Robert Bagg, Theodore Baird, John Bookwalter, John Cameron, G. Armour Craig, Jan Dizard, Walker Gibson, Thomas Looker, Dale Peterson, William Pritchard, Roger Sale, Geoffrey Shepherd, John Stifler, and Douglas Wilson for generously making their time, their resources, and their memories available to me.

I am greatly indebted to Daria D'Arienzo and her staff at the Amherst College Archives for helping me to use the materials in their care. I am also indebted to Douglas Wilson at the Amherst College Office of Public Affairs and to Daniel Lombardo at the Jones Library for making photographs available to me.

Finally, the book would not have been possible without the love and support of my family, Juris, Sofija, and Marija Zagarins.

CHAPTER ONE

A Maverick Course

*F*encing with Words is a social and cultural history of the two-semester freshman writing course, generally listed as English 1–2, which was directed by Theodore Baird at Amherst College from 1938 to 1966. By Baird's estimate, the course engaged some fifty instructors and six thousand students during its almost thirty-year span, yet perhaps because it flourished during a period when the teaching of writing had not become fully professionalized, little has been published about it. Even so, as one of the men who taught the course has noted, it "enjoys a certain vague reputation and is known to have influenced a number of college teachers" (Gibson 1985, 137). In a 1985 historical article, Ann Berthoff referred to those whom English 1–2 has influenced as an "Amherst Mafia," noting that by the date of publication of her article, the members of this "Mafia" had dispersed themselves across the country (72). What is perhaps most immediately remarkable about English 1–2 is that Baird and the members of his staff devised a new series of sequenced writing assignments each semester and used them in common. They also required their students to write frequently and from experience, and they brought what their students wrote to class for classroom discussion. My story concerns how Baird and the members of his staff understood their mission as teachers of writing, how they argued with one another about translating that understanding into practice, and how their students responded. My story also has to do with intellectual politics and with the ways individuals use and learn to use language to gain control of social situations. What I have to say should have implications both for contemporary composition pedagogy and for current intellectual politics.

Conflicts and political disparities exist at every level of academic culture. Teachers may challenge departmental or institutional policies. They argue with students about grades, with administrators about teaching loads, and with colleagues about the use of shared facilities. Students may resist a teacher's methods in class or drop out of class altogether. Students, moreover, compete with one another for grades and for the attention of their teacher and classmates. Faculty in one department or division compete with faculty in other departments for scarce institutional resources. Within most English departments, the teaching of composition is not so well rewarded as the teaching of literature. The humanities in general do not enjoy the same advantages as the sciences. Higher education, as most academics in the public sector would agree, is not sufficiently valued by the American taxpayer. Some combination of these and other conflicts will have a bearing on the circumstances in any particular classroom. At Amherst College, in English 1–2, conflict served as a spur to learning. Sometimes it was a subject of learning as well. In the fall of 1948, English 1–2 students had to address an entire series of assignments on the question "What is conflict?"

Amherst College, which is a private, now coeducational, liberal arts college in Amherst, Massachusetts, has seen its fair share of conflicts over the course of its 175-year history. A particularly heated series of conflicts attended the admission of women in 1976 to the previously all-male student body. During the nineteenth century and well into the twentieth, as Amherst historian Thomas Le Duc (1946) has recorded, the college was shaken by conflicts between religious faith and scientific or intellectual values. Theodore Baird, writing in 1978 about the 1821 founding of Amherst College, observed that "wherever you touch the record of a New England town, just before or just after this extraordinary community effort of making a college, the most obvious fact is the high degree of sustained and bitter antagonisms with which extremely irritable individualists maintained lifelong, acrimonious disputes over every possible subject" (1978a, 84). Baird was a strong and argumentative individualist himself.

In 1938, the year Baird began directing Amherst's freshman writing course, he disagreed publicly with his colleague from the biology department, Otto Glaser, about the aims of liberal education. Glaser was both the chairman of Amherst's Curriculum Committee (of which Baird was a member) and the principal author of the *General*

Report issued by that committee on November 10, 1938 (reprinted in Babb et al. 1978, 117–127). Glaser had reported that the faculty of Amherst College "remains committed to the ideal of a liberal education" (121), and Baird concurred. But Baird objected to Glaser's use of the terminology of behavioral science, to his assertion that human inquiry was "prompted by instincts" and rewarded, when successful, with "pleasure and satisfaction" (121–122), and to his implication that human beings were subject to the same kinds of conditioning as Pavlov's dogs. When Glaser observed that "from the naturalism of our own creation and age, there is little opportunity to escape" (121), Baird appended a footnote to the text of Glaser's *Report,* protesting that

> It is for me a matter of faith that Amherst College exists to combat (not escape, least of all accept) the naturalism of our own creation and age. I also believe that human beings are unlike all other creations of nature in their intelligence. This faith, which I know is central to the teaching of some of my colleagues, I had supposed was commonly shared by the Faculty. Furthermore, I believe that there is certain experience which is peculiarly human, and that it is knowledge of this experience which is called liberal, as belonging to a free man. . . . What freedom of mind is this which Professor Glaser mentions if the mind is a slave to heredity, environment, economic forces, glands, the spirit of the age, neuroses, nature itself? (122–123)

Despite Baird's aloofness from what he calls the spirit of his age, I do not regard either his position on freedom of mind or his pedagogy as independent of its context. I take his position to be rooted in the spirit of 1938, prewar America and to reflect a distinctly American and masculine ideal. His pedagogy seems to have been modeled on combat and reflects American culture during the war years and the period of the Cold War. It was designed to spur student self-determination, to empower student resistance to normative pressures, and to promote a student's growth as a responsible personal agent. In a passage from a memorandum Baird circulated to his staff on July 19, 1960, and whose impetus I take to have been similar to the passage quoted above on freedom of mind, although here he speaks of wildness instead of freedom and of imagination instead of mind, Baird suggested, "Perhaps writing may be seen as somehow the expression of the imagination, and imagination itself may be mysterious and wild."[1] By 1960, however, some of the younger instructors on Baird's staff had begun to question the notion of a free imagination. Some of them have told me they now understand the imagination to be constrained by both nature and culture and by such factors as gender, ethnicity, and social class.

Baird's memorandum of July 19, 1960, is a good one with which to introduce the course because in it he stresses the importance of both individual self-development and argument. In carefully qualified terms, he told his staff:

> Again we are concerned with placing the student in a position by means of our assignments and classroom discussion where he may learn something about himself as a writer. It may be there is not much for him to learn, although this in itself seems to me to be something. For I believe as a teacher that there may be some connection between self-knowledge and writing—and everything else for that matter. I am myself sure of this connection and assert it as an article of faith. I say, a writer who wants to write may be better off if he knows who he is. . . . We understand my simple remark, though it is not always illuminating for the freshman, since for him the question "Who am I?" can be answered simply by his name, as if that settled the matter. We ask him to be introspective, to look within for just a moment, and generally speaking he complies with reluctance. After all, who is this freshman? We do pay him the highest compliment, if he only knew it, by insisting over and over again that he is an Individual. Who are you? Why can't you talk in your own voice?[1]

The student, however, would not discover his voice on his own. He needed to wrestle with others and to oppose his ideas to theirs in order to find himself. In his July 19, 1960, memorandum, Baird explained:

> This is the way it works for me. By looking at others and the expressions of what they see I find points of reference and so go on constructing a map of the universe. I find what I can and cannot put on it. I come to see what I can and cannot do. And so there is self-knowledge.[1]

In the same memorandum, Baird described the writing assignments which were the chief vehicle of both teaching and learning in English 1–2. He told his staff:

> Every set of assignments for over twenty years has been one more freshly imagined attempt to make some communication work between teacher and student. So we have asked them questions about themselves. Again and again in different terms we have asked, How do you read? How do you see shapes and colors? How do you operate a machine or play a game? How do you solve a math problem? What does it mean to be in conflict with another person? How do you see the sights as a sightseer? No one I know has anything more than a tentative answer to any of our questions. Yet they are asked at higher levels and in more difficult vocabularies by eminent persons, and I think we are dealing with matters that concern the acutest minds I know. Of course we deal humbly with epistemology, ontology, perception, and never use these big words.[1]

Baird and his staff dealt humbly with matters of rhetoric also and did not advertise their use of dialectical methods. Nevertheless, what they did on a day-to-day basis was to ask questions and invite answers and engage in the give-and-take of combat. In using sequenced assignments, they put students in the position of having constantly to acknowledge new complications and revise their thinking. And by exposing each student's writing to the criticism of both his instructor and his peers, they put him in the position of having to test his words and ideas against those of others. Baird frequently insisted that dialogue was fundamental to the learning process.

He also insisted that the members of his staff talk to one another. He required them to meet together once a week to discuss the coming week's agenda. In 1939, reflecting on his first year of directing Amherst's freshman writing course, Baird described his weekly staff meetings and said he had set them up in the hope that "by an exchange of ideas, by self-criticism, by argument, we can define our objects more clearly and use the best methods for achieving them that we know about" (1939, 334). Twenty-one years later, in his memorandum of July 19, 1960, Baird complained that staff meetings were not producing as much debate as he would have liked. His memorandum indicates something of the nature of his relations in 1960 with colleagues both on and off his staff and with students:

> I was told not long ago that some of the more obvious misunderstandings among the teachers of English 1–2 could be cleared up if only I would write a history of the course showing just how we reached our present position. But do these misunderstandings even exist? Of course we have our critics, but I am satisfied that nothing we can ever do will make it right with them and that they know with complete certainty just what we are up to and they don't like it. And we have been put more and more in the position of being made to feel that we ought really to be pleasing our clients more than we do. Is clients the right word here? What is the metaphor for education? A Caribbean Cruise? But as for misunderstanding among the teachers of the course I do not feel this is a danger. Is there not understanding to the point of silence? This seems to me not good.
>
> Once upon a time we argued bitterly. A major issue was this: Is education limited to the expressible? Should we not go on teaching what cannot be taught?[1]

Except for two articles he published in the Amherst alumni magazine, Baird never did write the history of English 1–2 that he says some members of his staff wanted him to write. And except for an article entitled "Theodore Baird," which Walker Gibson published in 1985, no member of Baird's staff ever wrote that history either. To date, the only extended accounts of the course to have appeared in the professional literature are two dissertations, Gibson's 1985 article, and a 1958 article published by James H. Broderick in the *Harvard Educational Review*. In the latter, Broderick reported that as a matter of policy, "English 1–2 instructors try not to explain anything; they ask questions and can wait embarrassingly long periods for an answer" (46). He reported also that "the originators and practitioners of English 1–2 disclaim any philosophy; for them the course just happened, it evolved, it is their changing ways of handling certain problems in class" (44). In his 1985 article, Gibson acknowledged that the course had had "its epistemological biases," but he argued that it was "an English course and not a course in philosophy" (150). He reported that the members of the English 1–2 staff had resisted articulating their assumptions. They had regarded English 1–2 as an ongoing activity and not as a body of knowledge to be laid out on paper. Gibson conceded that there may have been "some smugness in the Amherst position that advertising to the wide world would do no good," and he noted that, partly as a result of the diffidence of its staff, the course had "received precious little professional notice" (137).

This lack of notice, however, is attributable to larger professional and historiographic matters as well as to the diffidence of those who taught English 1–2. One reason why the course has been overlooked is that it flourished during a period when the teaching of composition was supposed (wrongly, I believe) to have been governed by an obstructive "current-traditional paradigm." This negative characterization of the period has worked to deflect attention from it. At an even broader level, I would argue that the kinds of materials historians have chosen to examine and the lenses through which they have examined them have kept them from seeing some of what was to be seen. Much of the existing historical corpus in composition is either focused too narrowly on epistemology or based too exclusively on data from old textbooks. The tendency among composition historians has been to look at practice in the classroom, or at the materials and ideas presented there, without acknowledging the larger forces that created the classroom itself.

As Stephen North has observed in *The Making of Knowledge in Composition* (1987), composition historians have tended "to focus on a very limited number of features relevant to a history of the *idea* of teaching writing, located in an intellectual context, with a few institutional coordinates, but pretty much stripped of place and time in other ways" (77). Thus, according to North, we have no answers to such basic questions as

> Who learned to write? How many of them were there? How much did their teachers get paid? What kind of living was that? Were these teachers politically active? In what ways? How did these things vary across the country? (77)

North might have cited James Berlin's 1987 *Rhetoric and Reality* as an example of the kind of history that separates ideas from their social and political contexts. *Rhetoric and Reality* is in many respects a very useful survey of twentieth century approaches to writing instruction. It certainly provided me with helpful background for my own study. It even contains a brief reference to Theodore Baird, acknowledging his influence on Walker Gibson and on William E. Coles Jr., both of whom Berlin considers to have been among the leading "expressionists" of the 1960s and 1970s (151, 153). But Berlin focuses on epistemology and on the theories (such as expressionism) which teachers bring into the classroom, and by doing so, he deflects attention from the ways that politics and policies outside the classroom often determine what teachers do in class. In a 1988 review of *Rhetoric and Reality,* Sharon Crowley pointed out that Berlin's epistemological focus deflected attention from

> the repressive institutional situations which have shaped composition instruction since its beginnings: what ideological strictures mandate that most teachers of composition are (and always have been) part-time, untenured and untenurable instructors or graduate students? What ideological strictures have worked, historically, to confine research in composition to inferior status? (1988, 247)

Questions of epistemology, I would add, are less likely to concern a teacher than the question of how many students (particularly if it is more than twenty-five in each of several sections of composition) she has to deal with on Monday morning. A teacher's theoretical views may have less impact on her students' writing than the institutional realities within which she and they operate. The teacher may not have been free, especially if she is an adjunct, to choose the textbook she and her students use. She may not have been given an office in which to meet students after class. She may not have access to secretarial support or to photocopying facilities. On the other hand, her students are likely to have been required to enroll in her class. The fact that a semester or two of composition has been required for most freshmen at most institutions since shortly after the Civil War has probably had as profound an effect on what happens in composition classrooms as anything teachers have done or said in those classrooms.

The epistemological assumptions embodied by English 1–2 at Amherst College were probably spelled out most clearly in a course description dating from the mid-1950s, which warned students, in effect, that writing could be learned but not taught and that, in English 1–2, they would find themselves "in a situation where no one knows the answers."[2] These assumptions shaped the course in important ways, but the social context in which the course evolved and the institutional character of Amherst College also shaped it and may even have shaped the epistemological assumptions upon which, from another point of view, it seems to have been based. The college at mid-century was a relatively isolated, almost monastic institution. Its select, all-male student body was relatively homogeneous with respect to age, ethnicity, and social class. The curricular plan which governed Amherst from 1947 to 1966 required all freshmen to register for English 1 in the fall and for English 2 in the spring. This requirement, in combination with the English 1–2 staff's practice of employing a common set of assignments and administering them at the rate of one every class period for a total of thirty-three during the first semester and twenty-two during the second, resulted in a situation compelling every member of each year's incoming class to address the same intensive sequence of writing assignments. Each new assignment in the sequence thus represented a sort of campuswide event and was discussed in dormitories and dining halls as well as in classrooms. This situation, which interests me more than the epistemological assumptions underlying the course, turned English 1–2 into an obligatory rite of passage for students and made it enormously instrumental in forming the identity of each new Amherst class. It also kept instructors too busy to do much writing of their own.

In constructing my history of English 1–2, I have tried to take account of social and political forces, operating outside the classroom, which shaped what happened in class. I have looked at English 1–2 within its local institutional contexts, its larger educational and disciplinary contexts, and such still larger national and international contexts as World War II, the Cold War, and the civil disturbances of the 1960s. By looking at the course within these contexts, I have hoped to come closer than those who have focused narrowly on epistemology to answering the kinds of basic questions (at least with respect to a particular place and time) that both North and Crowley say composition historians have yet to answer. My focus on contexts, however, is only one of what I believe are the three chief virtues of my account. The other two are that I have consulted new kinds of historical resource materials and that I have reconsidered a period in the history of composition that has largely been ignored.

Too much historical scholarship in composition, it seems to me, is based on composition textbooks. In a field notorious for the nebulousness of its "content," the ironic result of such scholarship is to place disproportionate emphasis on the "content" of instruction. Such historiography also presumes that textbooks determine practice. In a 1982 article, Susan Miller noted that

> Most histories of composition teaching are histories of the use of textbooks—of their printings, adoptions, rises and declines. Such histories inadvertently imply that composition pedagogy, classroom practices and methods, and writing courses in general have slavishly followed textbooks and that the way to change the teaching and learning of composition necessarily depends on changes in composition textbooks. (22)

Miller urged historians to consider such materials as teachers' records and student papers, even though these might prove "difficult to locate or systematize," and to ask questions whose answers might "represent only speculation" (23). Two years after Miller's article appeared, Robert Connors answered her criticism of textbook-based historiography by claiming that, although textbooks cannot tell a historian all that he or she wants to know, "they do provide the best reflection we have of what actually was taught as the subject matter of composition" (1984, 164). Connors described two models for historical scholarship in composition: the traditional "kings and battles" model, which he himself followed, and the model provided by Miller and by the *annales* school in France. Traditional scholarship was based primarily on textbooks and other published materials and was focused on "great events and identifiable figures." *Annales*-style scholarship entailed exhaustive analyses of "thousands of memos, journals, public records of all sorts, in order to draw generalizations that accurately reflect the activities of people of the period." Connors argued that *annales*-style scholarship could only be practiced "effectively after the major currents of the age, the important figures and theories, have been mapped out" (162).

Connors has argued elsewhere that composition pedagogy was shaped primarily by textbooks at least until the 1930s, when, he has claimed, professional journals also began to assert an influence (1986,178). However, since, as he has also pointed out, textbooks are "conservators of tradition" (1984,164), I would argue that the view of history they provide is a more conservative one than might be derived from other sources. Textbook-based histories tend to characterize composition as a static and rule-governed field. Connors himself, after observing that "very little was added" to textbooks between 1900 and 1940 "that was novel," concluded that the teaching of composition stagnated during this forty-year period (1986, 189). Such a conclusion fails to take the nature of textbooks into account. Textbooks, according to Mike Rose in "Sophisticated, Ineffective Books," are "by nature, static and insular approaches to a dynamic and highly context-oriented process" (1981, 65). Rose has also claimed that "good" teachers know "writing is simply too complex and unwieldy a process to be taught from a textbook" and that therefore "they continually skip around in texts, qualify pronouncements, and supplement with sheet after sheet of handouts" (70).

Even had I wanted to base my history of English 1–2 on a textbook, I could not have done so. Except in 1938, during their first semester of teaching the course that then was listed as English 1C, Baird and his staff never used one. Reporting in 1939 on that first semester's experience, Baird expressed his contempt for textbooks and implied he would not (as in fact he did not) use one again:

> Until Thanksgiving we used a textbook, containing succinct remarks on spelling, analysis of sentence structure, punctuation, usage, construction of what are called good sentences, followed by exercises. We had the students do the exercises, and then the fun began. No one can say these classes were dull, for as the argument grew more and more abstract it increased in noise. There was much heat, but little light. The students quickly found fault with the succinct remarks. After a few weeks both students and instructors were convinced that the English language cannot be so silly as the three authors of our textbook seemed to require. The authors took a mechanical or legalistic view of language and a depressed view of human nature. . . . We demolished the book, tearing out pages (it had a ring binder) as we went, analyzing the conception of grammar and of language implied on every page. (1939, 329–330)

The absence of a textbook is one feature of English 1C, or of English 1–2 (as it was listed after 1942–43), that makes the course interesting to me. But in the absence of a textbook, I had no choice but to adopt the *annales*-style of historical scholarship that Connors describes and Miller recommends. What I have to say about English 1–2 is based on a wide range of published and unpublished materials—including assignment sequences, student papers, staff memoranda, and curricular reports—and on the memories of fourteen men, including Theodore Baird, who either taught the course or undertook it as students. Some of these men made their personal materials available to me. I also went through the five large storage boxes of materials in the English 1–2 Collection at the Amherst College Archives. The collection, which represents the chief physical legacy of English 1–2, includes between forty and fifty sequences of writing assignments, or (because the sequences were never repeated) two per year for most years between 1944 and 1966.

The third virtue I claim for my history of English 1–2, in addition to my looking at new resources through new lenses, is that I have tried to look closely at a set of instructional practices from an era which is not well understood. The writing course which Baird directed for thirty years belongs to the immediately preprofessional period of composition's history. When Baird retired from Amherst College in 1969, composition studies was only beginning to emerge, mostly within university English departments, as a recognizable field of specialized research and teaching.[3] Only Walker Gibson among the seven former English 1–2 instructors I interviewed would be likely to describe himself now as a composition specialist. Theodore Baird describes himself as a teacher. Throughout his career, Baird taught literature courses as well as composition. Except for the one textbook and seven articles listed at the end of Gibson's "Theodore Baird" (1985, 152), Baird published very little. His chief intellectual monument is the still largely unpublished collection of assignment sequences he wrote for English 1–2. For Baird, as for other members of his generation, particularly those who taught at colleges rather than universities, research publication was not a significant professional issue. During the time he was teaching there, moreover, Amherst College constituted virtually a world unto itself. Although Baird wielded enormous power within that world, his very original voice was scarcely heard beyond its cloistering halls. He has said of English 1–2 that "I never felt anything but happy to be able to teach this course. This is all I wanted. I didn't want anything more. I never used it for any purpose of my own, and I never discouraged anyone else who wanted to use it, as a considerable number did, going about making speeches and writing about it" (1978b, 26).

The professionalization of composition in the 1960s has shaped the way scholars in the field have come to see (or not to see) what happened before 1960. The emergence of the field was attended by a series of turf battles in which aspiring composition specialists competed with established literary scholars for power, tenure, and research funds. In order to legitimate their concerns, these first composition specialists rewrote history and, in doing so, provided a clear illustration of the way that history can be made to serve political ends. In *Textual Carnivals,* Susan Miller has identified two strategies which these first specialists used in order to further their agenda. The first was to find composition's roots "in a buried ancient past" and to proclaim its logical derivation from classical rhetoric (1991, 36). The second was to claim that composition possessed a "paradigm" like those used to organize research in the physical sciences (105). The view of history resulting from the first strategy fails to explain how composition evolved within specifically American institutional and disciplinary contexts in shifting relation to the adjacent fields of rhetoric, communications, literary studies, linguistics, cognitive psychology, and philosophy. The view resulting from the second, premised as it is on the notion of a "paradigm shift," has made it difficult for those who began teaching writing after 1960 to appreciate either the variety or the professional value of instructional practices employed before that date. It deprives them of the wisdom and experience of teachers like Theodore Baird.

The paradigm-shift account of composition history was first articulated by Richard Young in his 1978 article entitled "Paradigms and Problems." Young conceded, incidentally, that "seen through the historian's eyes, revolutions are more likely to appear as stages in the growth of a discipline" (46). Even so, he characterized the professionalization of composition as a revolution. Young borrowed the metaphor of the paradigm shift from Thomas Kuhn (1970), who had developed it in order to explain theoretical revolutions in the sciences. Kuhn, as Robert Connors later observed, had used the term "paradigm" in two distinct ways: in one sense meaning "disciplinary matrix," or a system of values and beliefs, but in another sense meaning "exemplar," or the kind of model that can serve as the basis for solutions to problems. Connors, who concluded that composition studies has a disciplinary matrix but lacks exemplars, argued that Young had overlooked this distinction (1983, 2, 9). Young's own argument was that, while one paradigm had governed the teaching of composition until approximately 1960, it was no longer viable, and a new, process-centered paradigm had emerged in its place. According to Young, the features of the old, or "current-traditional" paradigm had included an "emphasis on the composed product rather than the composing process; the analysis of discourse into words, sentences, and paragraphs; the classification of discourse into description, narration, exposition, and argument; the strong concern with usage (syntax, spelling, punctuation) and with style (economy, clarity, emphasis); the preoccupation with the informal essay and research paper; and so on" (1978, 31). Young based his characterization of current-traditional rhetoric upon an examination of composition textbooks, claiming that "textbooks elaborate and perpetuate established paradigms" (31). He did not consider either the conservative nature of textbooks or their limitations as sources of information about composition teaching.

Four years after Young's article appeared, Maxine Hairston seconded his notion that a "revolution" or "paradigm shift" was occurring in the field of composition. To Young's list of the features of the old, "current-traditional" paradigm, Hairston added the following three: "[I]ts adherents believe that competent writers know what they are going to say before they begin to write; . . . that the composing process is linear, . . . that teaching editing is teaching writing" (1982, 78). Hairston claimed that the new paradigm, by contrast, was rhetorically based, was informed by other disciplines, notably by linguistics and cognitive psychology, and was grounded in research into the writing process (86). Other historians also joined Young in using the paradigm-shift terminology. James Berlin and Robert Inkster declared that "the current-traditional paradigm represents a danger to teachers, students, the wider purposes of our educational enterprise, and even our social and human fabric" (1980, 13). Elsewhere, Berlin described current-traditional rhetoric both as "the manifestation of the assembly line in education" (1984, 62) and as a "compelling paradigm," making it impossible for the majority of composition teachers "to conceive of the discipline in any other way" (1987, 9). Donald Stewart expressed his conviction that "a writing teacher's development can be measured by the degree to which that person has become liberated from current-traditional rhetoric" (1988, 16). All of this should be read as a sort of power play or struggle for academic territory. Susan Miller observes that "'current-traditional' or 'product' theory appears to have been created at the same time that process theory was, to help explain process as a theory pitted against old practices" (1991, 110).

The unfortunate effect of polarizing old and new developments in composition, however, has been the devaluation of much that occurred before 1960. The notion that writing used to be taught in one tired old way has prevented many of those who currently teach writing from seeing the dynamic vitality of an era which, if the case of English 1–2 at Amherst College is at all representative, was as lively as any other. But in order to resee what happened before 1960, it is necessary to see what happened in the 1960s as the culmination of a process that had begun with such early moves toward professionalization as the founding of the Conference on College Composition and Communication in 1949 and the appearance of journals such as *English Journal* in 1911, *College English* in 1939, and *College Composition and Communication* in 1949. For the record, Fred Newton Scott began offering graduate courses in rhetoric at the University of Michigan shortly before the turn of the century (Kitzhaber 1953, 118). Organized freshman composition programs first appeared in significant numbers between 1920 and 1940 (Berlin 1987, 65). English 1–2 at Amherst College, incidentally, was one of these.

By looking here and there in existing histories, one can demonstrate that a number of alternative ideas and practices, including several that are now associated with the "new" or post-1960 paradigm, were introduced in composition classrooms during the early and middle decades of the twentieth century. No monolithic current-traditional paradigm ever dominated the teaching of writing. Anne Ruggles Gere has compiled a "small but steady list of publications" from 1900 through 1970 advocating the use of writing groups (1987, 28, 126–133). Kenneth Kantor has listed publications from 1900 through 1971 extolling the value of creative, experiential, and self-expressive writing tasks (1975, 5, 27–29). Kantor's list includes John Dewey's 1934 *Art as Experience* and the 1935 NCTE-sponsored *An Experience Curriculum in English* (Kantor, 14, 16–18) but not, as it fittingly might have done, Theodore Baird's 1931 *The First Years*. David Russell has shown that cross-curricular writing programs were introduced at the turn of the century and subsequently proliferated (1990, 52). During the 1920s and 1930s, writing instructors initiated the use of student-teacher conferences, of editorial groups, of journal-keeping assignments, and of courses in creative writing (Wozniak 1978, chapter 5; Berlin 1987, chapter 4). The project method, which was first outlined in 1917 and which entailed building curricula out of a series of projects students were to complete or problems they were to solve, came to be seen as an especially useful approach to the teaching of writing (Applebee 1974, 108–109). Empirical research studies which were conducted as early as the teens in such areas as remediation, error, and the use of grammar drills provided a new kind of evidence of the futility of teaching rules for correctness (Connors 1985, 69–70). For his *Current English Usage,* published in 1932, Sterling Andrus Leonard conducted the first large-scale survey of opinion about usage and grammar, thus producing an impressively scientific indictment of the pedagogy of correctness (Brereton 1985, 96–100). Standardized testing was introduced in the first decade of the twentieth century (Applebee 1974, 81; Resnick and Resnick 1977, 382). After World War I, a number of colleges instituted placement tests and ability groupings in the hope of providing more effectively for individual student differences (Wozniak 1978, 187, 198; Applebee 1974, 91). The first college-level communications courses, which linked instruction in writing to instruction in speaking and reading and to media studies, were introduced at the University of Iowa in 1944 (Connors 1985, 70).

The conclusion I draw from this survey of early and mid-century developments is that the climate for teaching writing during this period was far from stagnant. Different individuals promoted different methods and approaches. Progressive teachers contended with those who insisted on standards for correctness. Teachers who valued scientific methods contended with those who upheld humanistic or literary values. Teachers who linked writing to personal growth argued with those who linked it to clear thinking or to academic or commercial success. Those who advocated writing about literature argued with those who advocated writing about issues or about personal experience. Those who wanted students to learn to write by writing argued with those who wanted them to study model essays or to memorize rules.

Two additional points remain to be made about the teaching of writing between 1900 and 1960. The first is that it was closely connected to the teaching of literature, and the second is that it was strongly affected by developments in other disciplines. Most of those

who taught composition during this period had been trained in literature and either taught or aspired to teach it. In many composition
classrooms, literature served as the subject material for writing. The
preeminent rhetorical theorists of the period, I. A. Richards and Kenneth Burke, were also prominent as literary critics and critical theorists. Thus literature and composition did not seem as distinct from
one another as they have come to seem since 1960, and developments
in either of the two fields often influenced the other. The critical
approach known as the New Criticism, which Richards and others
introduced in the 1930s and which emphasized the words on the page
rather than the context for writing, shaped the teaching of both writing and reading. There was an explosion in the 1950s and 1960s in the
number of doctorates awarded for literary studies in English (Graff
1987, 155). This explosion coincided with the postwar enrollment
boom and with the rise of the modern (or postwar) research university. It preceded a parallel explosion in composition doctorates by
roughly twenty years.

Developments in the teaching of writing in the early and middle
decades of the century were influenced not only by developments in
literary studies but by those in various nonliterary disciplines as well.
The emerging social sciences served as an especially fertile source of
ideas and methods, but rhetorical theorists also derived insights from
the physical sciences. In their groundbreaking 1923 study of *The
Meaning of Meaning,* C. K. Ogden and I. A. Richards acknowledged a
special debt to anthropologist Bronislaw Malinowski for the support
his field research in the Trobriand Islands had lent to their context theory of reference (ix). In his subsequent *Practical Criticism,* published in
1929, Richards experimented with research methods—including
using his students as a sample population, asking them to respond in
writing to unidentified poems and analyzing their anonymous
responses or "protocols"—that had been pioneered in the social sciences. In *A Rhetoric of Motives,* first published in 1950, Kenneth Burke
expanded his conception of audience situations to include the internal
dialogue of ego confronting id and superego (1969, 37–38). He also
redefined rhetoric as "the use of language as a symbolic means of
inducing cooperation in beings that by nature respond to symbols"
(43). The founder of the General Semantics movement, Alfred
Korzybski, traced the rhetorical implications of Einstein's revolution
in physics. According to Korzybski in a work he first published in

1933, Einstein not only provided a new model for explaining the universe, he demonstrated that any such model, his as well as Newton's, was necessarily a "conceptual construction" (1948, 86). At Amherst College, Theodore Baird was strongly influenced by the writings of Nobel Prize-winning physicist, P. W. Bridgman. This evidence of cross-disciplinary interchange supports my conclusion that during Baird's era the teaching of writing was neither stagnant nor dominated by any single paradigm.

Two historians who published at the dawn of composition's professional era, Daniel Fogarty in 1959 and Albert Kitzhaber in 1963, provide evidence of theoretical and methodological pluralism which does not square with the notion, to which both nevertheless contributed, that a monolithic "current-traditional" paradigm governed the teaching of composition at that time. Fogarty pointed out that three new theories of rhetoric—namely, those of I. A. Richards, of Kenneth Burke, and of such general semanticists as Alfred Korzybski, S. I. Hayakawa, and Irving J. Lee—had emerged during the quarter century preceding his publication date (3). Fogarty hoped that his analysis of these new theories would "provide educators and formulators of general education courses with most of the elements, old and new, that promise to make rhetoric a better classroom instrument" (4). It was Fogarty, however, who actually coined the term "current-traditional" rhetoric. He used the term as a label for a dummy category he set up in contrast to his three new rhetorics and to Aristotelian rhetoric (118–119). The rhetorical elements he listed in the current-traditional category, Fogarty explained, were those which "time and expediency have added to the teaching rhetoric, now variously called composition, writing, speech, communication, and the like" (120).

Kitzhaber, drawing upon course syllabi and other material used at ninety-five different institutions in 1960–61, observed in *Themes, Theories, and Therapy* that "freshman English has assumed an enormous variety of forms" (1963a, 4) and that "what goes by the name of freshman composition on one campus may bear little resemblance to a course of the same name on another" (12). He noted that the course might be based on any of such subjects as grammar and usage, structural linguistics, literature, rhetoric (either the classical rhetoric of Aristotle and Quintilian or the nineteenth century rhetoric of paragraph development and forms of discourse), logic, semantics, communications and mass media, public speaking, propaganda analysis, or "a kind of watered-down social science survey based on collections of essays drawn for the most part from current magazines" (12–13). Nevertheless, despite his discovery of what Richard Young would later call an "extraordinary variety" of approaches to the teaching of composition (Young 1978, 30), Kitzhaber drew conclusions from his data which resulted, like the conclusions of the paradigm-shift theorists who followed him, in flattening the distinctions between different approaches. None of these approaches, according to Kitzhaber, was demonstrably successful in teaching students to write. He complained that "the people who plan and run freshman English courses" and "those who write textbooks for these courses" were "still doing business in the same old way at the same old stand" (Kitzhaber 1963a, 26).

In many ways, *Themes, Theories, and Therapy* can be seen as a logical outgrowth of ideas Kitzhaber had introduced in 1953 in his groundbreaking dissertation on *Rhetoric in American Colleges, 1850–1900*. In his dissertation, after declaring that the latter half of the nineteenth century "can hardly be called a particularly distinguished time in the history of rhetoric" (97), he concluded that much American rhetorical theory had remained frozen "in the form it had half a century ago" (261).

Susan Miller describes *Themes, Theories, and Therapy* as a "locus classicus for many common complaints about the transgressions of composition" and accuses Kitzhaber of engaging in a game of blaming the victim. She also points to his appeal for greater consensus regarding the aims of freshman English as evidence of his underlying hegemonic purposes (1991, 10). Although Kitzhaber was careful "not to suggest that variation itself is undesirable," he argued that "in a required course offered in many sections, if there is not considerable uniformity in all sections, the students who must take the course cannot be sure of getting the training or the knowledge that the course is supposed to give as a condition of its being required" (1963a, 53–54).

In point of fact, Kitzhaber played a major role in the effort to professionalize the field of composition. His conclusion in *Themes, Theories, and Therapy*—that "freshman English in the nation's colleges and universities is now so confused, so clearly in need of radical and sweeping reforms, that college English departments can continue to ignore the situation only at their increasing peril" (1963a, 26)—constituted an important challenge to aspiring composition professionals. In 1964, Kitzhaber served as president of the National Council of Teachers of English, having served previously as chairman of the Conference on

This view of the hills in the Holyoke Range was taken in the 1950s from the then newly constructed War Memorial on the Amherst College campus. In the fall of 1954, English 1 students were asked to make a line drawing of the Holyoke Range skyline.

College Composition and Communication (CCCC). In 1963, he not only published *Themes, Theories, and Therapy,* which Stephen North describes as "the first book-length study of college writing" (1987, 14), he also scolded CCCC for not having "consistently exerted the kind of intelligent and courageous leadership in the profession that alone, I think, can justify its existence in the long run" (1963b, 135).

One conclusion I could draw about the outcome of the professional struggles of the 1960s is that Albert Kitzhaber and others like him won the battle to set a composition agenda and that Theodore Baird lost or, more strictly speaking, did not deign to fight. At Amherst College at the time when Kitzhaber, at Dartmouth, was conducting his research for *Themes, Theories, and Therapy,* Baird was not interested in accounting to any outside reformer for his practices in English 1–2. Accordingly, Kitzhaber made only one brief reference to the Amherst course. He characterized it as a "maverick course" that did not fit any of his categories and as a "course at a distinguished men's liberal arts college that, at least until recently, required each student to buy a box of colored crayons to use in preparing some of the assignments" (1963a, 13). The particular assignments to which Kitzhaber alluded were written by a young Amherst instructor named

John Butler and used in the fall of 1954.[4] Among the assignments in this sequence were the following:

> Make a line drawing of three or four simple objects in your dormitory room. What did you do to make this drawing? What did you have to see to draw what you did? Define, in this context, *drawing.*

> In your dormitory room, make a drawing of a simple object which casts a shadow. What did you do to draw the object? What did you do to draw the shadow? What were you trying to show in your drawing? Were you able to show it? Define, in this context, *shadow.*

> From someplace on the campus, make a line drawing of the Holyoke Range Skyline, and *nothing but* the Holyoke Range Skyline. (Keep a copy or tracing of this drawing.) What did you do to draw the skyline? What did you have to see to draw what you drew? Define, in this context, *Holyoke Range Skyline.*

> Take your drawing of the Holyoke Range Skyline and put in the sky. How did you add the sky to your drawing? To add the sky, did you draw anything that is *not* sky? Define in this context, *sky.*

Needless to say, these are difficult assignments, and Kitzhaber's description gives no sense of that. When I asked him about Kitzhaber, Baird told me, "I remember his calling me up and wanting to come down from Dartmouth and spend a day. I was less than cordial, and he took his revenge in ridicule. This was naughty of me, but there were moments when sitting down once again to try to explain what we were doing was more than I could bear" (letter to R. Varnum, March 18, 1992). Butler, the author of the assignments Kitzhaber had ridiculed, had left Amherst in 1959, shortly before Kitzhaber began his research for *Themes, Theories, and Therapy.* Butler told me that "when Kitzhaber was in the middle of his very uneasy stay at Dartmouth, he sent to a lot of colleges a questionnaire about composition. TB didn't respond, which of course annoyed Kitzhaber, who knew, through others (including me), that something of great interest was going on at Amherst." Butler added that he and Kitzhaber had previously been colleagues at the University of Kansas and noted that "Kitzhaber, by the way, treated me very well, and I admired what he was trying to do" (letter to R.Varnum, August 4, 1992).

If Kitzhaber had persisted with his inquiry into English 1–2, despite Baird's rebuff, he might have learned something about the course from James Broderick's 1958 "A Study of the Freshman Composition Course at Amherst." Among other things, Kitzhaber might have learned more about Butler's 1954 assignments on line drawings, shadows, and the Holyoke Range Skyline.[4] Broderick had called them "unusual assignments" and explained that, in the first few assignments of the series, "the student is asked to consider the way he sees objects and their shadows; and he questions the way in which lines on a paper can be said to be like the objects he tried to draw." The next group of assignments in the series, according to Broderick, called "the student's attention to the influence his interpretation of one line on a paper has on his interpretation of another line on that paper." Subsequent assignments asked "students to draw an object about to fall, a man running, a man standing still, and to say how they indicated that the object was ready to fall, that the man was running or standing still." These assignments, Broderick claimed, "while introducing new points and complications, ingeniously make use of the same drawings to dramatize the student's growing ability to distinguish between what he sees and his interpretation of what he sees." A later assignment called on the student to draw the front of his dormitory from memory, and questioned him "closely about the number of windows" until he could be made to acknowledge the uncertainty of his memory. Finally, Broderick reported, "[T]he students are asked to explain, as if to a friend, that English 1–2 is not an art course, and to tell the friend what they've been doing in the course" (48–49).

Kitzhaber could also have found information about English 1–2 in the *Amherst College Bulletin*. According to the volume for 1960–61, which is the one he would have consulted, English 1, "Composition," carried two credit hours and entailed "three hours of classroom work per week." The course was required for freshmen and was offered during the first semester. English 2, "Composition," also carried two credit hours but entailed only "two hours of classroom work per week." English 2 was required for freshmen and was offered during the second semester. English 1 was a prerequisite for English 2. The staff for both English 1 and 2 consisted of eleven men in a sixteen-man English department and included Professors Baird (chairman), Craig (on leave in 1960–61), and DeMott; Visiting Professor Atherton; Assistant Professors Heath, Revard, and Sale; and Messrs. Cameron, Coles, Guttmann, and Pritchard (75). This eleven-man staff was responsible for the 271 members of Amherst's freshman class (191).

Despite the sketchiness of Kitzhaber's treatment of English 1–2, his survey of composition programs in the early 1960s is a rich source of information against which to measure the Amherst course. Most of the ninety-five colleges and universities Kitzhaber surveyed allocated two semesters or three quarters to an introductory course in English composition (1963a, 23) and required it of from 55 to 97 percent of their freshmen (21). The first term of the course, in 80 percent of these institutions, was devoted to the reading and writing of expository essays; in the remaining 20 percent, the emphasis was more literary (21–22). The second semester or third quarter of the course, in the majority of cases, was given to reading and writing about literature (23–24). The amount of writing required during the first term varied from 3,600 to 10,000 words, but the mean was 6,000 words or eleven 500-word themes. During the second semester, students wrote some ten papers, but as one of these was generally a "long" or research paper, the total number of words could approach 8,000 (24).

The amount of writing required of Amherst College freshmen during the same period was greater than either the mean or the high figures Kitzhaber cites. During the fall semester or English 1 portion of the Amherst course, students wrote from 30 to 32 short papers, each averaging some 400 words, a longer, five-page paper, and a two- or three-page essay exam. During the spring semester, or English 2, when class sections met less frequently, students wrote some twenty short papers, a longer paper, and an essay exam. Thus an average Amherst freshman wrote 14,000 words for English 1 and 10,000 for English 2.

At Dartmouth College, where Kitzhaber was teaching in the early 1960s, the academic calendar was divided into three ten-week terms, and the study of freshman English occupied two such terms. The students in most sections wrote seven papers during their first term of the course (each paper averaging 700 to 800 words) and sat for an exam. During their second term, these students wrote three or four short papers, at least one long paper of 1,500 to 2,000 words, and sat for an exam. Thus Dartmouth students were writing about 6,000 words for each term of freshman English (1963a, 29–32). The freshman course at Dartmouth is an interesting one to compare with English 1–2 at Amherst because the two colleges fit the same institutional profile. In the early 1960s, Dartmouth and Amherst were both private, liberal arts colleges for men. Both were located in the Connecticut River valley of central New England—Dartmouth in Hanover, New Hampshire, a little over one hundred miles north of Amherst, Massachusetts. Kitzhaber describes Dartmouth as "a restricted-enrollment college" whose average student was "noticeably superior both in intelligence and in preparation to his counterpart at less favored colleges and universities" (27). The Dartmouth English staff, according to Kitzhaber, was "composed entirely of full-time teachers with a high degree of professional competence, educated at the best universities and already experienced in teaching before they are hired" (27). Although beginning instructors at Amherst taught three sections of English 1–2 with twenty to twenty-five students per section (Gibson 1985, 139), instructors at Dartmouth never taught more than two sections of freshman English and never had to deal with more than twenty students per section (Kitzhaber 1963a, 35). According to Kitzhaber, institutions like Dartmouth were "the bellwethers of American higher education, so that developments in their curricula often are significant to other kinds of colleges and universities as well" (28).

The Dartmouth freshman English program, according to Kitzhaber, was "a striking example of that particular variety that is centered on the study of standard literature, with writing assignments growing out of this study" (28–29). The first-term English course at Dartmouth, entitled "Literature and Composition for Freshmen," was described as follows in the college catalogue:

> The course aims, through the study and discussion of selections from Shakespeare and Milton, to increase the student's capacity for enjoying and appreciating great literature. It also aims to develop clear thinking and correct and clear expression. Frequent themes are required, and no student will receive credit for the course until he has demonstrated his ability to write satisfactorily. (Quoted in Kitzhaber 1963a, 29)

As examples of theme topics for this first-term course, Kitzhaber cited the following: "The Role of Enobarbus in *Anthony and Cleopatra*," "Richard III—'Hell's Black Intelligencer,'" and "Who Was at Fault: Adam or Eve?" (30). He observed that the term's work was organized "not by linguistic or rhetorical considerations but (loosely) by the literary works being read—the Shakespeare plays first, with the least difficult usually beginning the course, and *Paradise Lost* at the end" (30). Except for scheduling one writing conference with each student in each section and for routinely returning marked themes to students for revision, Dartmouth instructors gave little direct instruction in writing. According to Kitzhaber, a departmental policy specifying that several class hours during the first term be "designated as 'composition meetings' at which writing problems will be discussed" was generally not observed (30–31).

The catalogue description for Dartmouth's second-term English course, entitled "Freshman Seminar in English," indicates that

> The course is designed to provide the student the maximum opportunity for responsible, independent study, and to offer him experience in the use of the library. Each section may be divided into two seminar groups. Topics for study are chosen by the instructor (e.g., an important figure or theme in English or American literature, representative figures of a period, a literary genre, or a major work). (Quoted in Kitzhaber 1963a, 31)

Freshman seminar topics were subject to the approval of a Steering Committee for Freshman English. As examples of seminar topics, Kitzhaber listed "The Concept of Tragedy," "Hardy and Conrad," "Literature of the 1920s, English and American," "Initiation as a Theme in Fiction," "The Irrational in Literature," "The Spiritual Journey," and "The Fall of Man" (31–32). He reported that writing during the second term was taught much as in the first term: the teacher assigned and marked papers, the student revised them, and occasionally teacher and student met in conference to discuss the student's writing. No class time during the second term was given to "composition meetings" (32–33). Kitzhaber raised the question of whether this emphasis on specialized research during the second-term course served the best interests of novice student writers (40–41). He also wondered whether the study of Shakespeare's plays and of *Paradise Lost* during the first term was "entirely appropriate to the task of teaching expository writing to freshmen" (37).

Kitzhaber's tone throughout *Themes, Theories, and Therapy* strikes me as dismissive. His complaints about freshman English at Dartmouth and the other ninety-five institutions he surveyed, together with the complaints he had made in his earlier *Rhetoric in American Colleges, 1850–1900* about what Daniel Fogarty was calling "current-traditional" rhetoric, served as a foundation for the paradigm-shift theory of the history of composition that was put forward in the 1970s and 1980s. The result has been that composition programs from the 1950s, like the one Kitzhaber described at Dartmouth and like English 1–2 at Amherst, are now presumed, when they are considered at all, to have employed "old paradigm" practices. I believe that a reappraisal of the Dartmouth course, as well as of the Amherst course, might be in order. At the 1993 meeting of the Conference on College Composition and Communication, John Brereton argued that

> One important part of composition's history that has been left unexplored is one of the oldest, most pervasive, and most popular forms of college composition instruction, learning to write through reading literature. This approach, what Wayne Booth called LitComp, is the way most of us learned to write and still dominates in many colleges and universities. (1993)

Brereton was arguing for a reappraisal of "Hum 6," a LitComp course that was offered at Harvard in the 1950s and early 1960s. And while I agree with him that LitComp courses are deserving of renewed historical attention, I believe that other neglected writing courses from roughly the period of Hum 6 or of Kitzhaber's Dartmouth course should be reevaluated as well. The course which is the focus of my own study, English 1–2 at Amherst College, was not a LitComp course. Instead of centering on literature, it centered on student writing and on the tricky sequences of assignments that occasioned that writing. It was more squarely a general education course than the course at Dartmouth that Kitzhaber described.

The volume of the *Amherst College Bulletin* for 1960–61, the year Kitzhaber was conducting his research for *Themes, Theories, and Therapy*, identifies English 1–2 as a core course within a general education curriculum which had been adopted at Amherst College in 1947. This curriculum, known then as the "New Curriculum," had instituted a series of core courses in each of the three divisions of the humanities, the social sciences, and the natural sciences and thus served as an important context for English 1–2. The aim of the New

Curriculum was "to provide a body of common knowledge that would serve as a basis for later specialization in any field" (*Amherst College Bulletin, 1960–61,* 19). Its aim was also, as Roger Sale (who was then a member of the English 1–2 staff) said in his address to the 1962 graduating class, "to preserve the ancient notion of the whole man." According to Sale:

> One of the oldest and most admirable ideas that there is about education derives from the dream of the whole man, a dream which imagines it possible for an individual to learn and a school to teach about the breadth of human knowledge when that knowledge is considered abstractly as a series of disciplines. The dream is for a man to know in miniature what all men can know, and who, because of that knowledge, can be free of all pettiness because he knows Truth. This dream is ancient, and attempts to make that dream fact were being made long before the schools had become separate from the church; in this country, the great document about this dream is *The Education of Henry Adams,* one of the few books about which it is still possible to say that everyone should read it. But the dream also finds expression in the curriculum of this college; here Adams' hope of running unity through multiplicity is a present concern for everyone. (1962)

Amherst's New Curriculum was the product of a study completed in 1945 by a Faculty Committee on Long Range Policy. In its 1945 report, this committee claimed that "if a liberal education is to be comprehensive, it should be organized in such a way as to unify the most fundamental cultural interests of the society in which we live" (Kennedy 1955, 27). Theodore Baird, who had agreed that the unification of knowledge was desirable, wrote a statement about English 1–2 in 1946–47 for the Committee on Publicizing the New Curriculum. He declared, "In this belief English 1–2 operates, that in the act of expression knowledge can be unified."[5] Amherst's New Curriculum was one of several postwar, general education curricula developed at a variety of institutions across the country. These curricula, the most widely known of which was outlined in Harvard's 1945 plan for *General Education in a Free Society,* variously instituted new interdisciplinary courses, or systems of distribution requirements, or (as in Amherst's case) networks of core courses. The perceived danger

in the 1940s—in the face of academic specialization, of the proliferation of elective courses, and of a postwar enrollment boom which
brought the traditional conception of education as the mark of a gentleman into conflict with the democratic ideal of equal access to education—was that there would no longer be a common body of
knowledge, or a common intellectual heritage, uniting educated men
and women. General education curricula, however, were subject to
the criticism that they represented an authoritarian effort to determine what every educated person should know. Faculty members,
moreover, were often reluctant to teach the general education courses
because of the large commitment of time entailed. Educational historian Frederick Rudolph reports that, by the mid-1950s, general education everywhere, "even at Harvard," was running "out of steam"
(1977, 259).

Amherst's New Curriculum, which survived until 1966, was
exceptionally long-lived. But already by 1962, when Roger Sale delivered his "Senior Chapel Address" to Amherst's graduating seniors, the
New Curriculum was a source of increasing faculty dissatisfaction. A
1958–59 study conducted by a Curriculum Review Committee did
not lead to any significant change, but a study which would be undertaken in 1963–64 by a Committee on Educational Policy would result
in the demise of the New Curriculum (see Babb et al. 1978, 5–6, 9).
In 1962, when Sale spoke to Amherst seniors about Henry Adams and
the dream of educating the whole man, Sale acknowledged that
Adams's dream belonged properly to the eighteenth century:

> Those of you who have read *The Education of Henry Adams* know
> that Adams failed in his quest for unity and wholeness and that
> he found himself forced to conclude that the education he
> wanted belonged to a century earlier than his or ours. We know,
> furthermore, that he was right and that the only way Amherst
> could make the ancient dream into a present fact was to make
> many modifications and alterations in order to face the twenti-
> eth century. But it can be said still that the finest thing about
> Amherst is its insistence on maintaining the ideals of the ancient
> dream. The ideal has the power to make one believe in an intel-
> lectual strength above and divorced from money and sex and
> commerce, and to the extent that this ideal has touched and
> changed you, you are better men. In a democracy a dream such
> as Amherst's is obviously, in one sense, anomalous and anachro-

nistic, but Amherst has faced this and said that it would provide leaders for a democracy much as earlier sharers of the dream provided the educated gentleman as the model of an aristocratic largesse. (1962)

When Amherst's New Curriculum was finally superseded in 1966, English 1–2 was replaced by English 11–12. In a 1971 dissertation on *English 1–2 at Amherst College,* subtitled *Composition and the Unity of Knowledge,* John Carpenter Louis observed that "the course developed at a time when Amherst College, and other schools, were concerned to reinvigorate and restructure general education" (14). Louis was an alumnus of Amherst College and of its freshman composition course and claimed to have "abundant testimonial evidence that Amherst freshmen found English 1–2 particularly provocative and intellectually stimulating" (2). He argued that a course like English 1–2 could best have flourished at a small, liberal arts institution, where the notion that it was possible to "know about knowledge in general" persisted, despite challenges from "research professionalism" and "specialist educational imperatives" (22). What Louis did not acknowledge was that by 1971, when he published his dissertation, research professionalism had largely supplanted the older, generalist ideal. He may not have known in 1971 that composition was beginning to take on the character of a specialized field. But it must have been clear to him that research professionalism was a driving force at the University of Massachusetts at Amherst, where he was then teaching. It was also driving a number of changes at Amherst College.

Louis wrote the first of two dissertations on English 1–2. I wrote the second. I filed my dissertation twenty years after Louis filed his and so was able to draw on a much larger body of materials than either he in 1971 or Kitzhaber in 1961 had been able to consider. Louis's dissertation, of course, and the previously cited articles by James Broderick and Walker Gibson were invaluable to me. Gibson, who taught in the English 1–2 program from 1946 to 1957, suggests that the aims of the course were to encourage students to adopt a critical attitude toward language, to lead them to recognize that the world is created of words, and to help them gain control of their lives by gaining control of language (1985, 146). Broderick, on the other hand, concludes that the aim of English 1–2 was to force the student "to think for himself in a radical and honest way" (1958, 47). According to Broderick, the student was also supposed to gain "a flexibility and sophistication in the use of concepts" and to learn "that a word means only what he makes it mean" (52).

The focus of Broderick's article is on the ideas and philosophical assumptions underlying English 1–2. Broderick argued that "the carefully selected order in which the assignments are given" could be seen as "a manifestation of the basic epistemological slant of the course" and that "from the repeats, the overlappings, and the reviews in which the student is asked to tell what he has been doing so far in the course the sense of a real, though unexplained, method is maintained" (1958, 50). Broderick claimed that English 1–2 might "be considered an original reflection of the American pragmatic, positivistic, and operationalistic philosophic temper" (44), and he described it as "a typically American course" (57). According to Broderick, English 1–2 combined the insights of operationalism, as set forth by physicist Percy W. Bridgman in *The Logic of Modern Physics,* with the linguistic and critical theories of I. A. Richards (Broderick 1958, 50). Broderick also claimed that English 1–2 shared "with progressive education an emphasis on the student's learning to work out his own problems, to find solutions when the problems have been made immediately real to him" (1958, 57). Both Louis and Gibson concurred with Broderick in detecting the influence of Richards and Bridgman upon English 1–2. Gibson also noted the influence of Alfred Korzybski and Henry Adams (1985, 149).

The focus of Gibson's article, however, is less on philosophical matters than on Baird's character, on the structural features of English 1–2, and on the influence of the course. Gibson claims that even if English 1–2 has not attracted much notice from historians, it cannot be dismissed as obscure. It has had an important, if not easily traced, influence upon those who taught it and upon their students. Among the men who taught the course, according to a list Gibson published in his 1985 article, were

> a number still at Amherst—G. A. Craig, Benjamin DeMott, John Cameron, William Heath, William Pritchard—as well as a larger number who have taken some part of Baird with them to other pastures—Reuben Brower, C. L. Barber, W. V. Clausen, Julian Moynahan, Roger Sale, William R. Taylor, Jonathan Bishop, John F. Butler, William Coles, myself. (147)

Gibson lists himself and William E. Coles Jr. as one-time Amherst instructors who went on to publish textbooks employing Amherst-like sequences of assignments (148). The particular textbooks Gibson cites are his own *Seeing and Writing* (1959) and Coles's *Composing* (1983; first published in 1974).

Gibson, who became prominent in the field of composition studies as the author of *Tough, Sweet and Stuffy* (1966) and *Persona* (1969) and as the president, in 1973, of the National Council of Teachers of English, is one of the seven former members of the English 1–2 staff whom I have interviewed about the course. The others are Theodore Baird, John Cameron, G. Armour Craig, Dale Peterson, William Pritchard, and Roger Sale.[6] Gibson has retired from the University of Massachusetts at Amherst. Baird and Craig have both retired from Amherst College. Pritchard, who has published literary biographies of Randall Jarrell and Robert Frost, is currently teaching at Amherst College. So are Cameron and Peterson. Sale, who published *On Writing* in 1970, teaches at the University of Washington.

It was Gibson's article on "Theodore Baird" which provided me with my initial introduction to English 1–2. When I first read the article, in 1990, I was a graduate student at the University of Massachusetts (UMass) at Amherst and very slightly acquainted with Gibson, who had retired from UMass three years earlier. I was searching for a dissertation topic and my advisor, who knew I had published a couple of short papers on the history of composition, handed me a copy of Gibson's article and suggested I talk to him. My advisor pointed out that since the course Gibson described had been offered at nearby Amherst College, I was well situated to study it.

Perhaps I should make it clear that although both UMass and Amherst College are located in Amherst, and although Gibson has taught at both, they are separate and very different institutions. UMass, with 23,000 undergraduate and graduate students, is the flagship campus of what has become a five-campus state university system. Its mushrooming assortment of parking lots, high-rise dormitories, and architecturally eclectic educational facilities sprawls messily over several acres of north Amherst. Amherst College, which is forty years older than UMass, is a private, highly selective, and now coeducational, liberal arts college. Its traditional brick buildings and the spires of its Mead Art Gallery and its Johnson Chapel crown the hilltop immediately south of the Amherst Town Common.

Center, *Johnson Chapel, surrounded by College Row at Amherst College in 1940.*

After speaking with my advisor, I visited the Amherst College Library, which is named for the poet and former member of the Amherst faculty, Robert Frost, and learned that its archives house a wealth of material relating to English 1–2.[7] I leafed through several sets of English 1–2 assignments and quickly came to see that the course must have been both a difficult and an interesting one to teach. I also found the transcript of a tape recording titled "Reflections on Amherst and English 1" that Theodore Baird had made in 1978 for the Amherst College Oral History Project. I decided I could feasibly write a thick description of English 1–2 by using the archival materials and collecting additional oral histories. I contacted Professor Gibson, and he not only agreed to talk to me, he offered to introduce me to Professor Baird.

Gibson warned me that I would find Baird, who in 1990 was nearly ninety years old, to be formidable. Gibson reminded me that, in his article on "Theodore Baird," he had described Baird as always having "suffered from the handicap of saying what he thinks" (1985, 151). I remembered that, in the same article, Gibson said that although Baird had made genuine efforts to involve the junior members of his staff in decision making, he had been the senior man, and "he did direct" (138). As it happened, Baird welcomed my inquiries. He granted me two interviews, wrote me letters, undertook to pose as both my teacher and my antagonist, and engaged my imagination. Several of the other men whom I wished to interview, however, resisted my overtures. When I first telephoned John Cameron, he expressed his consternation that anyone should still be interested in "*that* course." When I first telephoned Roger Sale, he expressed his amazement that any woman should want to study what had amounted to an "astonishingly masculine" enterprise. Both Sale and William E. Coles Jr. (of whom the latter ultimately declined to be interviewed) displayed their strong loyalties to Baird. Both expressed concern lest I attribute information to them that might upset him.

My age and my experience as a writing teacher seemed to serve me advantageously, however, as I went about soliciting interviews. I am younger than all the men I interviewed, in fact almost fifty years younger than Baird, but I am not much younger than either Dale Peterson or the two youngest English 1–2 alumni I talked to. I was a freshman composition student at the University of California at Santa Barbara in the fall of 1968, the same fall that Peterson began teaching at Amherst College and the last fall Baird ever taught there. I was a student of Sale's at the University of Washington in 1974. I earned a master's degree in English from the University of Washington and then, before beginning my study of English 1–2 in 1990, I spent a dozen years adjuncting in composition at sometimes one and sometimes two small colleges.

Early in the course of my dissertation project, I became convinced that English 1–2 was never the sort of current-traditional composition course said to have been standard at its time period. On the contrary, it employed practices and ideas which are not supposed to have been introduced until the 1970s or 1980s. I began to question the commonly held notion that a current-traditional paradigm had dominated composition teaching until 1960 and to suspect that such a paradigm had dominated only the composition of composition textbooks. I now believe that the history of composition teaching in the 1940s and 1950s and of the professionalization of composition in the 1960s is badly in need of revision. A new conception of this history would give those of us who teach writing at the close of the century new ways of conceptualizing our professional identity. We need to know where we have been in order to know who we are and where we are going. The successes and failures of our predecessors can and should inform our teaching. We need to be able to draw on our heritage from the 1940s or 1950s in order more effectively to answer detractors, compete for resources, evaluate the appeals of reformers, and guide our students and our discipline wisely into the twenty-first century.

This is not to say that a teaching ethos which evolved during the Cold War era can be revitalized for new contexts in the post-Cold War world. American colleges and universities have changed considerably and so in particular has Amherst College in the more than quarter century since English 1–2 was canceled. The ideal of the whole *man* no longer seems viable. Both research professionalism and feminism have supplanted it. The quest for unity seems less compelling than the need to honor diversity. From the vantage of the 1990s, the Amherst College of the early post–World War II years seems both elitist and authoritarian. And yet that Amherst also seems more hopeful and more sure of its mission than the Amherst of today. In the 1940s and 1950s, an Amherst teacher could suppose himself to be preparing students to lead the free world. Today, both the dream of a free world and the image of American leadership seem badly tarnished. I find much to admire in Theodore Baird's notion that education can liberate the imagination, and yet my own conviction is that the imagination is constrained by both culture and society.

CHAPTER TWO

Running Orders through Chaos

*I*n 1927, at the age of twenty-six, Theodore Baird accepted the position of instructor at Amherst College. A native of Warren, Ohio, he had received his bachelor's degree in 1921 from Hobart College in New York and his master's degree in 1922 from Harvard. At Harvard, he had studied with Irving Babbitt,[1] among others. Baird's academic interests were in eighteenth century literature and in Shakespeare. Once he had earned his master's degree, he combined doctoral studies at Harvard with brief teaching stints at Western Reserve and at Union College. When he arrived at Amherst, he was still two years shy of completing the Ph.D. degree he would receive from Harvard in 1929. He later speculated that he was hired at Amherst at least partly because he knew Roy Elliott, a senior professor in the English department. Baird was hired initially for only a year, at a salary of $2,700, to replace Elliott while he went on leave and to teach Elliott's Shakespeare course and two sections of freshman English (1978b, 1).

English A, as the freshman course was then called, was a required course at Amherst in 1927. Freshman enrollment in the late 1920s and early 1930s fluctuated between approximately 160 and 175 men, and English A was usually taught in eight sections (1978b, 8). Baird recalls that on the evening of the day he arrived at Amherst, he called on a senior colleague in the English department, George Whicher. One of the questions Baird put to Whicher was, "Well now, what am I to do in Freshman English?" Baird says he expected Whicher to give him a textbook because in similar circumstances, when he had asked for direction at both Union

College and Western Reserve, he had been told to teach a particular book. To Baird's surprise, Whicher merely said, "Why, do anything you want to." Baird says he thought about this for a week and finally decided he would spend the semester with his freshmen reading *The Education of Henry Adams* (8).

In 1927, according to Baird, *The Education of Henry Adams* was not yet a popular textbook in American colleges. Baird recalls that the Houghton Mifflin salesman with whom he placed his book order expressed surprise that he should want to teach such a difficult book to freshmen (1978b, 8). Nevertheless, Baird made his course out of Adams's *Education* not only that first semester, but for a number of semesters thereafter. Many years later he acknowledged that "I've always thought it an influential book, a book that changed your mind. It changed mine" (8). Baird's younger colleague, Walker Gibson, speculates that *The Education* "was surely formative in Baird's own education, and one can perhaps feel in his own prose style some echoes of Adams" (1985, 149).

From Henry Adams, Baird learned to see education as an enterprise in running orders through chaos. In the early stages of my own research into the composition course that Baird directed at Amherst College, as I was reading assignments and other materials relating to English 1–2 or to Baird's career, I began running into one sentence-long passage from *The Education of Henry Adams* with remarkable frequency. The passage, which occurs in Adams's first chapter, asserts that

> From cradle to grave this problem of running orders through chaos, direction through space, discipline through freedom, unity through multiplicity, has always been, and must always be, the task of education. (1973, 12)

I found this passage quoted, for example, in Baird's 1931 anthology, *The First Years* (48). It was also quoted in various assignment sequences for English 1–2. Roger Sale, in his "Senior Chapel Address," said that Adams's dream of running "unity through multiplicity" had found an expression in the Amherst College curriculum. I think I hear echoes of Adams's "discipline through freedom" in Baird's assertion, in his footnote to Otto Glaser's 1938 *Report* (reprinted in Babb et al. 1978, 122–123), that a liberal education must promote freedom of mind. I think it was Adams whom Baird was invoking when he expressed the wish in 1952 that his students might "recognize as the marvel it is the human being's power of making order out of chaos" (1952, 196). I know that "order" and "chaos" have been literary buzzwords since at least the 1930s and that Robert Frost, among others, spoke frequently of order and chaos, but I think it was Adams's use of "orders" in the plural that specifically appealed to Baird. Your order, the plural form indicates, is not the same as my order. When I asked Baird if I were right in assuming that Adams's definition of "the task of education" had particular significance for him and for English 1–2, he replied, "Yes, that's the classic passage; that's what we had in mind when we put together a lot of our assignments." I came to think that "running orders through chaos" could be a central metaphor for Baird's enterprise. As the director of a teaching staff, he ran an order through chaos by organizing a group of disparate individuals with different aims and teaching styles into a working unit. As a teacher of writing, he taught student writers to run orders through chaos by defining themselves in relation to their experience, their language, their audience, and their writing problem.

In assignment 25 of a sequence Baird wrote for English 1 in the fall of 1959, he not only quoted the Adams passage, he also explained something of his own thinking on the opposition of order and chaos in human experience. According to Baird:

> When we write or talk and use words and symbols and signs, what we are doing is making sets, composing, organizing, ordering similarities. This act of ordering (a metaphor for all sorts of things that happen) is an extremely difficult one to express in general. Nevertheless it is at the heart, in the center, of our experience.[2]

In assignment 27 of the same sequence, Baird explained that

> The existence of chaos is a fact of experience. We encounter it daily, hourly. We know it is, even though when we begin to talk about it we make some kind of order. It can be referred to and pointed at by many different sets of words, many different metaphors.[2]

In assignment 26, Baird had pointed out that "order" and "chaos" were relative terms and that "one man's chaos" could be another's order. His fall 1959 sequence culminated in assignment 33, in which, as was his practice with end-of-term assignments, he asked students to make sense of what they had been doing in English 1. His specific directive was to "make an order out of the assignments you have done this semester, an order, that is, of thinking which you have made for yourself in doing these assignments."[2]

In Baird's account of his early experience at Amherst College, he initially encountered, if not chaos, then at least "no organization at all" in the teaching of freshman English. He claims to have had "no idea what the other teachers were doing" (1978b, 8). His first task, necessarily, was to work out methods for himself. After devoting his first semester of English A to *The Education of Henry Adams,* he spent his second semester reading a selection of poems from a poetry anthology, plus a novel and a couple of plays, one of which he thinks was by Shaw. In 1928, Baird was hired for a second year at Amherst College, and during that year he married Frances Titchener (whom he calls Bertie). The following year, he was not only rehired at Amherst, he was promoted to the rank of assistant professor. At some point in these early years, he began experimenting with autobiographical writing assignments. In 1931, he published an anthology of selections from Henry Adams, Marcel Proust, and others concerning the experience of childhood and youth. Entitled *The First Years: Selections from Autobiography,* it is the only book Baird has ever published.

Its introductory pedagogical essay reveals much about his early thinking on the teaching of composition and makes a strong case for asking students to write from experience. This introductory essay also gives an indication of Baird's classroom methods at around the time of its publication. Baird reported he began each new year by asking his students to read several brief autobiographical selections of the sort he had included in *The First Years,* plus parts of *The Education of Henry Adams,* of *Father and Son,* and of the *Autobiography of John Stuart Mill.* Each student then had to write about these readings, "not Book Reports however," but papers "in which he considers the method of autobiographical writing and in which he makes some judgments of its success" (1931, 10). During the last month of the course, each student was required to write an extended autobiography. Baird insisted that his course was not merely a course in autobiography, but was a course in writing (10–11). He concluded that

> In the process of writing autobiographically the student ought to make some interesting discoveries about himself. . . . This self-discovery, intimately connected with the processes of writing, furnishes the student with present proof that the art of writing is more closely connected with straight thinking than it is with rules and rhetorics, and that it may have value and importance for its own sake. (22–23)

Roger Sale, who taught at Amherst from 1957 to 1962 and who has spoken to me at length about the course, told me in 1991 that he had recently reread Baird's introduction to *The First Years*. He said, "I was just struck—I had read that before, when I was here in Amherst—by how clear Baird was in 1931 about things which I was only beginning to learn in 1958 and which an awful lot of our colleagues don't know now."

In his introduction to *The First Years*, Baird stated that he intended his book to serve as a textbook "for a course in the writing of English" (1). Its method was to direct "the student's attention to his own resources of experience," and Baird hoped it might "help the student to remember his own past experience and to convey that experience in writing" (1). Noting that the use "of the student's experience as subject matter for his writing has been for many years a conventional device of the teacher of composition," Baird refrained from claiming that his book or its approach offered anything that would seem particularly new (1). What he did claim was that by attacking "the problem of writing with subject matter rather than form as the end in view," his approach would engage the interest of students.[3] He explained dryly that no student writing about his experience could, "except by admitting his own deficiencies as a human being, ascribe his lack of interest in his subjects to his opinion that they are dull and uninspiring" (1).

Baird went on to list what were then the other common approaches to the teaching of writing and to give his objections to each. The first of these was to drill the student "in diction, syllabication, letter writing, and the correction of faulty sentences," with the aim of cultivating what Baird saw as "an artificial and academic standard of 'correctness'" (1931, 2). Another, which he ascribed to John Franklin Genung, his nineteenth century predecessor at Amherst College, was to provide the student with sample essays for imitation, arranging these so as to illustrate either such rhetorical properties as "ease, force, and unity" (2) or the various modes of exposition (4). Still another was to introduce "a tricky numbering system," whereby "not only is the 'comma-splice' bad English, but it is to be remembered as error number 91b" (2). In Baird's view, the problem with all these approaches was that they attempted to come at writing by means of principles and forms rather than content (2). He argued that "if at college age a student has not learned how to spell *receive,* how to punctuate, how to write sentences of greater complexity than those of [sensationalistic journalist] Arthur Brisbane, he has so successfully resisted the pressure of former teachers that he ought to be considered immune and be allowed the precious privilege of discovering these intricacies for himself" (5). "Let the student find out by experiment and observation some of the qualities of good writing," he advised, "and the memorized characteristics of exposition are unimportant" (11).

Speaking from his vantage point at an elite New England college at a time when a relatively small proportion of the nation's population enjoyed access to higher education, Baird noted that

> After all the nearly illiterate student is not the problem in college courses in composition. The real problem is the student who with painfully spidery handwriting completes his assignment of three hundred words without a word to spare and without positive errors or positive virtues, the student whose imagination and interest have never been aroused by anything so tenuous as the art of writing. (1931, 5)

Baird added that the student's interest would not easily be aroused by such writing topics as "My Philosophy of Life, What I Think of Bertrand Russell, How Public Utilities Should Be Financed, My Religion, How I Think the United States Senate Should Be Reformed" (1931, 3). In response to such topics, students were all too likely to produce what Baird called the "Perfect Theme," with its introduction, three body paragraphs, and conclusion (3–4). He warned, however, that it was not enough for the teacher who hoped to avoid the tedium of reading endless "Perfect Themes" simply to assign autobiographical topics. The teacher must also give a student "training in remembering, encouragement in looking objectively at his relations with his family and friends, and most of all guidance in distinguishing the significant from the insignificant memory" (6). To a student's anecdote of a camping trip in the Adirondacks, the teacher should ask, "What of it?" so that the student might "look at that camping experience in an entirely different manner" (6). Only when the student had ascertained his purpose, could he successfully run orders through chaos and make sense of his experience.

Sixty years after publishing *The First Years,* Baird told me that his idea of making childhood memories the focus for a writing course had grown largely out of his reading of Proust. I knew from having read his introduction to *The First Years* that Baird regarded *A la recherche du temps perdu* as a model of perfection in autobiographical writing, showing "just how well the human memory can work" (1931, 20). Baird told me he had read Proust and thought, "Here's a subject for them; have them write about their childhood memories." When I asked him why this had seemed a worthwhile approach, he explained, "It always seemed to me that the most interesting thing about teaching was to see if you could move a student so he wanted to express himself. This is where it all began for me, and all that happened in English 1–2 was just techniques to try to arrive at this wonderful relationship where a student feels a desire to express himself, to express something, and not just to write a theme."

I interviewed Professor Baird twice, both times in his home, once in November of 1990 and once in May of 1991, three months after he had celebrated his ninetieth birthday. I found him a spectacularly intimidating personality, still imposing in both stature and carriage, with a prominent, bulldog thrust to his lower jaw. The first thing he said to me in November was, "I hope you have questions; otherwise this will be a waste of time." Despite this frosty greeting, he invited me into the living room of his home (which, because it is the only Frank Lloyd Wright house in Massachusetts, is a distinct part of his persona), ensconced himself in a deep leather chair, bade me sit opposite him, and lit a cigarette.

Theodore Baird in 1986 outside his home.

Although he continued to display his gruff manner and to smoke one cigarette after another, he also revealed a dry wit, a disarming flare for self-mockery, and a ready excitability. At the close of our session, he said, "I find the course arouses a great deal of emotion in me still."

In Baird's account, most of his own significant actions were in fact reactions against what others were doing or saying. He claims he formulated his teaching methods largely in rebellion against what his own teachers had done at Hobart and Harvard, against what he saw his senior colleagues doing at Amherst, and against the notion that an English department "should be teaching spelling, it should be teaching good English." Despite the fact that he had studied with Irving Babbitt while at Harvard and the fact that he has acknowledged learning a vocabulary from Babbitt with which to discuss those areas of experience that "could be talked about" (1978b, 11), Baird was short with me when I asked him about his education and indicated my interest in pursuing questions of influence. He told me, "Teachers for me were people I reacted against."

He added, "That doesn't mean that I didn't borrow a lot of the ideas for English 1–2, but I was not anybody's disciple." Later, when I suggested that he may have been influenced negatively by his teachers and senior colleagues, or repelled from them on a course of his own, he said, "Oh, yes! That [kind of influence] is discussed in *Henry Adams;* he calls it 'Negative Force.'" One of Baird's chief criticisms of his senior colleagues at Amherst was that they never talked to one another, except at cocktail parties. His opposing idea, which he says was "all I really had in mind for English 1–2 and all I ever had," was that a group of teachers involved in a common enterprise "should try to establish a conversation" (1978b, 7, 23).

Baird's senior colleagues during his early years at Amherst were George Whicher, Roy Elliott, and David Morton. In the tape he made for the Amherst College Oral History Project, Baird paints relatively unflattering portraits of all three of them, though he says he respected Whicher and Elliott. Whicher is remembered chiefly now for his 1938 biography of Emily Dickinson, *This Was a Poet.* He was a graduate of Amherst College and was, according to Baird, the most conventional and academic of Baird's three seniors. Baird says Whicher was a cultivated man and an orderly teacher. He was a man "you could talk 'books' with," but "temperamentally he was not given to speech." He gave well-organized lectures on literary history. Elliott had taught previously at Bowdoin and had written one of the first academic essays on Robert Frost. He had come to Amherst with the understanding that he would not be required to do much teaching and would be free instead to write. He taught a course on Shakespeare for several years, but eventually handed it over to Baird, which Baird says "was a great mistake on his part and a great opportunity for me."[4] He says Elliott was a high Episcopalian and "very interested, as in the old days of the College, in the spiritual life of his students." He was paid more than either Whicher or Morton, which made for ill feelings among the three of them. Morton was a football player and a boxer, interested according to Baird in "demonstrating that he was very much a manly man." He was also a poet, and according to Baird, "wrote really lovely poems, technically exquisitely done, the most delicate sentiment." Baird says Morton preferred Sara Teasdale and Edna Millay to *The Wasteland.* Morton's title for his course on modern poetry was "Moods of the World Today," which Baird says "created a good deal of hilarity among the faculty who didn't particularly go for that sort of talk." Morton's purpose, according to Baird, was to show "the rather philistine Amherst student that there was beauty in the world." In Baird's opinion, pleasing Morton "wasn't hard for some primitive Deke or whatnot and he could always say, 'Yes, I, too, have known beauty. Dave Morton introduced me to it.'" Baird concludes, "It's easy to laugh at this, and I do" (1978b, 2–5, 7).

Baird's younger colleague, Walker Gibson, characterizes Baird as a "fighter" and says he often antagonized others needlessly. Gibson told me there was no reason why Baird should have had difficulties with Whicher, for example. According to Gibson, Baird could have made Whicher an ally.

Baird, however, says he was dismayed to see that his seniors never asked one another what they thought they were doing as teachers. According to Baird, no one ever asked Morton, for example, why he was teaching Sara Teasdale or why he dismissed his classes early, as he frequently did. Baird says, "I had no idea what the other teachers were doing except by accident; you'd pick up the information that so and so is now reading drama or something. But we never had a meeting in which we confessed and said: 'I'm going to do this, this year'" (1978b, 5–8). One year, however, under pressure from the Instruction Committee and President Stanley King, Whicher got the several men who were teaching freshman English to agree on a common reading list. Baird remembers that everyone agreed to read the "Prologue" and "The Pardoner's Tale" from *The Canterbury Tales,* and *Lycidas, Don Juan,* and several works by Shakespeare and Boswell (1939, 326; 1978b, 9). However, when it came time to address the problem of making an examination for the freshmen, Baird says it proved impossible to agree on a common set of questions "since each one of us was using this reading for his own peculiar purpose. . . . [W]e could not even agree as to whether it was a course in reading or in writing, or what the proportion of one was to the other" (1939, 326). Whicher's compromise was to devise an examination form on which "each instructor's questions were listed separately, so that you had 'Professor Baird's students will answer the following questions,' and so on." Baird says, "I found this very disheartening. It seemed to me that this was not a common examination at all. It was a common piece of paper that was handed out to all the freshmen" (1978b, 10).

Left, *Theodore Baird;* center, *Armour Craig;* right, *Robert Frost in 1958.*

In addition to Whicher, Elliott, and Morton, a fourth figure who was already an important presence in the English department and on the Amherst campus when Baird arrived was Robert Frost. Frost was associated with the college intermittently from 1917 until his death in 1963, sometimes as a member of the regular faculty, sometimes as a visiting lecturer. He held a full professorship at the college from 1926 to 1938, but the terms of his appointment required him to be in residence only for ten weeks of each academic year (Pritchard 1984, 174). His published prose from this period—especially his 1929 "Preface" to *A Way Out,* his 1931 "Education by Poetry," and his 1935 "Letter to the *Amherst Student*"—expresses ideas that were echoed in English 1–2. His "The Figure a Poem Makes," which first appeared in 1939, does so as well. I can only speculate as to the nature of Frost's influence upon Baird, but several of the younger men who taught English 1–2 have acknowledged a considerable debt to Frost.

"Education by Poetry," originally delivered as a lecture at Amherst College and then published in the *Amherst Graduate's Quarterly,* is now available in *Selected Prose of Robert Frost* (1949,

33–46). Early in the essay, Frost explains his title, declaring that "education by poetry is education by metaphor" (35). He then argues that metaphor is at the root of all education and all thinking, including scientific thinking. Darwin's model of evolution, for example, is an extended metaphor (38–39). The Heisenberg paradox, whereby one cannot know the speed and position of a particle with equal accuracy, results from trying to mix metaphors (37–38). Still another metaphor, the one equating the universe with a machine, is useful in some respects but breaks down in others, as when one asks whether the universe is driven by an operator (40–41). We use metaphors, Frost says, every time we say "one thing in terms of another." Equating one thing with another, or "just putting this and that together," is what it means to think. Frost notes, however, that although teachers often aim at teaching their students to think, they seldom tell students what thinking means (41).

Baird and the members of his staff may not have told their students what thinking means, but they regularly phrased assignments in such a way as to move students to put things together or to say one thing in terms of another. Robert Bagg, an alumnus of the course, told me that an examination of metaphor was "one of the centers of English 1," and Baird himself has acknowledged that metaphor sometimes seemed to be its central preoccupation (1978b, 28). Historian Ann Berthoff says that men who taught English 1–2 and alumni of the course can be identified by their use of the term "metaphor" in a manner that she says reflects the thinking of I. A. Richards (Berthoff 1985, 72) but which may more directly reflect that of Robert Frost. Baird's own indebtedness to Frost is suggested by the fact that he published a 1946 essay on "Darwin and the Tangled Bank," in which he discussed, in much more detail than Frost had done in "Education by Poetry," Darwin's creation of the metaphors of the struggle for existence and of the survival of the fittest (Baird 1946, 481, 483).

At the close of "Education by Poetry," Frost linked the impulse to create metaphors with the imperative for forming order out of chaos. "The lost soul," he claimed, "is the man who gets lost in his material without a gathering metaphor to throw it into shape and order" (1949, 41). Frost spoke of "order" and "chaos" again in his 1935 "Letter to *The Amherst Student*."[5] In this "Letter," Frost suggested that the background of human life is "hugeness and confusion shading away from where we stand into black and utter chaos" (reprinted in Frost 1949, 107). Against this background, one might counterpose "any small man-made figure of order and concentration," such as a poem (107). In "The Figure a Poem Makes," however, Frost observed that no poem could offer more than "a momentary stay against confusion" (reprinted in Frost 1949, 18).

Although Frost was twenty-seven years older than Baird, Walker Gibson remembers that the two were great friends. Baird remembers an afternoon in 1937 when he was on sabbatical leave from Amherst College, when Frost was visiting him and Mrs. Baird in their temporary home in Missouri, and when he and Frost stood side by side, throwing stones into the Mississippi River. Gibson says, however, that Frost dismissed English 1–2 as "kid stuff" (1985, 148). When I asked Baird about Frost and in particular about Frost's practice of reading with "the ear of the imagination," he replied, "I am not in the least interested in talking about whether we owed a debt to Frost when we talked about 'voice.' I don't think I ever did; why should I?" (letter to R.Varnum, March 16, 1991).

William Pritchard, who is both an Amherst alumnus and an Amherst faculty member, remembers "Baird reading aloud a soliloquy from *Hamlet* in a rather self-consciously loud, deliberately unactorish way, yet one that was scrupulously observant of the syntax and sense of the lines," and Pritchard contends that behind Baird's performance "was the example of Frost" (1991, 128–129). Frost had declared in 1929, in his "Preface to *A Way Out,*" that "everything written is as good as it is dramatic," that writing is "drama or nothing," and that any passage of prose or poetry worth a reader's attention would necessarily have "the speaking tone of voice somehow entangled in the words and fastened to the page for the ear of the imagination" (reprinted in Frost, 1949, 13–14). According to Pritchard, Frost's view "of the primacy of voice in poetry was the cornerstone of what theorizing he did about the act and the art of reading" (1991, 129). Pritchard tells me, moreover, that Frost's influence on the Amherst College English department is "pervasive." In "Ear Training," he says his own education at Amherst, both in English 1–2 and in subsequent literature courses, "was essentially a training in ear reading, whether the bit of writing under scrutiny was (as it often was) a lyric of Frost's, or the opening of Henry James's *Portrait of a Lady* . . . or one of the unwittingly fatuous sentences I turned out in my papers. Do you want to sound like *that?* was the direct or implied question we were invited to put to our own prose" (130). It seems to me that echoes of Frost's views on voice may be found in various assignment sequences for English 1–2, most notably in Baird's sequence for the fall of 1960, and that attention to voice, like attention to metaphor, was one of the centers of the course. In assignment 11 of the fall 1960 sequence, for example, Baird asked students:

> What tone of voice do you assume for writing a theme? What attitude toward your subject do you adopt in order to talk this way? Why is this an easy attitude to adopt? Where do you hear this tone of voice?[6]

And in assignment 23, he told them:

> In the last few assignments you have been asked to characterize a writer's "voice," to construct a personality for the character you "hear talking" in a piece of writing. Suppose you now try doing this with your own work.[6]

In addition to those in Baird's fall 1960 assignments, other echoes of Frost may be found in Pritchard's "Ear Training," in Reuben Brower's chapter on "The Speaking Voice" in *The Fields of Light* (1951), in Walker Gibson's analysis of tough, sweet, and stuffy voices in *Tough, Sweet, and Stuffy* (1966), in William Coles's account of a classroom discussion of "voice" in *The Plural I* (1988a, 20–22), and in Roger Sale's suggestion in *On Writing* that teachers ask their students, "Why do you want to talk that way?" (1970, 49).

William Pritchard told me that, although Frost's influence is difficult to pin down, the poet informally "dropped the kind of hints or used ways of talking that got assimilated, maybe sometimes almost unconsciously into exercises and teaching matters." Roger Sale, who taught at Amherst from 1957 to 1962, told me that "I found myself in the years since I left Amherst saying sometimes, 'Frost was greater than Baird'; sometimes I said, 'Baird was greater than Frost.' I go back and forth on that, but they are very much alike." John Cameron, another former member of Baird's staff, told me that "to my mind, Frost epitomized the heritage of American, nonsystematic thought in which English 1–2 was grounded." Cameron, I believe, gets at something which is larger than either Baird or Frost, which was no doubt characteristic at that time of small, liberal arts colleges like Amherst and which expresses itself in a distrust of systems, tidy summations, plodding scholarship, and, for that matter, simple-minded studies of influence. The heritage that Cameron has identified is reflected in Frost's and Baird's wit, in Baird's tough-minded pragmatism, in his idiosyncrasy, and in his fascination with puzzles and paradoxes.

Although several of the men I spoke with, including Cameron, Pritchard, and most notably Armour Craig, talked to me at length on the subject of the course's intellectual context, Theodore Baird seemed to me to be reluctant to consider questions of this type. An alumnus told me he had found English 1–2 to be curiously "ahistorical" in that those who led it had tended to dismiss the notion that different approaches to teaching and learning are historically situated. This tendency may have stemmed from the heritage of nonsystematic thought in which Cameron says the course was rooted. Or it may have derived from the New Criticism, which was the dominant critical methodology during the period of English 1–2 and which explicitly denied the importance of a text's external context. But whatever the cause, Baird has dismissed suggestions that English 1–2 grew out of any particular school of literary or philosophical thought. He has insisted, "It was homemade; that's the truth of the matter, and it was no better, no worse than we could make it at home." He added, "I was no philosopher. I never have been able to keep my mind on a piece of philosophical writing; I have tried. Armour Craig was good at this; he knew names, and he knew what the philosophers stood for. Regularly we would hear from someone that this [English 1–2] was logical positivism, and indeed I had read Ayer's book, but this seemed to me, and it still seems to me, wide of the mark." To the suggestion that the course owed something to Wittgenstein, Baird retorted, "I never, I think ever, read a word of Wittgenstein, and whatever connection there was there, I don't know" (1978b, 30).

On the other hand, Baird has acknowledged the influence not only of Henry Adams and of Marcel Proust, as I have noted, but also that of Harvard's Nobel Prize-winning physicist Percy Bridgman (letter to R. Varnum, December 8, 1990). Bridgman's name generally featured prominently on the lists of suggested readings[7] Baird circulated from time to time to his staff. One such list, from May 24, 1947, includes citations to works by Bridgman and by R. G. Collingwood, C. C. Fries, S. I. Hayakawa, William James, Alfred Korzybski, Irving J. Lee, C. K. Ogden, and I. A. Richards, among others. Another, circulated in April of 1946, has citations to Ogden and Richards's *The Meaning of Meaning,* Richards's *Interpretation in Teaching,* Korzybski's *Science and Sanity*, Hayakawa's *Language in Action,* Bridgman's *The Logic of Modern Physics,* and James's *Pragmatism.*

But despite their giving me an idea of what Baird was reading at particular times, these lists may not reflect the intellectual experience of his staff. Baird told me, "I used to give out a reading list, but I think only Armour Craig ever read it." Several of the former members of Baird's staff told me they made little use of Baird's lists. Gibson said he had "read a little Bridgman at least," but "very little Korzybski." Sale said he had resisted the notion "that if I just read Auguste Comte, for example, or Wittgenstein, I would finally understand what the assignments were about." Cameron said that other than some Richards and some Hayakawa, "I never read the works on Baird's lists." Cameron explained that "one of the reasons I didn't read them was that in more immediate conversation, Baird would tend to deny that there was any specific influence behind the course, which was a way of denying his own relationship to authority, which denial always has been troubling to me. He embodied authority and yet denied that he did embody it or that authority played any role."

But even if only a few members of Baird's staff, such as Gibson, actually read Bridgman, it seems clear that, through Baird, Bridgman exerted a considerable influence upon English 1–2. Bridgman was the originator of the concept of the "operational definition," whereby words are to be defined in terms of operations whose results can be measured. In one account of the operational definition, Julienne Ford has explained that "a hypothesis like 'Those rabbits will be afraid' is regarded as meaningless. However, the statement 'Those rabbits will be seen to be emitting more fecal boluses per hour than is normal for rabbits' is perfectly meaningful as far as Bridgman and his men are concerned" (1975, vol. 1, 149).

In another account, Amherst College alumnus Charles Kay Smith has observed that "until the late philosopher of science, Percy Bridgman, made popular the term *operational definition* in 1938 to explain Einstein's procedure in defining the concept of simultaneity by describing simple, measurable operations, it did not occur to researchers outside the sciences to define their terms measurably" (1974, 198). Bridgman himself, in an essay which appeared originally in 1950 and which Walker Gibson later reprinted in his *Seeing and Writing* (1959, 148–157), noted that Einstein's work with relativity phenomena had led to the realization that "the common sense meanings" of such physical terms "as length and time were not sharp enough to serve in the new physical situations" and that in order to sharpen meaning it was necessary "to specify the operations which were involved in concrete instances in applying the term" (148). Bridgman contended that adopting the "operational attitude toward meanings" would entail seeing "the world in terms of activities rather than in terms of things" (153). Bridgman added that "the most revolutionary of the insights to be derived from our recent experiments in physics" was

> the insight that it is impossible to transcend the human reference point.... The new insight comes from a realization that the structure of nature may eventually be such that our processes of thought do not correspond to it sufficiently to permit us to think about it at all.... We are now approaching a bound beyond which we are forever estopped from pushing our inquiries, not by the construction of the world, but by the construction of ourselves. The world fades out and eludes us because it becomes meaningless. We cannot even express this in the way we would like. (157)

Bridgman's position has been described as one of radical empiricism and as highly critical of the ways language is encumbered with metaphysical assumptions. And yet it seems to me that the philosophical center of Bridgman's thinking is not so much a hope of purifying language or of seeing things as they are more clearly as it is an acknowledgment of the impossibility of transcending the human reference point. Bridgman's insight leads naturally to the further insight that human reality is a human construction. It is *an* order, not *the* order.

Bridgman's influence on English 1–2 can be detected in the many assignments which called on Amherst freshmen to define their terms operationally and to explain step by step what they had done to reach a particular conclusion. Bridgman's influence can also be seen in Baird's 1952 account of "The Freshman English Course," in which Baird reported that

> we try to put the student in the position where he will see for himself what his subject may be and how this subject can be talked about as an order. For example, when the student writes about his activities as a historian he may begin with something as apparently remote as his memories of his own grandfather and then by taking describable steps he translates his personal recollections into statements about American history. Or he may begin his account of his activities as a scientist by reading the instruments in the campus weather station and again by taking describable steps make a larger statement which might be called scientific. Our art as teachers lies in finding examples so simple that when we talk about them we are reasonably sure that we are all talking about the same action. (195–196)

Bridgman's influence can also be detected in Baird's concern with the limits of language or, as he sometimes phrased it, the "inexpressible." This concern, more than either the concerns with metaphor or with voice, both of which it subsumes, seems to have lain at the very center of Baird's thinking and of English 1–2. Baird spoke frequently about the dichotomy between the expressible and inexpressible and sometimes linked it to parallel dichotomies between the public and the private, between sense and nonsense, or between order and chaos. The "inexpressible" seems for him to have represented that chaos beyond the point at which, as Bridgman said, "the world fades out" and human inquiry becomes meaningless. Within the bounds of human reality, which both Baird and Bridgman saw as narrow, language could serve as a means for creating order. The challenge for any speaker or writer, and certainly for the teachers and students in English 1–2, was— through operational definition, metaphoric extension, the adjustment of voice, and other measures—to extend the limits of language and invent new ways of organizing the world.

Many of the assignments used over the years in English 1–2 asked students to confront their own limitations as language users. Assignment 12 of a series Baird wrote for the fall of 1948 asked students to "Locate the point where you reach your Speechless Level about the following: Russia, Boogie-Woogie, Burial Customs among the Carthaginians, the Feudal System, Trigonometry, Proper Dress for an Amherst student."[8] Assignment 16 of a series used in the fall of 1956 asked students to

> Select from your recent experience at Amherst an example where a question was asked and an answer was given and you were more than ordinarily concerned. Do not take the first that occurs to you but consider how your example may be written up, what you (or any writer) can make of it. Your example may be taken from your conversation between classes, in the dormitory, and so on, or from the classroom, laboratory, playing field. It should show you when you were unable to express what you wanted to say. This does not mean that you remained silent. You may have talked a good deal. Yet you were never able to say what you wanted to say.
>
> a) Tell what happened in the form of an anecdote writing out this dramatic situation, answering the usual questions, who, what, where, how, why.
>
> b) What does it mean to say, "I talked but I was unable to say what I wanted to say"?[9]

Assignment 33 of a series that John Butler wrote for the fall of 1958 asked students to

> Reflect on the "power" you have as a user of language. You have been writing for several weeks about what language cannot do, about the inexpressible, about the unexpressed, about your own limitations as a speaker and writer, about the inadequacies of various systems. Now look once more at the other side of it. What power do you have as a user of language? What is so amazing about it? Do not search your memory for a perfunctory answer to these questions; consider them freshly, by looking once again at yourself as you go through a day, by looking at the people and things you see around you. What evidence do you see as you look within and around you of the astonishing power of language?[10]

Baird wrote to me about the inexpressible in a letter that I have reproduced in Appendix C. He said:

> I think the course over the years at least for me developed the capacity to stand outside a problem, to see it as a matter of how language is used, of what language can do in solving it. How much of experience anyway, can be expressed in language? Five per cent? What about in music? In other symbols? What then was the 95 per cent unexpressed? Can you be aware of that while talking and writing? What does the awareness of the inexpressible do to your own conviction in what you are saying? Will you, say, die for these words? No? Then What? Here we fade off in each one's belief. And will. I used to try to say, finally, *I exert my WILL.* I'm, say, patriotic, finally. Not reasonable I know. Lots of faults.
>
> I wonder if I am saying something about the unsayable? This was for me the heart of my teaching. I say this in so many ways. (Letter to R. Varnum, December 6, 1990)

What I construe Baird to be saying here, although he says it in such a way as to mock both himself and human nature, is that the human condition entails a perpetual struggle with the chaos that individuals encounter both within and outside themselves. In order to see anything or do anything purposefully, individuals must draw upon the tools available to them, of which language is one, and try to determine the relationship between their will and their problem. With an effort of will, they may succeed in finding a language to suit their purpose. I accept Baird's statement that a focus on the limits of language and on the relation of the expressible to the inexpressible was at the heart of the approach which he gradually developed to the teaching of writing. That approach, as I have been characterizing it, also included asking students to write from experience, asking them to formulate operational definitions, and pushing them both to recognize and to employ a wider range of metaphors and voices. I have been arguing that Percy Bridgman, Robert Frost, and Henry Adams provided important pieces of the intellectual context for this approach. But there is another very important part of that context which I have not yet discussed, and that is the part provided by Amherst College itself. I suspect that

Baird's concern with free will, with human limitations, and with order and chaos has roots in Calvinist doctrine.

Baird's relation to the traditions of Amherst College is as difficult to characterize as his relations to Frost, Bridgman, or Adams. On the one hand, Baird has claimed that English 1–2 "was in the best tradition of Amherst and Amherst has had a long tradition of teaching. I think that you could look back and find one man after another who was concerned about how you reach a class" (1978b, 31). On the other hand, when I pressed him for details about this teaching tradition, he replied, "Teaching is a mystery. Nobody knows how to teach. Nobody knows how to learn. I suppose there is a tradition that exists somewhere, but it doesn't exist in the minds of very many people." And when I asked him whether he thought he had inherited a tradition from Amherst's distinguished professor of rhetoric, John Franklin Genung, Baird said, "I think it would be very hard to trace local influences, back to Genung, back to George Whicher, except by reaction. No one wants to do what his predecessor, his teachers did. You get forgotten in five minutes flat" (letter to R. Varnum, December 8, 1990). And in "A Dry and Thirsty Land," an essay which Baird published in 1978, ten years after his retirement, and which seems as much an expression of perplexity about his own place in history as a reflection on his connection to nineteenth century predecessors in the Rhetoric Room at Amherst College, Baird wrote:

> As for the past, it is not only dead, it is stupid. So even though you may feel the past is just within your reach while standing where others have stood, while teaching where others have taught, there is also the strong awareness that any sense of a tradition in teaching is simple egotism. Teaching—and learning?— has no history, at least when places like the Rhetoric Room are considered. (1978a, 81)

The "Rhetoric Room," located in Amherst's 1827 Johnson Chapel building, had served throughout much of the nineteenth century as a place both for the delivery of student declamations and for prayer meetings. Amherst College itself had been founded in 1821 by orthodox Congregationalists who, acting under the conviction that the establishment of a college was the surest method for "civilizing and evangelizing the world," had hoped to provide "for the Classical Education of indigent young men of piety and talents, for the Christian Ministry."[11] Noah Webster played a leading role in the founding of the new college, and so did Samuel Fowler Dickinson, the grandfather of Emily Dickinson. According to Amherst historian Thomas Le Duc, Amherst's founding fathers intended the college to serve as an alternative both to Williams College, whose location in the Berkshire hills of far western Massachusetts they perceived as too isolated, and to Harvard, which they perceived as a hotbed of Unitarianism (1946, 4–5).

Baird himself, in "A Dry and Thirsty Land," has written about the founding and early history of Amherst College. His essay is interesting both for its historic details and for its expression of Baird's views on the combativeness of human nature. He says that nearly all those who involved themselves in the founding of Amherst College "were Calvinists, and they could fight bitterly" (1978a, 109). He says that their quarrels were local and relatively insignificant but nevertheless demonstrated

> the surging energy of the human will. A single agent, with the support of those who more or less share his determination, strives with all his might to impose his will on others, and he does this for their own good so that they will conform to his idea of what they ought to be and are not. Immediately, as if by the release of a spring, other wills are set in opposition. (134–135)

Baird reports on several conflicts which interfered with the establishment of Amherst College, including the quarrel between the First and Second Congregational churches of Amherst and other quarrels within the First Church, whose parishioners, despite their differences, took a leading role in financing and building the college. According to Baird, when the first college building was completed on the hilltop south of the Amherst Town Common, only some forty houses existed within a mile of the center of town, and woods stretched in every direction (1978a, 83). The sermon preached at the dedication of this first building was entitled "A Plea for a Miserable World" and purported that

> This college was to be unlike any other: here an education could
> be had free of expense to those who would enter the gospel
> ministry. And this ministry was to bring joy to the destitute and
> hope and salvation to perishing millions. Such was the language
> used. (83)

Baird, who himself more than a century later exercised considerable authority over students, reports that the instructional staff of the fledgling college consisted of a "small number of ministers" who "became professors, exercising intellectual, spiritual, and paternal authority over a few green and ignorant country boys" (1978a, 83). These boys in their turn became ministers and missionaries. One of Amherst's early graduates died in the cause of Christ and became known as "the Martyr of Sumatra" (83).

Amherst historian Theodore Greene reports that one half of all Amherst graduates before 1860 entered the ministry, and he says that, in the early days of the college, "students rose at 4:45 a.m. for morning prayers and two recitations before breakfast" (1992, 5, 9). Student enrollments grew from 47 in 1821 to 252 in 1836, by which time Amherst was the second largest college in New England, behind Yale, but ahead of Harvard, Dartmouth, and Williams (4, 14). By 1883, Amherst had 321 students and, after Harvard's, the second fastest rate of enrollment growth in New England (Peterson 1964, 69). During the first four decades of Amherst's history, the curriculum at the college was entirely fixed, and although in 1827, in one of the first faculty-initiated curricular reports in American higher education, Professor Jacob Abbott proposed a parallel curriculum which would both have introduced courses in the pure and applied sciences and substituted courses in English literature and the modern languages for the established courses in Latin and Greek, the trustees of Amherst College elected not to fund Abbott's proposal (Rudolph 1977, 83–84; Babb et al. 1978, 3). Electives were not introduced at Amherst to any significant degree until the 1876–1890 administration of President Julius H. Seelye (Babb et al., 3). Although Harvard removed Greek as an entrance and graduation requirement in 1886 (Rudolph, 186), Amherst retained both Latin and Greek as graduation requirements until 1900, after which date students were required to study only one or the other of these ancient languages (Le Duc 1946, 64n).

The responsibility for teaching the collective subjects of rhetoric, oratory, and English literature at Amherst College devolved upon the tenant of a single professorial chair until the 1880s, during which decade an English department began to emerge. By 1885, the fledgling department was staffed by three individuals, one of whom, John Franklin Genung, was responsible for teaching rhetoric.[12] Genung, who taught at Amherst College from 1882 to 1917, was unlike most of the men hired there before 1890 in not having graduated from the college. But like one third of his colleagues, he had received graduate training in Germany, and like the majority of them, he was an ordained minister (Le Duc 1946, 49–50). I consider Genung the most significant of Baird's predecessors in Amherst's "Rhetoric Room."

Genung, along with Adams Sherman Hill and Barrett Wendell of Harvard and Fred Newton Scott of the University of Michigan, has been identified by composition historian Albert Kitzhaber as one of the "big four" who, through their authorship and publication of rhetoric textbooks, did the most to shape the theory and practice of composition teaching in the final third of the nineteenth century (1953, 97). Genung (like Hill, Wendell, and Scott) belonged to the academic generation which, partly as the result of a rapid proliferation of print media, experienced the shift from a predominantly oral rhetoric to the rhetoric of written expression. Genung reported in an 1887 pamphlet on *The Study of Rhetoric* that "English instruction is groping for a method" (9), and I would guess that his primary motive for writing textbooks, several of which were first printed in the shop of the local Amherst newspaper, was to supply materials for his own classes. Genung's textbooks included most notably his *Practical Elements of Rhetoric,* published by Ginn & Company in 1886, and the revised and expanded version of the same text issued in 1901 as *The Working Principles of Rhetoric.* According to one historian, the popularity of Genung's textbooks "may partly be inferred by the length of their publication: his shorter rhetoric was kept in print by Ginn & Company until 1931, and the longer one until 1942" (Rockas 1981, 56). Kitzhaber attributes the popularity of *Practical Elements* to its "well-planned organization" and says that the book "is perhaps one of the most systematically ordered textbooks on rhetoric ever written" (1953, 107).

In addition to the *Practical Elements* and the *Working Principles,* Genung published a *Handbook of Rhetorical Analysis* in 1889 and *Outlines of Rhetoric* in 1893. The former, an early example of a rhetorical reader, provides a selection of exemplary essays for students to analyze. The latter, an early example of what would now be called a rhetorical handbook, includes a list of 125 numbered rules for correct grammar, punctuation, and usage. In *The First Years,* as I have already noted, Baird made fun of Genung for his "tricky numbering system" (1931, 2). Baird also wrote a series of assignments for the fall of 1963 in which he invited his students to examine the elitist assumptions underlying Genung's concern with correctness (see Gibson 1985, 143).

Genung was a teacher as well as a writer of textbooks. In an obituary piece for the *Dictionary of American Biography,* Genung's student, George Whicher, reported that Genung was "always the gentlest of teachers" and that "his classes were both a haven of refuge for the unthinking many and a source of lasting inspiration for the few students capable of appreciating his fine scholarship and rich stores of wisdom" (1931, 211). Genung himself, in an 1894 article on "English at Amherst College," describes the yearlong elective course in rhetoric he offered to sophomores. The first two terms of this three-term course were devoted to the study of rhetorical principles, the application of these principles in written exercises, and the analysis of exemplary essays. The third term was given to the writing of essays, which students were required to present at the rate of once every fortnight. Genung reports that he met each of his students in conference to give "careful individual criticism" to their essays (55). According to Genung, one of the "interesting and novel features" of the course was "the setting up in type of many of the students' written productions and the reading and criticism of them in proof" (55). In his 1887 pamphlet on *The Study of Rhetoric,* Genung describes additional features of his course, including a system of in-class publications, which seems to have been very much like the system later employed in English 1–2. Noting that he liked to provide students with the "opportunity to estimate and criticize each other's work" (25), he reported that during the third term he regularly gave the first hour of each two-hour class period to the reading and criticism of essays and exercise pieces his students had written. Over the course of the term, every student in the class had his work subjected to this kind of treatment. Before each class meeting, Genung selected four or five representative papers from those he had most recently looked over, then he read them aloud in class, without identifying their student authors or telling them beforehand that their papers would be published. After reading a paper, Genung invited students to criticize it on such points as "faithfulness to fact, vividness, consistency, and . . . style" (29–30). Years later in the writing course Baird directed, instructors also selected and published anonymous specimens of student writing, but unlike Genung, these instructors had the advantage of a mimeograph machine.

There was one outstanding difference between Genung's course and the one Baird later directed: Genung's course was elective and Baird's was not. In his 1894 article on "English at Amherst College," Genung had declared that "as a required study in the midst of electives, English is at a disadvantage; the very fact that it is compulsory weights it with an odium which in many colleges makes it the bugbear of the course" (54). His method of dealing with this "disadvantage" had been to decline to teach those students who did not freely elect his course. Baird, by contrast, seems to have been happy when the course he directed was designated as a universal requirement. This may indicate that he was a stronger teacher than Genung or that his will was stronger.

Baird never knew Genung. The older man had died in 1919, eight years before Baird came to Amherst College. Although Baird's senior colleague, George Whicher, had been a student of Genung's, Baird told me that he never heard Whicher mention his former teacher (letter to R. Varnum, December 8, 1990). It is quite possible, therefore, that the apparent similarity between Genung's system of in-class publications and Baird's is an illusion. Yet it seems clear from various references Baird has made to Genung, that Baird saw his predecessor not only as a figure to react against, but also as an authority to invoke when it served his purposes to do so, and as a fellow traveler. In a lengthy memorandum that he circulated to his staff in August 1946, for example, Baird quoted a passage from Genung's *Practical Elements of Rhetoric,* construed it as a confession of "helplessness," and concluded that "our confession of failure [in English 1–2] is not unusual."[13] And in the final examination he wrote for English 1 in the fall of 1961, Baird quoted Genung's opinion that rhetoric is concerned "with the whole man" and then observed that "much the same language could be used today and with universal agreement and understanding."[14]

The Amherst which Genung knew, however, was different from Baird's Amherst. The population of the town grew from around 4,000 residents in 1870 to 5,000 in 1900, and to 7,000 in 1945 (Longsworth 1978, 147; Abramson and Townsend 1978, 191, 193). Although half of all Amherst College graduates before the Civil War had entered the ministry, by 1871 three quarters of the men in each new graduating class were entering other professions (Longsworth, 148). The college was gradually moving away from its Calvinistic past, and in Baird's words, history "proved to be on the side of an increasing confidence in the goodness of the human heart" (1978a, 130). When Genung arrived in Amherst in 1882, the town was served by rail and illumined by gaslight, and Emily Dickinson was living in the house her grandfather had built on Main Street. In 1882, Amherst College was, although the oldest of the four, nevertheless only one of four colleges in its immediate region. One of the other three, Massachusetts Agricultural College, was a public, land-grant institution and was located in Amherst itself. The other two, Mount Holyoke in the nearby town of South Hadley and Smith in nearby Northampton, were both private women's colleges. In 1931, soon after Baird began teaching at Amherst College, Massachusetts Agricultural College became Massachusetts State College and enlarged its curricular offerings. And by 1931, in view of the 760 students at Massachusetts State (Cary 1962, 148) and the 670 students at Amherst College (Kennedy 1955, 176), education had become a leading industry in the town of Amherst. The economic importance of this industry both distinguished Amherst from the nearby manufacturing towns of Springfield, Chicopee, and Holyoke and enabled Amherst to weather the Depression in relatively good shape (Abramson and Townsend, 191).

One account of Amherst College in the 1930s suggests that the college both felt itself superior to Massachusetts State College and held itself aloof from the outside world (Abramson and Townsend 1978, 205). Whereas Massachusetts State College prided itself on its ever-expanding agricultural extension service (226), Amherst College, with its principal buildings arranged in a quad-

rangle on its secluded hilltop, focused inward on its own intellectual life. The members of the Amherst College faculty concerned
themselves much more with teaching than with publishing—
despite the examples of such individuals as George Whicher, who
published an important biography of Emily Dickinson in 1938,
and of Roy Elliott and Robert Frost, who did little teaching. Generally speaking, publication did not emerge as a significant professional issue for American academics until after World War II (Graff
1987, 59). Baird himself gave his foremost concern to teaching and,
except for *The First Years,* published very little. He has said of
Amherst College, "I thought that this was a very fine place. I felt
privileged to be here, and I always have" (1978b, 6).

During the decade of the 1930s, Amherst College undertook a
significant number of curricular changes. Some of these changes
apparently generated friction, because early in 1939 a group of five
faculty members, including Baird's senior colleagues Roy Elliott
and George Whicher, sent a letter to President Stanley King urging
him to preserve Amherst's character as a small and selective college
(reprinted in Babb et al. 1978, 138–139). At the beginning of his
tenure in 1932, President King had led a successful effort to free
the members of the freshman class from the requirement that they
study an ancient language (Babb et al., 4). Freshman English, or
English A, was dropped as a curricular requirement in 1933–34, but
in practice most of the freshmen continued to elect it, and in
1937–38 for example, 220 out of 237 did so (Baird 1939, 327n). A
curricular plan adopted by the faculty in 1935 eliminated virtually
all specific course and distributional requirements and established
sequencing requirements in their place (Babb et al., 11–13; 110n,
124n). But by the spring of 1937, the faculty had decided that curricular review was once again in order and appointed three of its
members—Otto Glaser (chair), Theodore Baird, and Charles W.
Cole—to serve on a Curriculum Committee. Baird served on this
committee for two years, until 1939 (Babb et al., 4, 107). He
appended a dissenting footnote, as I have already noted, to its
Report of November 10, 1938.

According to the authors of a 1978 study of the Amherst curriculum, the curricular changes resulting from the recommendations of the Glaser Committee and initiated between 1938 and
1940, although overshadowed by subsequent changes which were

undertaken after World War II, "were among the most important in the College's history" (Babb et al. 1978, 107). The most significant of these changes was the introduction of a distributional system whereby students were required to elect courses from among each of the three broad areas of "Mathematics and Natural Sciences," "Social Studies and Philosophy," and "Language, Literature, and the Arts" (8, 11). This tripartite division was to become an organizational foundation for the curricular plan which would be adopted by the college in 1945 and would require first- and second-year students to take core courses in each of the three areas (13).

In the spring of 1938, soon after the Glaser Committee had begun its deliberations, the English department appointed a committee to report on the freshman English course, or English A. One of the three members of this committee, Gilbert Hoag, put together what Baird calls "a political deal," securing Associate Professor Baird's agreement only after first securing that of Professors Whicher and Morton. Hoag, whom Baird remembers as "a friend of mine," was preparing to leave Amherst, having accepted a deanship elsewhere. According to the proposition Hoag put before the English department, an introductory course, English 1, would be required of all freshmen but offered in three variants as English 1A, 1B, and 1C. Upon arrival at Amherst College, freshmen would be given a placement test. Those who placed within the lower two thirds of the score range would be required to take "English 1C: Composition." Those who placed in the upper third could elect either the composition course or Professor Whicher's "English 1A: Survey of English Literature," or Professor Morton's "English 1B: Introduction to the Study of Poetry and Prose Fiction" (Baird 1939, 327). English 1C would be taught in sections by the junior members of the English faculty, of whom Baird was the most senior. Like all courses then offered at Amherst College, English 1C would be a two-semester course (Babb et al. 1978, 145n). Hoag's proposal was accepted not only by the English department, but by the entire Amherst faculty and was scheduled for implementation in the fall of 1938. Baird says, "This was the beginning of English 1. We were given the privilege, we were to be allowed to teach composition to the freshmen if we sacrificed all the best students as measured by this test" (1978b, 12).

When I asked Baird to speculate on the reasons why Gilbert Hoag may have wished to institute a composition course, he said, "I think he was just practicing being dean." When I then asked Baird whether I was correct in assuming he had personally had an interest in teaching composition, he said, "It is an interesting thing to do, you see" and "Oh yes, I was interested." And when I asked him whether he had wanted to teach the composition course Hoag had proposed, he said, "Oh yes," and added that Morton and Whicher "had nothing to do with my teaching that composition course, except they let me do it. They let me do it!"

The way that the Amherst English department chose to deal with the issue of freshman English was not unusual in the 1930s. According to John Michael Wozniak's survey of *English Composition in Eastern Colleges, 1850–1940*, a freshman composition course was required throughout the whole decade of the 1930s at 28 out of 37 private eastern colleges and required for portions of this decade at seven others, including Amherst (1978, 186). By the end of the decade, Allegheny, Brown, and Colby, as well as Amherst, were exempting students from composition on the basis of their perfor-mance on a placement test (187). Wozniak cites a survey, prepared in 1942 for the National Council of Teachers of English, of 290 col-leges and universities, of which 213 required a year of composition and 187 grouped composition students according to ability (198).

At Amherst College in the fall of 1938, it fell to Baird to select the placement test which was to be administered to the incoming freshmen. The one he chose took the students about an hour to complete and consisted of questions on vocabulary, sentence struc-ture, grammatical error, punctuation, and spelling. As he explained, "The virtue of this kind of examination is that we are clear about what we are testing and certain that we judge all papers by the same standard." He added, "I do not know how to separate 240 stu-dents into three groups by exercising subjective judgment in the course of a few hours" (1939, 328n).

That first fall, 160 students either elected or were assigned on the basis of the test to take English 1C. These students were then divided into eight sections of twenty students each (Baird 1939, 328). But on Wednesday, September 21, 1938, the day before the fall semester at Amherst College was scheduled to commence and the first sections of English 1C were scheduled to meet, Baird's

Right, *Johnson Chapel; fallen trees on the Amherst College campus after the hurricane of September 21, 1938.*

orderly arrangements were disrupted by a hurricane which devasted Amherst and most of southern New England, downed more than 150 trees on the Amherst College campus, tore the roof off the east end of Johnson Chapel, and claimed some 700 lives in Connecticut, Rhode Island, and neighboring states. Classes were canceled at Amherst College until the following Monday, and students joined enthusiastically in the effort to clear fallen trees. If any student found time to listen to a radio on September 22, he might have heard that Neville Chamberlain, in Munich, had attempted to secure "peace in our time."

When the fall semester finally got under way, Baird took up the work of directing English 1C. His initial staff consisted of Messrs. McKeon, Theobald, Wood, and Hutcheson (1939, 327). Baird had at least three key ideas to implement. Two of these were that students should write from experience and that they should write frequently. The third was that the members of his teaching staff should engage in a conversation about their collective enterprise. From the very outset, Baird insisted upon a common teaching strategy, on common assignments and examinations, and upon weekly staff meetings.

During the first year, as Baird reported in an article he wrote for the Amherst alumni magazine in 1939:

> We met about once a week to discuss our immediate program, constantly subjecting our aims to criticism, trying to define our purpose. Whatever success the course may have we owe to these meetings. . . . The meetings kept the course alive in our minds as something always to be thought about. Ideally the course would be as good as the instructors in it, working together. Ideally no one person would dominate. It would be a common action, subject to our control and direction, even as it happened day by day. (1939, 329)

Baird also claimed that "the only virtue of English 1 C is that five teachers are engaged in a common effort to see to it that two-thirds of the freshmen do as much writing as we can read and that the writing is as decent, as clear, as sensible, as intelligent as we know how to make it" (333). When I asked Baird to confirm that it had been his goal from the beginning to have teachers work on the course together, he said, "That was our trade secret, really. People would come around and say, 'What are you doing?' The trade secret really was we were trying to talk about how to teach composition. That doesn't sound like much. That isn't what you would call a very well-developed program."

The immediate question Baird remembers having to address in the fall of 1938 was "WHAT on earth were we going to do?" (1978b, 12). No longer could one teacher decide to read Shaw and another to read Eliot or someone else. Baird remembers, "This was a wonderful freedom that we were sacrificing, and what were we sacrificing it for? What could we possibly agree on?" (13). He called a meeting and proposed to "begin at the beginning and do the most stupid thing we could think of doing . . . to take a textbook, as I had done when I began teaching years before, and see if we could do anything with these questions of good English, and split infinitives, and spelling, and things like that. And this was agreed to and this we did and it was a discipline for us all" (13–14). Baird and his fellow teachers spent their first semester diagramming sentences on the blackboard. As Baird acknowledges, "That wasn't a very original beginning." He adds, "But I think I was deliberate enough about this to say, 'Well, we'll just have to begin as stupidly as we can and see what results we feel we get from being really stupid teachers.' At least that is the way I began to explain it" (14). Baird's opening gambit may not have been very original, but it was a step toward organizing chaos.

Baird says he and his staff chose "the most sensible textbook we could find" (1939, 330), but after that first year, they never used a textbook again. In the process of going through their text, Baird and the other teachers had concluded that "this is no way to teach, divorcing the technique of writing from the act of composition." They decided, "Next year we shall make our own book as we go along, from the specific needs of our own students" (329–330). In fact, already by November of their first year, they had left their textbook behind. After Thanksgiving, each teacher gave several weeks of class time to the reading of what was, according to Baird, "a comparatively difficult book, either *Walden* or *The Education of Henry Adams,* analyzing the ideas, and using them as material for writing" (330). Later, the staff tried what Baird called "an experiment in practical criticism, owing our inspiration in general to I. A. Richards in his *Practical Criticism* and *Interpretation in Teaching*" (331). In the spring, they worked with their students on "the writing of short autobiographical fragments and one long autobiography. Here the subject matter was given by experience. The student's problem was to sort out from his own memory those scenes or atmospheres or events which were clear and which were capable of expression in words" (333).

In the I. A. Richards phase of the course, students were given parallel passages and, without knowing where the passages came from, asked to make critical distinctions between them. Baird impressed upon me that "this took hours, you know. Imagine trying to find a good poem; you'd get a good poem in Frost about a bird, and you'd say, 'Let's find another bird.' You'd go to the library, and you'd find something in James Russell Lowell or somebody, and you'd put them together. You'd say [to students], 'One of these is better than the other.'" Baird told me that in giving students parallel passages, he and his staff had made a great advance over Richards, whose protocols consisted of single, unidentified poems. According to Baird, "Richards was a fake. He could give you, or give me, a poem, and you'd look at it, and it might be John Donne, and it might be Woodbine Willy, and you didn't know which was which, and so you would praise it, or you would blame it, and you would hit the wrong author, and he would say, 'See! What bad readers they are!'"

English 1C students were required to write frequently; during the second semester the norm was between two and four papers a week. Even so, Baird says that "every paper was carefully read and commented on." None of these papers was given a grade; instead, he says the instructors "watched for signs of improvement" (1939, 331). Baird was far from satisfied with the first year's efforts, and at the end of the year, he declared that "at least half the course next year will be entirely revised" (333). He was careful to note, however, that "there are no methods which will succeed in teaching everyone to spell correctly and to think straight. They are means to an end, and come to life, if at all, only because of the energy which they generate in teacher and student" (333).

In the spring of 1939, near the end of his first year of directing English 1C, Baird was promoted to the rank of professor. In the fall, perhaps owing to the increase in his salary, he and Mrs. Baird bought a lot on a piece of high ground in south Amherst and began negotiating with Frank Lloyd Wright to build them a house. The three-bedroom "Usonian House," which Wright completed for them in early 1941, cost the Bairds approximately $8,000 to build.[15] The house is small and functional, which seems to have suited the Bairds, who had no children. To my eyes, however, it is anything but modest. The large expanse of glass along its south wall affords both the benefits of passive solar heating and a commanding view of the hills in the Holyoke Range.

In 1940, Baird says, house building was a distraction. His primary concern remained focused on his college duties and on English 1C. He and his staff were actively seeking ways to improve the course.

CHAPTER THREE

Charting the Course

During the ten-year period from 1938 when English 1C was initiated, through 1942 when it was renumbered as English 1–2, until 1947 when it became a core component of Amherst's "New Curriculum," Amherst's two-semester freshman writing course gradually assumed a more and more definite form. Armour Craig told me that with the implementation of the New Curriculum in 1947, "the shape of the course" and "the way the course was conducted" became fully established. It was then, Craig said, that "English 1–2 began, really fully, with all the assignments—a whole sequence of assignments." During the ten preceding years, Baird and the instructors on his staff, including Craig, had experimented with devising their own materials and assignments. They had relied heavily on their departmental mimeograph machine, planned out their course from week to week at staff meetings, and argued vociferously with one another about the phrasing and sequencing of assignments. They had worked out a way of getting students to write about their learning across the curriculum. They had adapted what may roughly be described as New Critical methods to the analysis of student papers, and they had developed a method for publishing student papers in class. During this same period they had had of necessity to deal with the exigencies created by World War II.

In addition to Baird, the two men who played the most active roles in the early development of English 1C, or English 1–2, were Reuben Brower and G. Armour Craig. According to Baird, both Brower and Craig in their different ways contributed "many new ideas and approaches" (1978b, 14). Both were graduates of Amherst College and both, like Baird, had graduate degrees from Harvard. Brower began teaching at Amherst in 1939 and Craig in 1940. Craig, like Baird, was to devote his entire professional life to teaching at Amherst, and like Baird, he has spoken to me at length about Amherst's freshman writing course. Brower followed a different path, concerning himself not only with teaching, but also with professional publication. In 1953, he left Amherst to seek what he must have seen as wider opportunities. He died in 1975.

Brower graduated from Amherst College in 1930, then went on to complete a second baccalaureate and a master's degree at Cambridge University, where he studied with F. R. Leavis and I. A. Richards. He earned a doctorate in classics at Harvard and wrote a dissertation on Dryden's *Aeneis*. Baird takes some credit for Brower's appointment at Amherst. The senior professor of Greek was retiring, and a trustee of the college asked Baird, in his capacity as a member of the Instruction Committee, whether Amherst College still needed two men in Greek. Baird recalls that he replied, "Well, this is a very simple matter—it's just a matter of feeling that when you are privileged you have obligations, and Amherst is a privileged college and not poor—there's no question about money here—and no question either of a need for two teachers of Greek. It's just a matter of pride. We're a proud place and we can afford two teachers of Greek" (1978b, 14–15). The trustee apparently responded positively to this argument, for Brower was hired with a dual appointment in Greek and in English.

Brower contributed to English 1–2 not only by teaching the course itself but by designing and directing a course in literary criticism for sophomores. He did not teach composition during his first few years at Amherst and is not listed in the *Amherst College Bulletin* as a staff member for English 1 until 1941–42. Throughout the war years, however, he and Baird and Craig are the three individuals most commonly listed as teaching English 1–2. Brower's sophomore course, entitled "Reading Poetry and Prose," or English 19–20, appears in the *Bulletin* for the first time in 1942–43. It became a course in close, or as Brower termed it, "slow" reading and employed the methods of Richards, Leavis, and the New Criticism. Baird told me Brower's sophomore course grew out of what had been the practice, during the second semester of English 1C, of using reading as material for writing. The introduction of the sophomore course meant that English 1–2 relinquished its literary concerns and became more distinctly a

Reuben Brower about 1950.

writing course. While sophomores in English 19–20 analyzed literary texts, freshmen in English 1–2 analyzed the texts which they and their classmates composed.

Both the freshman and sophomore courses were staff-taught by more or less the same people, and for a while not only was Brower a member of Baird's staff, but Baird was a member of Brower's. Baird recalls attending weekly staff meetings for both courses (1978b, 15). Walker Gibson told me that he found no inconsistency between English 1–2 and Brower's sophomore course and that "many of us taught both courses comfortably and simultaneously." The staff of the sophomore course, like that of the freshman course, agreed (although not without argument) on a common reading list and a common set of exercises. These exercises, as William Pritchard reports in a 1985 article on "Reuben A. Brower," never took the form of a "free-floating invitation to 'discuss'" (something Pritchard says Baird would have termed "an invitation to chaos"), but called on the student to locate himself "in relation to specific expressions in the text" (242). Pritchard says the exercises consisted of "a carefully planned series of questions; queries about parallel words and phrases . . .; an invitation to the student to make connections, and eventually to conclude with a generalization about the kind of literary experience he had undergone" (242). Careful sequencing of both exercises and readings was essential for, as Brower argued in a 1962 essay on "Reading in Slow Motion," every stage of a literature course should be "planned with a view to how the student reads the next work, whether poem or play or novel" (15).

Brower left Amherst for Harvard in 1953, taking course materials with him to use in the introductory literature course he would organize and direct at his new institution. His Harvard course, entitled "Humanities 6: The Interpretation of Literature" and familiarly known as "Hum 6," involved two hundred or more Harvard freshmen a term from 1954 until 1973. It was similar in many ways to the sophomore course Brower had directed at Amherst. Hum 6 was staff-taught, with Brower supervising the work of the six or seven junior instructors or graduate students who served as his section leaders. Its freshmen met all together once a week for a lecture, generally delivered by Brower himself, and twice a week additionally, in groups of twenty-five or so, for discussion sessions with their section leaders. It was a two-term course and called upon students to address a series of some twelve carefully sequenced "exercise" essays per term. Historian John Brereton has described Hum 6 as "one of the best-known and most influential literature courses of its time" (1993, 1). Speaking more precisely, Brereton characterizes it as a "LitComp" course rather than a literature course (1) because, he says, it combined instruction in reading with instruction in writing and did so "in a number of explicit ways: by the demonstrations Brower provided in the lectures; by the remarkably narrow, highly directive assignments; by intensive discussions in sections; by examples from other student papers read or given out in class; and by the instructor's comments on the papers themselves" (2). Brower himself, in his essay on "Reading in Slow Motion," contends that the "teaching of reading is necessarily teaching of writing" because "the student cannot show his teacher or himself that he has had an important and relevant literary experience except in writing or in speaking that is as disciplined as good writing" (1962, 7).

Other introductory English courses at Harvard at this time, according to William Pritchard (who was a section leader in Hum 6 in the middle 1950s), had "titles such as 'Epic and Novel' or 'Ideas of Good and Evil' or 'Man and the World' or 'Crisis and the Individual,' and they covered a lot of ground, doling out great ideas about Western civilization to the freshmen—with Dostoevski as the inevitably featured star—and concerning themselves very little with critical method and scarcely at all with the activity of reading" (1985, 243). Hum 6 seemed different and, Pritchard testifies, was "looked at with condescension and annoyance by other teachers of literature at Harvard" (243). Moreover, because many members of the Hum 6 staff[1] had, like Armour Craig and William R. Taylor, also taught at Amherst or had, like Pritchard himself and like Richard Poirier, done their undergraduate work there, the course was considered to be an Amherst operation (243). Pritchard says that those who taught Hum 6 "were arrogant (I was, anyway) and defensive about the course, feeling that—unlike the rest of benighted Harvard English—*we* were vehicles of truth, bringers of light, at least of the Right Method for going about things" (243).

Hum 6, like Brower's earlier course at Amherst, employed the methods of New Criticism. One of Brower's frequent practices was to present students, as Baird had done in the early days of English 1C, with paired texts and to invite students to compare them (see Brower 1962, 14). Brower also asked students to define terms "by context" and to see "how words are given rich and precise meaning through their interrelations with other words" (11). But unlike New Critics elsewhere, Brower (with his background in classics and in philology) was deeply interested in the historical contexts of literary works. Pritchard says that Brower was interested particularly in the "history of genres" and that if he began a course "by focusing minutely on the sonnet or quatrain," he would go on "not only to a consideration of other genres, such as poetic drama and the novel, but would trace the fortunes of pastoral or the heroic through a sequence of writers and literary periods" (1985, 241). Richard Poirier, who like Pritchard served as a section leader in Hum 6, points out in a 1990 article on the course that the term "New Criticism" is "exasperatingly inexact" and that to him at Harvard in the 1950s it had designated "an ideological mutation of I. A. Richards that was occurring not at all in Hum 6, but rather to the south of it at Yale" (24). For Brower, Poirier contends, "reading ideally remained *in* motion, not choosing to encapsulate itself as New-Critical readings always ultimately aspired to do" (21). Poirier links Hum 6 with its parent courses at Amherst College and says that its intellectual context included the ideas of "Emerson, Pierce, William James and John Dewey, Wittgenstein, Kenneth Burke, and F. R. Leavis, most of whom have been afforded little or no place in the history of contemporary theory" (16). Poirier also acknowledges the considerable influence which Robert Frost exerted upon Brower's thinking (25–29). Pritchard, for his part, says that Brower learned from Frost to value the quality of "voice" in writing (1985, 244).

Brower graduated from Amherst College at a time (1930) when Frost was a regular member of the Amherst faculty. At some point during Brower's undergraduate years at Amherst, Frost heard him read an Elizabethan poem aloud, marveled at "the way his voice fell into those lines, the natural way he did that very difficult poem," and told Brower, "I give you an A for life" (Poirier 1990, 27; Pritchard 1985, 241). In 1951, while he was teaching at Amherst, Brower published a collection of critical essays entitled *The Fields of Light,* in which he acknowledged debts both to Theodore Baird and G. Armour Craig, whom he believed would "see at many points how much I have learned from their teaching," and to Robert Frost (vii). The epigraph to the first essay in *The Fields of Light* is Frost's statement that "Everything Written is as good as it is dramatic" (Brower 1951, 19; Frost 1949, 13). In this first essay, entitled "The Speaking Voice," Brower asserts that "a poem is a dramatic fiction no less than a play, and its speaker, like a character in a play, is no less a creation of the words on the printed page" (19). In order to support this assertion, he explicates Frost's "Once By the Pacific," contending that for any reader the experience of reading this poem will consist not only of seeing ocean, storm, and land through Frost's eyes, but of hearing Frost's special voice. According to Brower, this voice takes its character from a "speculative way of talking, from the flow and arrest of American speech" but has "other strains sounding through it—pronouncements of the Old Testament, talk about the end of the world, and echoes of older mythological styles" (22). Brower concludes his essay by contending that readers hear the drama of a poem through the voice of the poet (29).

If Frost inspired Brower, Brower in his turn inspired many of the younger instructors who taught with him at Amherst and Harvard. William Pritchard, who was Brower's student at both Amherst and Harvard as well as a section leader in Hum 6, remembers that what Brower did "to me, and what so much of his teaching did, was to instruct by example, especially by the example of the performing voice making a piece of old poetry come alive" (1985, 240). Walker Gibson, who taught under both Brower and Baird at Amherst, told me in response to my questioning him about Baird's influence on his subsequent teaching that "I'm sure that whatever happened to my teaching after I left Amherst College was not just English 1, but was the Brower, literature, I. A. Richards kind of thing as well, and that I was putting these together in some shape or form." Specifically, Gibson told me that his 1950 article on "Authors, Speakers, Readers, and Mock Readers," which is often cited as an early example of reader-response criticism, came "far more directly out of the Brower, sophomore literature course" than out of Baird's English 1–2.

John Cameron, on the other hand, told me that, from his perspective as a young instructor, Brower had seemed like just a big fish in a small pond. Cameron, who came to Amherst from Yale in 1958, after Brower had already moved on to Harvard, remembers that when he began to entertain the notion of coming to Amherst, friends at Yale referred him to Brower's *The Fields of Light*. Cameron, to whom Brower's name was new, remembers that soon after joining the Amherst faculty "I was informed that Reuben Brower was one of the leading critics in the world, and that to me epitomized Amherst College. I'm not putting him down at all, but at Yale I'd never heard of him."

Richard Poirier, who now teaches at Rutgers, acknowledges in his article on "Hum 6" that "I am acutely aware in all my references to Amherst that the credit I give to Hum 6 at Harvard, and to its founder Reuben Brower, could be differently distributed so as to give more prominence to some teachers at Amherst, . . . who were Brower's colleagues when he taught there, who initiated with him the parent courses of Hum 6, and who helped fashion many of the assignments used in the course after Brower started it at Harvard" (1990, 16). Poirier, who was an undergraduate at Amherst in the late 1940s, notes that alongside Brower's sophomore literature course at Amherst there was a freshman writing course that "was an even more radical immersion in the waywardness of language" (21). Incidentally, Poirier credits Armour Craig,[2] who was his instructor in English 1–2, with being the individual "from whose teaching at Amherst I profited most as an undergraduate" (18).

Craig, like Baird, was above all a teacher. And like Baird, he published very little. Poirier notes that Craig "did nearly all of his critical work for and in his classes" (1990, 18). Craig, as I said above, joined the Amherst faculty in 1940, the year after Brower arrived, and like Brower, he contributed significantly to the early development of English 1–2. He had graduated from Amherst College in 1937, earned a mas-

G. Armour Craig, mid-1940s.

ter's degree from Harvard in 1938, and was working on a Ph.D. at Harvard when he received a telegram from Amherst, asking him to return to teach at the college. Craig told me that upon receiving the telegram "I thundered 'Yes!' so loud that they heard me." He had not yet finished his dissertation, and in fact would not do so until after the war. During his first year teaching at Amherst, he taught two sections of English 1C.

I interviewed Professor Craig twice, both times in February of 1991. Craig, who was born in 1914, retired from Amherst College in 1984, having officiated during 1983–84 as its acting president and having given the whole of his professional life to its service. Walker Gibson, speaking of Craig, told me that English 1–2 had been "absolutely central to his life." Douglas Wilson, an alumnus of English 1–2, created an analogy for me, saying that "if Baird was the president of English 1, Craig was the vice president." Baird himself, acknowledging that he could not single-handedly have kept English 1 going for thirty years, told me that "Armour Craig's support was very powerful support."

Craig told me he had majored in English and philosophy as an undergraduate at Amherst. He had taken freshman English from

David Morton at the time in the mid-1930s when Morton, Whicher, and Baird had agreed to a common reading list. Craig remembers reading *King Lear* and Boswell's *Life of Johnson* and not writing much. That year, Craig told me, "there were no common assignments; you gave whatever you wanted, and David Morton wanted to read as few papers as possible." Craig said he began to form an interest in composition during his junior year, as a result of having to struggle both to write good papers and to figure out what made a paper good. He remembered that "it finally dawned on me that a good paper in American lit, or on Kant, or whatever, had to answer a question, and a question furthermore that drove the asker to a particular passage or passages." He remarked that while this truism might seem obvious to me and to others of my generation, it had not seemed so to him because "most literary and humanistic education in those days was really being able to talk a certain kind of belletristic rhetoric. A good paper was an effusion."

Craig had his first teaching experiences in the late 1930s when he was a graduate student at Harvard. He was responsible for two sections of English A, Harvard's freshman composition course, per semester. Craig remembers English A as "a course in which you would read something and then have the class write a theme on this." He remembers using a reader and having to operate from a belletristic theory of composition whereby a student should "write with some kind of grace" and "write like a gentleman." He remembers being irritated with senior professors at Harvard for speaking the kind of "double-talk that authority produces" and specifically with a professor of Renaissance literature who once asked him witheringly, "Don't you know what anti-rational fideism is?" During his second year of teaching English A, Craig had the idea that one way to get students to write would be to ask them to explain what they were doing in their other classes. He illustrated this for me by reenacting a dialogue with a chemistry student:

"You say you're a chemist? Tell me about being a chemist. What interests you? Tell me what you do. People tell me chemists sit around and watch pots boil. Come on! That won't do!"

This young man laughed and said, "Well, there's a lot to it, but I've never tried to explain it to anybody."

I said, "Well try to explain it to me. Tell me what you do when you do a particular chemical assignment."

Craig told me he tried this approach with several individual students during his final year at Harvard, though never with an entire class. He said, "I got interested in this. I got interested in it as a principle of composition." He would continue building on the approach at Amherst.

Baird remembers that soon after Craig joined the English 1 staff, he suggested asking students to write about their experience in other courses and that he interviewed faculty members in biology, chemistry, and other departments to solicit ideas for writing assignments. According to Baird, Craig wanted students to translate "their experiences as students in the science courses into English which would be intelligible to anybody. And we even had some subjects proposed in mathematics, and this was very interesting, to me, and still is, of where you draw the line between languages. Can you say that it is like music where you know it is not a verbal experience? Music is not verbal, even though people go on talking about it all the time and using metaphorical language: you hear someone commenting on a new recording by saying 'well, it lacks guts.'" Baird added, "And so we had assignments on music, we had assignments on mathematics, and you'd say what are the limits of English?, and you'd say what are the limits of these other subjects?, and this generally was Craig's contribution at this stage. His contribution was great all the way through this" (1978b, 15–16).

Craig told me he remembers talking to Otto Glaser, the head of the biology department, and saying, "We would like to make some assignments in English composition that will ask students what they know and how they get to know it, especially what is the experience of biology? What do you do?" Craig added that at the time "people were beginning to talk this way, to think this way; they were beginning to realize mathematics is a language. I collected a series of titles for topics that would compel a student who wrote any one of these to define certain key terms and to try to say what they were keys to. They were keys to doing something. If you understand 'cell,' you can make a certain number of particular observations in a lab."

Craig, who says he had serious intellectual interests in the history of ideas and the history of science, told me that "one of the things that got me really interested in the nonliterary approach to composition, if you will, was helping a friend of mine at Harvard with a book he was writing, the title of which was *Why Smash Atoms?* This was one of the first books about atom smashing and what it meant in modern science." Craig added that "important changes were occurring then in the philosophy of science. Einstein had sparked a revolution in physics which brought the human capacity for constructing a model of the universe into question. People of my generation had to unlearn many of the things they had been taught. It became clear that we live in a world of probabilities rather than certainties. We began to take it for granted that there were things going on that we did not understand. We accepted the subconscious, for example."

Unlike Baird, Craig discussed the intellectual context of English 1–2 with me at some length. Speaking of the history of teaching English, he told me that "English hasn't been a profession all that long, and for a long time most of the people that taught it were genre or century people—'he's the Melville man' and things like that—and they had a hell of a lot of information, but there were very, very few people before the 1920s, before Richards, who as practicing people tried to address the performance of the imagination." Craig said that the modern history of the profession "began in the 1920s as a rebellion against the terrible, terrible claims for literature that were made in conventional courses." When I asked about specific influences upon English 1–2, Craig gave most credit to the contributions of Robert Frost and of Kenneth Burke.

Craig said that English 1–2 "owes a great deal to Robert Frost and to his notion of the poem as drama." Craig affirmed his belief in Frost's maxim that "Everything written is as good as it is dramatic" (Frost 1949, 13) and explained, "What's profoundly true about it is that the dramatic speech demands a response from another consciousness and presupposes another consciousness that is ready to reply." For many people, Craig added, "It's very easy to live in a world in which there's only one consciousness, namely one's own and one's own fantasies." Craig remembers that students used to complain to Frost that "'sometimes poetry doesn't seem to give us the answers.' And he [Frost] would say, 'I'm not interested in answers; I'm interested in replies.'" Craig noted that whereas by "reply" Frost had meant a response in an ongoing dialogue, by "answer" he meant "doctrine" or "pretty much what the mountain says."

Uniformed students in a war-era classroom at Amherst College.

Craig told me that Kenneth Burke had had a major influence on his own thinking, and through him on English 1–2. In fact, when I asked Craig whether he thought of himself as a teacher of composition, he identified himself more precisely as "a teacher of symbolic action." He told me that "motive," in Burke's sense, "would be another name for what this course [English 1–2] was about. It was about motives for knowledge." Craig added that what Burke and Frost had in common, as he had discovered when, as he put it, "I was growing up and growing into my profession," was that "for both of them speech is dramatic." Craig told me that at a fairly early date in his own career he had written about Burke. Soon after Burke published *A Grammar of Motives* in 1945, Craig was invited to review it for *Foreground,* a small literary journal which enjoyed a brief publication history after the war. He told me he had read some Burke before, but this was the first of Burke's "Grammar" books and the one in which he first addressed the issue of motive. Craig wrote a nine-page review, concluding that "as a critical discipline Burke's dramatism can enlarge our awareness of action in language."[3] However, *Foreground* folded before Craig's review could be published. Later, in an April 12, 1956, article in the *Amherst Student* newspaper announcing an address Burke was to deliver on the Amherst campus, Craig was quoted as saying that Burke was "one of the most original thinkers in America today" (1). William Pritchard, who was a student in Craig's 1949–50 section of English 1–2, says that when he, Pritchard, subsequently read *A Grammar of Motives,* he recognized in reading it that Burke's "rhetorical/dramatistic way of thinking about communication" was something "I had taken in here and there in my freshman year, in my English 1 course. Craig had read Burke."

Richard Poirier, who like Pritchard is a former student of Craig's, also attests that Craig was "a devoted reader of Kenneth Burke, nearly as much as of Frost" (1990, 27). Poirier says that "Craig, at one time in the early fifties, proposed changing the vocabulary of English 19–20," which was Brower's sophomore literature course at Amherst, "so as to feature Burke's pentad of 'act,' 'scene,' 'agent,' 'agency,' and 'purpose'" (27). Poirier adds,

> The antipathy among Amherst people to any such proliferation of metalanguage prevailed, however. And even if the terminology had been adopted it would not have made the emphasis less Frostian, since Frost's insistence on the dramatic, on the drama of and among words, resembles what Burke's was to be, even in detail. (27–28)

Well before he encountered Burke, Craig had had to join with Baird and Brower in addressing the pedagogical challenges posed by World War II. Craig told me that during the war years, all three of them "taught around the clock," dealing with students as they came in, whether they arrived in October or in February or in the summer.[4] Baird remembers that "immediately after the war began, the College had to take on, to survive, one Army or Air Force program after another. The regular student body all but vanished" (1978b, 19). He adds, "This meant that the Dean would call me up at 7:30 in the evening and say, 'We're going to have about three hundred students here on Friday.'" As Baird recalls, "I'd say, 'All right. How many sections? How often does English meet?'" When the dean had given him the information, Baird would call a meeting with Brower and Craig and the handful of other teachers engaged in teaching composition, most of whom were employed on a short-term basis, and the staff would work out a plan for addressing the needs of these students in

Uniformed students on the Amherst College campus during the World War II years.

whatever time was available (19). Craig remembers they generally had a group of naval cadets in preflight school, a group from the United States Military Academy (USMA), and a group in training to become weather observers. According to Craig, the USMA students generally stayed for an entire year, and he told me that "we gave them in a year the equivalent of freshman and sophomore years at Amherst College." Baird remembers that the premeteorology students were at the college for forty-eight weeks, a preengineering group stayed only eight weeks, and a pre-West Point group, which had already seen combat, stayed for three months.[5] He says that although he and Craig and Brower had little more to work with than "a mimeograph machine and our wits," they took their work with these wartime groups "very seriously," regarding this as their contribution to the war effort (1978b, 19–20). The pace could be grueling. Baird told me, "There was one time there I taught three hours in a row, different sets of assignments. I don't know how I did it. I was exhausted, and so were Craig and Brower. We were all under great pressure." He has also noted that "I felt that we gave every one of these classes the best we had, as good as we ever gave an Amherst class" (1978b, 20).

Baird believes that the war played an instrumental role in the development of English 1–2, and it seems to have been during the war that he and his colleagues refined the practice, which was to become a hallmark of the course, of devising, mimeographing, and teaching from sequences of short writing assignments. It was also during the war, as Baird recalls, that they began mimeographing student papers and using them as classroom texts. Baird told me that "the war was the thing that shook us up." He explained that he and his staff were forced to develop great flexibility. They had to learn to make sets of assignments in very short order. They had to learn to work with adult students and also with what Baird describes as "high school boys from Flatbush." What was perhaps of most significance was that they had to learn to work with students who had their hands so full balancing the demands of their academic and military lives that often, as Baird told me, "the only writing they could do was when we had them in the classroom." Baird reported in 1946 that he and his wartime staff had "found that the students in uniform had the common knowledge of basic training, and that assignments dealing with techniques learned outside the schoolroom were unusually successful."[6] He reported in 1954 to a committee charged with reviewing the Amherst curriculum that, during the war, he and his staff had taught English to about 1,600 soldiers and had

> proved that we could confidently teach writing to almost any group of people so long as we could catch their attention for but a moment. All we had to do was tell them to go ahead and write, and when asked what about, all we had to say was, tell us what you know. (Kennedy 1955, 233)

The English 1–2 staff seems to have discovered they could most effectively engage their students by assigning writing tasks that teased students along through a series of short steps and ultimately brought them someplace other than where they began.

Among the course materials generated during these war years and now held in the English 1–2 collection in the Amherst College Archives is a set of twenty-two assignments on boundaries. It is the earliest extended sequence of assignments I can find, and it must have established the pattern for the even longer sequences Baird would develop subsequently. This wartime sequence indicates, moreover, that despite what Baird told me about the constraints on his military students' time, he and his colleagues were remarkably ambitious with regards to what they expected these students to accomplish. Baird's authorship of the sequence, which was apparently used in the fall of 1944 in all sections of English 1, can be adduced from a memo sent by Baird to Brower and Craig on July 4, 1944, outlining his preliminary ideas for a set of assignments on boundaries.[7]

According to this outline, the first seven assignments in the series were intended to show that lines and boundaries are made by men for particular purposes and that the nature and exactness of these boundaries depend on these purposes. The next three assignments were intended first to demonstrate the inadequacy of a general theory of boundaries to bring order out of the "chaos" which geographers encounter in the actual world. Baird hoped they would also prepare students to consider "the Language Problem which we find at the heart of everything, of course." Other assignments in the series had to do with how maps are made and used and with the building up of a vocabulary for geography. The actual assignments are built around a collection of mimeographed passages, including an account of a sporting event at which a ball was said to be "out of bounds," a legal record of a boundary dispute, a discourse on the territoriality of birds, discussions of the overlapping of climate zones and of cultural regions, a technical description of the Connecticut River Valley lowland, and parallel descriptions of the Arabs, one more scientific and the other, from Doughty's *Travels in Arabia Deserta,* more literary. The assignments tend to direct students to analyze the language of these passages by carrying out a detailed list of as many as four or even ten separate steps. Students are asked to make lists, for example, then to rearrange the lists according to some criterion, and finally to explain what they have done. They are asked to define terms "by context" and to trace how, in parallel passages, the meaning of a particular term can shift. They are asked at one point to translate a map into English and at another to make a map from a table of statistics. In the case of the legal dispute, they are asked first to define "boundary" in the terms of both the plaintiff and of the defendant, then to explain how the court establishes the true boundary, and finally to say what "true boundary" means in this context. In the case of the parallel descriptions of the Arabs, they are asked to list the uses they can see for each of the accounts and to say which is better, or "better" for which purposes. The series as a whole explores the ways in which geographers organize chaos by building fences with words.

When I asked him about the series, Baird insisted: "We weren't interested in geographers. We were interested in the way LAN-GUAGE makes order out of chaos. Over and over again we considered how language does this. We ran into opposition because many freshmen assumed that the order was there, out there, and all they had to do was look and they would see it" (letter to R.Varnum, January 9, 1991). With respect nominally to these boundary assignments but actually to English 1–2 assignments in general, Baird added, "In setting up examples of how language organizes our chaos, I think the assignments generally, but not always, showed great ingenuity. This is my claim. Also there was (for me at least) a lot of fun in it. I laughed a good deal" (letter to R.Varnum, January 9, 1991).

At the same time as Baird and his colleagues were teaching from these boundary assignments, a Faculty Committee on Long Range Policy was meeting under the chairmanship of Professor Gail Kennedy of Amherst's philosophy department to consider the curricular and policy directions the college might best take after the war. This committee, constituted originally in October of 1941, was reconstituted in February of 1944 after its work had been interrupted by the war (Babb et al. 1978, 4–5). The reconstituted committee (or Kennedy Committee) made a number of recommendations, the most daring of which, and the one which was to bring national attention to Amherst's New Curriculum, was that the college establish a series of core courses to be required of all freshmen and sophomores. In October of 1945, with the war freshly concluded, the faculty adopted most of the recommendations of the Kennedy Committee and directed that the New Curriculum be implemented by the fall of 1947 (5, 15).

Amherst's New Curriculum was one of a number of general education curricula instituted at colleges and universities across the United States in the immediate aftermath of World War II. Educational historian Frederick Rudolph credits the publication of the 1945 Harvard report on *General Education in a Free Society* with launching a general education movement (1977, 257–259). Rudolph claims that the authors of the Harvard report hoped to forestall social divisiveness and "to democratize what had once been the education of a gentleman and an aristocrat and make it the education essential to the responsibilities of every citizen" (258–259). At Amherst, I suspect that teachers toughened by the rigors of teaching under wartime conditions were reluctant either to relax discipline or to restore the measure of elective choice which students had enjoyed before the war.

Three Amherst College reports describe the curricular changes which were undertaken at the college during the New Curriculum years. The first two of these, the 1945 *Report of the Faculty Committee on Long Range Policy* and the 1954 *Report of the Review Committee on the New Program,* were published together in 1955 in a single volume edited by Gail Kennedy and entitled *Education at Amherst: The New Program.* The third, produced by Professor Lawrence A. Babb and five other members of the Amherst faculty, appears in a 1978 volume entitled *Education at Amherst Reconsidered.* Babb and his five colleagues charge that the 1945 *Report of the Faculty Committee on Long Range Policy* "ranks among the decidedly anti-electivist documents of American educational history" (20).

The aim which Kennedy and his co-authors of the 1945 report acknowledged at that time was to establish Amherst College even more consciously than before as "a college for students of superior intelligence" (1955, 56). Accordingly, they urged the college to "make it a first priority to secure an increasing number of students of high ability" (87). They recommended the adoption of a curriculum which would give each of these students "the sense that he has a community of knowledge and interest with all of his fellow students" (28). Thirty years later, Amherst College historian Theodore P. Greene observed that the framers of the New Curriculum did not "in 1945, feel any contradiction between their desire for a larger, brighter, more diverse pool of applicants and their insistence upon a new curriculum of 'general education' courses which was to be more demanding, more rigid in its requirements, and less tolerant of diverse student interests than the program of any competing liberal arts college" (1978, 301).

In 1945, Kennedy and the other members of the committee that designed the New Curriculum affirmed the Amherst faculty's traditional belief "that teaching is the most important function of the faculty of the college" (1955, 80). The committee had what it thought of as "two Big Ideas" to promote: "the laboratory method and the integration of previously separate subjects in one course" (204). They recommended dividing the curriculum into lower and upper division programs, the lower division portion of which was to be almost

entirely prescribed (39). Their plan called for freshmen and sophomores to take a heavy load of core courses in each of the three broad
curricular areas of mathematics and the physical and biological sciences; history and the social sciences; and the humanities. These would
include English 1–2, History 1–2, Science 1–2, and a humanities
course (170). In 1945, Science 1–2 and the humanities course had yet
to be developed. History 1–2, although renamed, would continue
from a course in Western civilization that had been offered at Amherst
for years (218). English 1–2, according to the Kennedy Committee,
"has proved itself an effective course and should be required of every
student" (48).

English 1–2 and the humanities course were to be taken concur-
rently as half-courses, which together would fulfill the freshman
requirement in the humanities (Kennedy 1955, 229). First, however,
there was some sparring over turf. Theodore Baird told me that Gail
Kennedy had hoped to model the proposed humanities course after
the famous great books course organized at Columbia University in
the 1920s (see also Kennedy, 57). Baird told me that "we wrangled
and we wrangled over that, and we said, 'Let us teach the literature,
and give us five hours a week, instead of having two courses, three
hours and three hours.'" In a formal protest, Baird and his staff
declared that

> We, the instructors in English 1–2, have worked out an "orienta-
> tion" of the Freshman mind and an "integration" of Freshman
> knowledge which we believe is a workable, teachable answer to
> the needs which the Humanities Course proposes to fill. We
> have developed our methods of orientation and integration by
> actual class-room teaching, and we use these methods every day
> that we teach. English 1–2, therefore, might well be officially
> designated as the Introduction to the Liberal Arts which it in
> fact is for those who take it now. (Quoted in Kennedy, 184)

The eventual outcome, as it was reported in 1954, was that Kennedy
prevailed, and from 1947 on, English 1 was scheduled to meet three
times and Humanities 1 twice each week during the fall semester. This
frequency of meetings was reversed during the spring semester, with
English 2 meeting twice and Humanities 2 thrice weekly (229).

Although the New Curriculum was formally adopted by the Amherst faculty in late 1945, its implementation was delayed for two years in order to give time both for the college to readjust to peacetime conditions and for the faculty to plan the mandated new courses (Kennedy 1955, 191). A complication arose when the number of potential students seeking admission to the college after the war was swelled by hosts of returning veterans. The freshman class of 400 students admitted in 1946 was nearly twice as large as the class admitted in 1940 had been (176, 191), and the total enrollment figures swelled from 850 students in 1940–41, to 1,163 in 1947–48, and to 1,201 in 1948–49 (195, 197). Meanwhile, those attempting to plan the new science course stumbled over a number of disagreements, with the result that Science 1–2 did not finally gel until Arnold Arons was appointed to the faculty in 1952 and made co-chairman of the course (209). Still another planning problem was posed by the fact that the proposed course load for freshmen was unusually heavy (185). No one knew whether the class admitted in 1947–48, the first to encounter the New Curriculum, would be able to handle its requirements, but according to those who reviewed the New Curriculum in 1954, "[T]he students did it. They did it because they had the ability, were challenged by the difficulty, and took a self-conscious pride in themselves as 'guinea pigs'" (197). According to the same report, "As the whole college gradually went over to the new program, freshman year seemed comparatively less difficult and the student body came to take a matter-of-course attitude toward the harder work" (197). Students who had hit the ground running after World War II not only took Amherst's demands in stride, they established a smart pace for their successors to follow. I suspect that Cold War militancy also operated to keep standards high.

In the English department, Professor Baird worked with an enlarged staff of eight instructors, some of whom like Walker Gibson were freshly decommissioned from the battlefield, to adapt English 1–2 to the requirements of the New Curriculum. Several documents which Baird wrote in 1946–47 indicate the nature of his preparations for the transition. One of these is a three-page statement which Baird wrote for the Committee on Publicizing the New Curriculum. Others are memoranda which he prepared for his staff.

In his public statement, Baird addressed the "two Big Ideas" of the New Curriculum, asserting that English 1–2 employed the laboratory

The faculty of the Amherst College English department in 1951–52. Seated, from left: *G. Armour Craig, associate professor; Reuben A. Brower, professor; George F. Whicher, professor; Theodore Baird, professor; Newton F. McKeon Jr., professor and director of Converse Memorial Library; Cesar L. Barber, associate professor.* Standing, from left: *W. Walker Gibson, assistant professor; Robert O. Preyer, instructor; Robert Ross Staley, instructor; Benjamin H. DeMott, instructor; Richard L. Waidelich, instructor.*

method and promoted the integration of knowledge. He described English 1–2 as a "laboratory course," noting that

> There are no lectures and the student does no required reading. Each student supplies his own subject matter for writing. That is, we ask the student to put into English what he has learned, both in and outside the classroom. In Term 1 we arbitrarily limit his material to physical activities, skills at the workbench, plays or strokes from games, many of them performed without any verbal accompaniment. We ask the student to become conscious of his particular ability, to sort out those actions which he knows he can do well, and to write about them. As teachers we encourage the student to believe that what he has learned to do he can put into words, and in the detailed criticism of particular papers we try to express the possible relations between the order of the wordless action and the structure of the English sentence.[8]

In the same document, Baird described Amherst College as "a universe of languages, among which English served as the common, or unifying, medium of communication" (2, see note 8). He declared that

> for the Amherst freshman, at least, communication ought to be possible. He ought to be able to talk and write about his experience with games and machines, with biology and chemistry and history and economics in such a way that a person of ordinary intelligence can understand him. In this belief English 1–2 operates, that in the act of expression knowledge can be unified. (3, see note 8)

In the summer of 1946, Baird for the first time employed the practice, which he and others would repeat, of drafting a series of assignments for the coming year of English 1–2. On August 5, 1946, having worked out a set of assignments for the fall and a partial set for the spring, he issued a twenty-four-page memorandum entitled "English 1–2, History and Content"[9] and circulated copies to his staff. The memorandum, consisting of a ten-page overview of the history of the course, a summary of its methods and objectives, and the sequence of assignments Baird had drafted, represented a sort of teacher's guide to English 1–2. Baird informed his staff that during the year ahead, which he described as a year of transition into the new curriculum, they would be responsible for teaching some 480 freshmen (2).

Baird expressed reluctance to define his theoretical assumptions too explicitly. He explained that "English 1–2 is not a body of metaphysical propositions, a system of logic and epistemology, complete, final and known as the truth. It is not a content course in which teachers transmit the laws, rules, principles of writing" (1, see note 9). Rather, it "is an instrument, created by purposeful effort, to do a particular thing, a means to an end, a force to motivate action" (8). It should motivate students to make connections, to relate new ideas to old, and to learn (9). Baird enjoined his staff, as he would continue to do long after 1946, not to give students ready-made answers. To do so might interfere with their learning. "See to it they make the comments," he insisted, "don't tell them things" (9). He likened the role of a writing teacher to that of an athletic coach creating "situations in practice which will form habits of successful performance" (1).

Baird began the historical overview section of his memorandum by stating that English 1–2 had evolved through trial and error over the period of eight years (1, see note 9). As the director of the course, he had always believed that it should be possible for the members of his staff to communicate, cooperate, and even learn from one another (2). He explained that he and those who had helped him develop the course learned early on that "we should always make our own exercises and find our own examples" (3). Baird was careful to give credit to the most senior of his colleagues, noting that the course took a positive turn when Armour Craig proposed having students write about what they were learning in their other courses (5). Arguing that it took another turn during the war years when teachers found that "assignments dealing with techniques learned outside the schoolroom were unusually successful" (7), Baird credited Reuben Brower with having developed "a fruitful series of assignments on the order of actions in a technique" (8). At the conclusion of this section of his memorandum, Baird declared that "English 1–2 now takes this shape: term 1, students write on subjects relating to particular actions which they have performed outside the classroom; term 2, the students write on subjects derived from their courses in Amherst" (8).

Baird then listed twenty-nine assignments for English 1 in the fall and eighteen of the thirty-two assignments needed for English 2 in the spring. He intended for his staff to use these assignments in common, and he expected every member of the staff to participate in revising them. Weekly staff meetings, as he explained in a memorandum on "Some Practical Matters,"[10] would serve as the forum in which to revise the assignments. On the second page of this memorandum, he instructed his junior colleagues that

> Whenever you see a possible improvement in the phrasing of assignments or a lead for new assignments make a note of it instantly and share it at the weekly meeting. Keep a part of your mind on the next week's work, for thus you control direction. I shall send you in advance of our meeting a tentative, a possible list of assignments. Any suggestions or changes which occur to you should be discussed at our meeting, and at the end of our discussion we must know what it is we are going to do for the next three or four classes. My part in all this will be in trying to maintain the kind of coherence which I have tried to express in that long paper [see note 9] I sent you.

The twenty-nine assignments Baird outlined in August were thus discussed and modified by his entire staff, and from time to time throughout the fall, Baird issued memoranda listing new or reworded assignments. By the time they were finally given to students, some of the assignments had been revised and re-revised three or four times.[11] Probably because of the curricular ferment at the college and because of the several new instructors on his staff, Baird provided his staff in the fall of 1946 with an unusual number of written suggestions for teaching. Thus it is possible to form a fairly clear idea of how his assignments for that fall were actually taught. The documents which are most useful are the above-cited memorandum of August 5 on "English 1–2: History and Content"[9] and a three-page memorandum dated September 15, 1946,[12] which contains revised assignments and directions for teaching the first six classes of the term. Baird's discussion of the fall 1946 assignments in his 1952 article on "The Freshman English Course" is also useful.

In his memorandum of August 5, Baird informed the new members of his staff that English 1–2 was "self supporting entirely," that it employed no textbook, and that his proposed assignments, together with students' responses to them, were intended to provide "the material for our classes" (9, see note 9). When a teacher had read the papers his students wrote in response to any particular assignment, he was to comment upon them and then to select exemplary papers, or portions thereof, to mimeograph and to discuss with his students at the next meeting of his class (9). He could call upon the departmental secretary for help with typing and mimeographing specimen papers.

The procedure that was actually established was to collect one assignment, give another, and discuss a third at each class meeting. A teacher who taught on a Monday-Wednesday-Friday schedule,[13] for example, began a Wednesday class by collecting the papers written to the assignment he had given on Monday. He then distributed mimeographed copies of specimen papers he had collected on Monday. These in-class "publications" were, for the most part, handled anonymously, and the point was for the class to judge how well each student author had faced the question put to him. At the end of the hour, the teacher gave a new assignment, which he expected his students to complete for Friday. Each teacher gave three assignments per week for eleven weeks, then assigned a long paper and administered a final exam. With twenty or more students per section, the teacher read sixty or more essays per section per week.

Students' essays were not graded. As Baird explained to his staff in his memorandum of September 15, "We do not put grades on their papers. We do correct and make comments. We do give grades when Dean asks for them" (1–2, see note 12). In his memorandum of August 5, Baird suggested that "the most sensible comment for many of the student's papers, week after week, will be that he doesn't know what he is talking about" (10, see note 9).

The nominal subjects of the assignments Baird had drafted for the fall of 1946 were "technique" and "learning," and they called upon students to describe the experience of performing a physical action. In his memorandum of August 5, Baird advised his colleagues to proceed by asking students to "tell what you did, you can always tell what you did,—that is, if you know what you did" (10, see note 9). The first few assignments in the sequence, he said, were designed to get the course going by encouraging the student to think about his audience and the context for his writing (10). In his memorandum of September 15, Baird explained that the first few assignments should serve to

> raise the question of what the individual student knows in general and in particular. . . . Then they concentrate on an example, here is something in particular I know. The words most used will be I know, I can do, I learned. The rest of the course will define these words. (1, see note 12)

At the first meeting of every section of English 1, students were asked to address a brief biographical exercise in class. They were asked to describe their previous schooling, their experiences in reading and writing, their interests, and the like. The purpose of the exercise was to generate information that would help instructors to learn students' names and faces. At the end of the hour, instructors gave students their first homework assignment:

> 1. a) Reflect on your resources for writing in English 1–2 and make a list of subjects—*from experiences outside the classroom*—you know you know.

b) Select one in which you claim special expertness.

c) Give reasons to support this claim.

d) Write a paragraph, one page, in which you write out a) b) c) as an "English paper."[14]

The directive to write a paper "as an 'English paper'" meant that the student was to write a coherent essay, not a series of answers to separate questions. The purpose of the assignment was to get students to begin thinking about actions they knew how to perform. As Baird later explained in his 1952 article on "The Freshman English Course," an Amherst freshman could "successfully perform a number of actions, some of them complex and subtle, all of them requiring some capacity to make a shape, to put in order, to see what to do next, to begin and end" (194). Any action the student could perform could serve as a subject for his writing. Moreover, as Baird explained, writing itself

> is an action, it is something the student does, and the teacher aims at putting the student in a position where he can do it. The assignments are our means of locating that situation in which the student knows what he is talking about, in which he feels the desire to express what he knows. When we make an assignment we do not say "Discuss—" or "Write a paper about—," but give such explicit directions that once they are followed the student will find himself saying something he did not know he could say. (194)

During the second class period, Baird suggested in his memorandum of September 15, instructors should describe "the conduct and machinery of the course." They should explain that English 1 was "not a lecture course, [or] a content course, and it has no required reading. It is an action."[12] The paper they would assign at the end of the hour was designed to get students to think further about actions they could perform and ways to write about these performances:

2. Write a paper, two pages, demonstrating or displaying this expertness which you claim.

It was important for the student to choose a fortuitous subject to write about. Otherwise, he might find it difficult to proceed with the next several assignments. The third class period, accordingly, was designed to give students the opportunity to change their minds. During this period, for the first time, instructors were to introduce the procedure of distributing mimeographed specimens of what students had written previously. In this case, the specimens were responses to assignment #1: select something in which you claim special expertise. Instructors would discuss these specimens with their students before giving them assignment #3. As a demonstration of teaching procedures, Baird mimeographed a paper a student had written on "My Hobbies" and distributed copies to his staff.[15] The student had asserted that

> My hobbies are mostly of the sports type, however, and I am interested too in model planes.
>
> In this last I think I am pretty expert because I know about many different types of plane. The thrill of flying your own model too is something not to forget, and I have had it many times.

Baird suggested that an instructor leading a discussion of this paper in class should ask: "Who would be interested in this?" or "Who would bother with this, except a parent?" The instructor should also ask his students: "What other names of hobbies could you substitute here without violating the sense of the paper?" Baird observed that the paper might as easily be about kite flying as about flying model planes.[15] It was an example of what, in his memorandum of August 5, he had called "themewriting," or "write anything about anything for anybody" writing (10, see note 9). In his memorandum of September 15, Baird suggested that an instructor dealing with a theme like the one on model planes should lead his class to recognize that the writing was "bad" and that it was bad because its subject was not, and perhaps could not be, supported. This discussion would prepare the students to address assignment #3, which would invite them to reconsider both the subjects they were claiming to know and their resources for supporting these claims:

3. a) Express again the subject of [the] paper just handed in.
    b) Redefine this subject so that it is manageable in this course.

Assignment #3 was the first of several invitations for revision built into the assignment series. Baird suggested that it might be done in the last five minutes of the second class period and handed in together with assignment #2. Ideally, the student would now claim to be an expert at some kind of physical action. The fourth assignment would make that explicit:

4. a) Write a paper on an action you have repeatedly performed with distinction.
   b) Tell exactly how you performed this action on a particular occasion.

The assignment, like others which would follow, called for narrative writing about a specific experience. Its subject, as Baird explained in his memorandum of August 5, could be "defined in terms of what I did with my body" (11, see note 9). In his memorandum of September 15, he directed his fellow teachers to steer their students away from writing about "something commonplace, like brushing teeth, [or] mowing grass" (3, see note 12). Serving a tennis ball would make a better subject. But even with a good subject, as Baird later pointed out in his article on "The Freshman English Course," the student was likely to have trouble explaining how he did whatever it was he was claiming to be able to do well:

> A student who is a good tennis player sets out to write a paper on what he does when he serves a tennis ball. He knows he knows what he is writing about, yet as he begins to address himself to his subject he immediately encounters the inescapable fact that his consciousness of his own action contains a large area of experience quite beyond his powers of expression. The muscular tensions, the rhythm of his body as he shifts his weight, above all the feel of the action by which he knows a stroke is good or bad almost before the ball leaves the racket, all this and much more lies beyond his command of language, and rendered almost speechless he produces a mess. (1952, 195)

A selection of sample paragraphs written by students in Walker Gibson's section E in response to assignments #2 and #3 of the fall 1946 sequence illustrates Baird's point.[16] One student found it difficult to write about sailing because "in addition to being a highly developed skill, it is also an art" and because "there is a certain 'Feel' to a boat and sailing which comes only with long practice and not always then." Another who began by defining fishing as a "science, or art, if you please," went on to say that in fishing "skill is at least 75% of the battle." He concluded that "fishing is still an unsolved mystery" and that "just when you think you have mastered it, something happens which completely undermines your pet theories." A third student declared that "the field of horseback riding, in which I have chosen to consider myself fairly expert, requires from its experts both a knowledge of horse and sport and the ability to control a horse with a great deal of skill."

One cannot help sympathizing with these students. And as if it weren't hard enough simply to describe how to sail a boat, or fish for bass, or ride a horse, the fifth assignment in the fall 1946 series asked students to explain how they had learned to do these things:

> 5. a) How did you learn this action?
>   b) What did you do to learn?
>   c) Define "learn" in this context.

The question of learning would come up again later in the series, but first, as Baird explained to his staff in his memorandum of September 15, he wanted to spend a few class periods building up the vocabulary of the course and complicating "the definition of the keywords *know* and *knowledge*" (3, see note 12). He suggested that an action "which a student knows how to do" and "has done repeatedly and successfully" might be called a *technique* and one "which he has done successfully only once" could be called a *fluke* (3). In his sixth assignment, Baird called on students to describe a fluke:

> 6. a) Write a paper on an action you performed once and only once with distinction, an action you performed once but were unable to repeat.
>   b) Tell exactly how you did it.

In his memorandum of August 5, Baird suggested that "falling down stairs and landing on your feet" could serve as an example of a fluke.[9] Students could be asked in class to distinguish between a case in which someone fell downstairs and landed on his feet and another case where he broke his arm. This would prepare them to undertake assignment #8. First, however, they had to address #7, which was another instance of an invitation for revision:

> 7. Rewrite assignment #4.[17]

Since assignment #4 was the one in which the student had had to describe a technique, assignment #7 allowed him to reconsider his description in the light of what he had written subsequently about a fluke. Assignment #8 asked him explicitly to

> 8. Contrast papers written for Assignments 6 and 7 (technique and fluke) and make a list of differences between a Technique and a Fluke.

Assignment #9 asked him to review what he had done so far in the course and to

> 9. Make a vocabulary (a list of keywords with definitions) for this course. Do not use [a] dictionary.

If frequent invitations for revision were one noteworthy feature of the assignment sequence for the fall of 1946, so were repeated calls for the building up of a course vocabulary. *Technique* and *fluke* were key words, of course. So were *know* or *knowledge, learn, action,* and *define.* One student in Walker Gibson's section E wrote that "as far as this course is concerned I believe it is safe to say that an action is any bodily movement." Another defined technique as "a systematic method of [a] series of actions, which, if carried out in the order required, will accomplish a successful execution of the desired end." A third student wrote that "a fluke is an action that gives a desired result, but the operator of this action is unable to explain how he did it, nor is he able to repeat this action successfully."[18] But however students managed to define *technique* and *fluke,* their definitions were sure to be complicated further by assignments #10 and #11:

10. "One man's fluke is another man's technique." Take a new personal example and show how an accidental performance of one man might reasonably be a matter of conscious skill for another.

Baird suggested in his memorandum of August 5 that the flukish case of falling downstairs and landing on one's feet might be reconsidered in the context of this assignment. Falling downstairs was an action which could be learned and which was often performed successfully by clowns and stunt men (11, see note 9). Assignment #11 called for a new contrast, and assignment #12 was another invitation for revision:

11. "One man's routine is another man's technique." Take an example and show how routine behavior of one man might reasonably be conscious and purposeful for another. [19]

12. Copy [assignment] 5b, "What did you do to learn?"
    b) Rewrite—using original or a new example?—in light of present knowledge of meaning of *learn*.
    c) Look at example of fluke and using the vocabulary of this course express what the difficulty is in learning how to perform a fluke.

Assignment #12 called for carefully focused revision. The student was to revise his assignment #5 paper "in the light of" what he had learned about learning since he first wrote it. He had written six new papers since that time and presumably had become aware of some of the complexities entailed by his original position. Assignment #14 called for a similar kind of focused revision, in this case of assignment #11. Assignment #13, by contrast, was an open-ended invitation to

13. Rewrite any paper you like.

14. a) Describe a technique that has become a routine.
    b) Briefly describe a situation where this routine performance would be unsatisfactory.

c) Tell exactly what you would do and how you would do it
to make your performance satisfactory.

Assignments #15 and #24 worked together as a pair. While #24
would call on the student to describe a teaching experience, #15
called on him to

15. Describe exactly the situation (circumstances, time, place,
persons) when you learned something from another person,
a coach or teacher, at the moment when you became aware
that you had learned it.
b) What had the coach or teacher done to teach you?
c) What did you do to learn?

In his memorandum of August 5, Baird suggested that a good
many students would respond to this assignment by saying that

they know they have learned because they were praised or got
rewards or were told they had learned by someone in authority.
Some will say, when I did it, it worked, it succeeded. What does
this refer to? Here we face a major issue of pragmatism, but our
purpose is achieved if we demonstrate to them that success and
failure is not an either-or proposition. Games are extremely useful here as illustrations, for they all have rules and, sometimes,
umpires to apply them. (12, see note 9)

In a memorandum he circulated on October 25 (see note 19),
Baird noted that the question asked in assignment #15c, "What did
you do to learn?" ought "to get words like *practice* and *try* out into the
open." Assignment #16 would ask students to reconsider their use of
such verbs:

16. a) Make a list of the verbs which you used in paragraph "c."
b) Write a new paragraph using these words [and] showing
how you learned this action.

Assignment #17 called on students once again to revise #4,
"Write a paper on an action you have repeatedly performed with dis-

tinction." They had had, for assignment #7, to revise #4 once before. In his memorandum of October 25 (see note 19), Baird referred to #17 as "an important assignment" which should show whether students had "made any advance."

> 17. Rewrite or [write] a completely new version of a technique and the process of learning it.

Assignment #18 asked students to consider alternative ways of describing a performance. A baseball player's performance, for example, might be described loosely as "good" or "bad" or "successful," or it might be described in terms of his batting average.

> 18. List three standards or scales of successful performance, omitting those used as examples in class, such as a batting average.
>   b) Select one and translate the figures standing for very good and very bad performance. By translate we mean, express in English.

Assignments #19 to #21 related to the controversial fifth down of a 1940 football game between Dartmouth College and Cornell. On a one-page document[20] that was mimeographed for all students in all sections, the game and its aftermath were described as follows:

> ON SATURDAY, NOVEMBER 16, 1940, Cornell defeated Dartmouth 7–3. With less than three seconds to play, the score Dartmouth 3—Cornell 0, Bill Murphy caught a pass in the end zone, sealing the doom of one of the fightingest Dartmouth teams in history.
>
> Cornell had advanced to the Dartmouth 6 yard line. There followed three line plays which netted 5 yards. Cornell was then penalized 5 yards for an extra time out period. Cornell passed and Hall of Dartmouth knocked it down instead of catching it as he might well have done. An official started to put the ball down on the 20 yard line, meaning it was Dartmouth's ball on downs, but he changed his mind and replaced it on the Dartmouth 6 yard line and gave it to Cornell. With 3 seconds to play Scholl passed to Murphy in the end zone and the game was over, Cornell 7—

Dartmouth 3. Coach Snavely supposed, it was said, that on the pass which was knocked down both teams had been offside.

After the game coaches and officials admitted that Cornell had five plays in the scoring series. Referee Friesell refused to make a statement.

ON MONDAY, NOVEMBER 18, Asa Bushnell, head of the Eastern Intercollegiate Football Association declared his association has no authority to change the 7–3 score. Nor, he said, do the officials have any authority to change their decision after it has been made. The Dartmouth–Cornell game was, he said, "a rather unique case."

Compiling records of football games is done by an organization that has no power to make any changes in the scores of games.

The whole point seems to revolve about the question whether there was a double offside on the pass thrown just before the final pass. Films of the game are being developed feverishly.

The Dartmouth Indians were hailed on the Dartmouth campus as "victorious heroes." The Dartmouth coach told a rally that Friesell was a "great referee" and that Dartmouth will abide by the decision of the Eastern Intercollegiate Football Association.

ON TUESDAY, NOVEMBER 19, Referee Friesell publicly admitted he had been in error when he gave the Big Red a fifth down. Cornell relinquished all claim to victory. Dartmouth accepted the triumph. Only by this combination of circumstances could the score be reversed, for there is no authority beyond the colleges themselves for correcting the error. Cornell in doing this removed itself from the list of undefeated teams, and it has had 18 straight victories.

ON WEDNESDAY, NOVEMBER 20, President Day of Cornell in speaking at a rally likened Cornell's tribulations to the ill fortunes of Job, and he said he has been "deeply resentful of some of the things the season has brought to the university and the team." The Captain of [the] football team is reported in the hospital with a stomach ailment.

ON NOVEMBER 21, Commissioner Bushnell of the Eastern Intercollegiate Football Association said that revising the score of the Dartmouth–Cornell football game should not establish a precedent. Only when an official reverses his decision on the last play of the game is it possible to accept a change in score.

ON NOVEMBER 23, the "fifth down" sundae is reported as setting the ice cream style at Hanover.

Assignments #19 to #21 asked Amherst students to grapple with the ambiguities inherent in the Dartmouth–Cornell game:

19. Make a narrative of events in chronological order and within the limits of a page.

In his memorandum of October 25 (see note 19), Baird suggested that before giving students assignment #20, instructors should spend a class period discussing the question of what a football game was. A football game might be described, he observed, as a contest. During the last fifteen minutes of the period, students could be asked to address the new assignment:

20. Write a definition of a game.

In Walker Gibson's section E, one student wrote that a game "always has a winner except for the case of a tie." Another student wrote that "it is not uncommon to have the inferior team win because of flukes (fumbles, penalties, etc.) and so success based on score is no accurate measure of the team's real ability." A third wrote that "the thing striven for is success or victory which is defined in the rules of the game." This student added that "the rules must be construed to meet the situation" and that "the authority to do this is given to the game officials."[21]

The instructor who led section E, Walker Gibson, was a friend of a friend of the man who in 1940 had been the captain of the Dartmouth football team. On November 13, 1946, Gibson wrote a letter to this former captain explaining that the English staff at Amherst College was very interested in the 1940 Dartmouth–Cornell game:

We have been assigning a series of freshman composition exercises based on that reversed decision, asking our students such questions as "Just what *is* a game?" "Who *really* won on Saturday?" "Who *really* won the following Wednesday?" etc. These questions, as I'm sure you perceive, are highly provocative and indeed almost unanswerable. We hope to get a useful kind of point across involving shifting concepts of Success and Failure.[22]

Assignment #21 asked students to look at the game from different points of view:

21. What went wrong with the famous Dartmouth–Cornell game? Wrong from the point of view of a) Scholl and Murphy, b) Referee Friesell, c) the Dartmouth Captain, d) Asa Bushnell, e) the Dartmouth Coach, f) the Cornell Coach, g) the President of Cornell, h) the Captain of the Cornell team.

In Gibson's section E, one student wrote that the Cornell coach had been "bitterly disappointed" because "his team had done their best and the last play had been perfect but in vain due to the referee's error." Another complained that "how the Cornell coach, captain, and President could differ is beyond my comprehension." A third student wrote that "the thing wrong from the C captain's point of view was that the referee had erred ... but so what?" He explained in capital letters that "REFEREE'S MISTAKES ARE PART OF THE GAME OF FOOTBALL and should be treated as such."[23]

Assignment #22 was an invitation to revise #20. Assignment #23, like #9, invited students to take stock of what they were learning in English 1:

22. Rewrite [your] definition of a Game.[24]

23. a) Make a list of keywords in this course.
    b) Do you want to add some? You don't have to do this.
    c) Arrange these keywords in a diagram to indicate relations.

Assignment #24 was paired to #15. For the earlier assignment, students had had to describe a learning experience. Now they had to

24. a) Describe exactly a situation (place, time, circumstances) in which you taught some one something he needed to know.

    b) What did you do to teach him?

    c) What did he do?

    d) How did you know he finally succeeded in learning?

    e) Point out those things which are unteachable (those things which no one on earth can supply for another person).

    f) What kind of experience can be taught?

In his memorandum of August 5, Baird told his staff that "we ought now to be able to sort out the element of imitation" (13, see note 9). An athlete could learn something by imitating his coach's movements, Baird observed, but not all that he needed to know. A student in Gibson's section E wrote about his experience teaching his sister to ride a bike. He explained:

> I found that I couldn't teach my sister how to keep the bike balanced. She had to feel it out for herself using her own sense of balance. What I could teach her were the actions themselves, the action of pedaling and of turning the bicycle. I could not control her actions, but I could show her how to do them.[25]

In his memorandum of August 5, commenting on the question "What can be taught?" Baird observed that "the answer here is not movement (for is not that inexpressible?) but the order of movement." At this point in the course, he suggested, instructors could "introduce slow motion, fixing the eternal flux in moments of time, breaking down sequence into steps or stages" and raise the matter they would "talk about nearly every day for the rest of the course,—order" (14, see note 9). Assignments #25 and #26 would deal squarely with this matter of order:

25. Make a list of five orders you know how to make.[26]

26. a) Select a particular order you know how to make.

    b) Make it in particular terms—and in manageable form.

c) Explain briefly your reasons for establishing each position in this order.

d) How else could this order be made?

e) How would you prove that one [(b) or (d)] is "right"?

Giving reasons for establishing nine places in a batting order,
Baird observed in a memorandum he circulated on November 22,
would "take pages"(see note 26). Assignment #27 asked students to
contrast an order with a mess:

27. Describe a mess of physical objects and tell how you
straightened it out, how you put it in order.

Assignments #28 to #30 had to do with making orders in the
library, and with them Baird introduced the practice, which thereafter
became standard, of building three or four assignments on the library
into each fall's sequence. He devised the fall 1946 library assignments
with the help of Newton McKeon, who had been a member of
Baird's initial staff in 1938–39 and then, in 1939, became the director
of the Amherst College Library. In conjunction with the library
assignments, McKeon and his staff would give each English 1 class section a tour of the library. Baird, in his memorandum of August 5,
explained that the library assignments would be especially critical for
students because

Here we connect in practical terms the subject of our conversation and assignments with their total experience as students, and
relate some instruction in use of the Library to our main ideas.
Here we take a number system and connect it with physical
movements, both in using the library and in maintaining the
library. (15, see note 9)

The first assignment in the library block called on students to
describe the arrangement of books in the library in terms of a user's
experience:

28. Go to the Library. Note the number of any card in the catalog. Find the book which the number designates. (If it is not

in its place, you may assume that it has been loaned. Return to the catalog and begin afresh with another number.) In writing, report a) the number, b) how you got from a number on a card to the book, c) the author and title of the book.

d) What, specifically, is signified when you say of this book that it is *in its place?*

e) What is demanded of anyone wishing to find the book?[27]

The next assignment asked students to look at the same arrangement of books through the eyes of a cataloguer:

29. Go to the library and follow the directions in the above assignment, taking another book number to start with. On finding the book examine the other volumes on the same shelf.

a) What subject do they appear to have in common?

b) What elements of their numbers do they have in common?

c) What inference can you draw as to the relation between the number and the subject?

d) With respect to other elements these numbers will all differ. By examining the backs of books as they sit on the shelf ascertain what relation these elements of the numbers bear to the books.

e) You have established two relationships between the numbers and the physical objects. How, then, would you describe the order employed in arranging books in the Library?

The third assignment in the library block asked students to contrast what a library user and a cataloguer would need to know about the arrangement of books in the library:

30. a) Assume that you have a newly purchased book and have the task of assigning it to its appropriate number. What decision would you first have to reach?

b) What means would you have for reaching it?

c) Your next operation would be to determine the proper number (which, you have observed, consists of two elements). What sort of information would you require in order to do this?

d) Which is the more complex, finding the book after it has been assigned to its place in the order, or placing the book where it may be found?

e) What does the phrase *in its place* signify to the Library? To the user?

At this point in the semester, there remained only time for one last assignment before the Christmas break. The term would not end until January, however, and when students returned from vacation, they would have to write a "long paper" for English 1 and to pass a final examination. Assignment #31 was similar to assignments #9 and #23 and was designed to prepare students for the kinds of summarizing activities they would be asked to undertake in January:

31. a) Make a complete vocabulary with definitions for this course.

b) Express the argument or order of this course in a paragraph.

The "long paper" assignment for January of 1947 followed very neatly from assignment #31. Students were asked to

1. Make a complete list of assignments.

2. Make a vocabulary for this course, i.e., make a list of words and define them in the context of this classroom.

3. Write an essay of not over five pages expressing the sequence of ideas you have perceived in this term's work.

GENERAL DIRECTIONS: Do not merely repeat your list in No. 1 in sentence and paragraph form. Do not make the sequence of ideas the sequence of time in which you did the assignments. What you should do is translate the list in No. 1 into terms of your own conclusions, as if you were telling someone who is interested what you have learned.

PARTICULAR DIRECTIONS: Your list in No. 1 should refresh your memory of what you have done. You should read over the papers you have written. Your list in No. 2 will lead to the "subject" of your essay if you decide which one of these words in your vocabulary is the keyword of the course. By keyword is meant the word most important for you to use and understand to get on in this course. Make a statement about this word, a statement of what you have done, and this ought to give you the "subject" of your essay in No. 3. Now write this essay, expressing the argument as it has been built up in your mind, the sequence of ideas, telling what you think and how step by step you came to think it.[28]

The assignment invited the student to make sense of the semester and put him in a position where he could hardly fail to recognize his active involvement in whatever he could claim to have learned. The subject for his writing had been his own know-how, and he had had to find ways to write about what he knew. Throughout the semester, assignments had been presented to him in a particular order, but he had constructed further orders among them.

The final hurdle of the semester was an examination.[29] Students were given two hours and told that

The purpose of this examination is to test your ability to reflect and to write under pressure of time and with no resources but your own. Connect your answers to the questions in part II to form a coherent essay. You must finish this examination.

The directions for part I of the two-part exam were simply to read two passages carefully. The passages had been taken from two of the "long assignment" papers written the week before:

A

The keyword of this course is thus "order." This is so because we have been learning to eliminate confusion from our thoughts and our writing, and this we must do if we are to succeed as college students. By our trips to the library, as I have shown, and by the other examples I have given, it will be seen that our instructors have been exposing us to the principle of orderly thought, the principle that underlies all the basic forms of knowledge.

This principle, now that I see it, is as simple as it is obvious. I have found that just as I eliminated confusion from my workshop by putting each tool in its proper place, so I eliminate confusion from my writing by putting each word and thought in its proper place. In this course I have thus learned first to consider the principle of order in my subject and then to write. In this way I am sure to write clearly and with the correct order of my subject in mind.

B

The keyword of this course, to sum up, seems to me to be "order." This word suggests the kind of answer we have agreed to give to the key question of the course: "What are you doing?" When some one asks me this question, I cannot tell him *all* I am doing, even if he had time enough and I had words enough. I must select *from* my action, I must talk *about* it. Now the answer to this question that communicates knowledge, we have seen, is the answer that enables the questioner to follow us in doing the action. We must therefore answer him in words that communicate some of the possible steps he can follow to perform the action himself. For it is a sequence of steps that really makes the difference between doing and not doing the action. A good football coach is one who can size up a prospect and give him a few, often a very few, instructions that turn the prospect into a valuable player. The coach knows, as my coach knew in the example I described earlier, that if a prospective guard can move his body so as to do this, then that, he can control the rest of the actions involved in "pulling out." A bad coach is one who fusses about little acts that don't help you to do anything else.

It would seem from all this that the "order" of any action is a varying thing. It varies from situation to situation and from person to person. It changes constantly and is constantly modified to meet new conditions. But that is only natural. It is still true that if I communicate the order of an action to some one, then he will know just what he *can* change and adapt. Order then means a describable relationship between individual movements I can direct and a successful result. And to describe this relationship has meant good writing in this course.

Part II, which was the written part of the exam, consisted of four questions about the two passages:

1. What meaning is given to "order" in passage A? Work it out and state it in your own words.
2. What meaning is given to "order" in passage B? Work it out and state it in your own words.
3. Which passage, A or B, do you find the more useful for your guidance in writing? Or do you find them equally useful? Or do you find neither useful? Why?
4. Illustrate your answer to 3 by showing how you would select and define a subject to write about from your own experience. This subject, preferably, should not be one you have used in a course assignment. Do not write the paper: merely show how you would go about writing it and why.

Applying the lessons of the course, most students would have seen that the second of the two passages provided the more useful advice. While the first writer had said little more than to "be clear," the second had distinguished between knowing how to perform an action and knowing how to communicate something of that knowledge to another. This was an important distinction for a student to make, as Baird observed in his 1952 article on "The Freshman English Course." Baird noted that a student who wanted to explain how to serve a tennis ball needed to recognize

> that a part or an element of his experience can be communicated to another person when he isolates the order in which he throws the ball into the air, raises his racket, and so on, and that the order of his action, as distinguished from the action itself is the subject of his writing. The student may even perceive that between the order of movements as he sees them and the order of words in a sentence some relation can be made, and that when he has made this relation he knows what he is talking about. (195)

At the conclusion of "The Freshman English Course," Baird argued in defense of the course that

> some decent writing does get done, and the student sees it happen. I am well pleased when he finds himself saying, as one surprised, "Why, I know what I am talking about." And there may

be by-products. The student may come to respect good writing, however plain. He may even recognize as the marvel it is the human being's power of making order out of chaos. (196)

Baird's assignments for the fall of 1946 became a model for sequences used subsequently in English 1. Similarly, his sequence for the spring of 1947,[30] except in one important respect, established a pattern for later English 2 sequences. Because they concerned techniques students were learning in school, the spring 1947 assignments followed neatly from the ones on techniques learned outside the classroom that had been used the previous fall. Students were asked to write about the operations necessary for generating knowledge in each of the four subject areas of the social sciences, the laboratory sciences, English, and mathematics. In the area of history, they had to make a list of key words for a history course. They had to select a historical period, specify its terminal dates, and explain whatever procedure they had followed in doing so. They had to select a building on the campus or in the town, determine its period, and explain how they had made the determination. Given a collection of statistics arranged in long columns, they had to identify a trend and to explain it in English, without using figures. Finally, students had to write a paper about the language they had been using as historians and the operations this language stood for.

English 2 in the spring of 1947 was anomalous, however, in that classes met three times a week and students addressed thirty-three assignments for the semester. The following spring, with the New Curriculum fully in effect, the mandated Humanities 2 course took a class hour away from English 2, and English classes met only twice a week. Thus a typical English 2 assignment series after 1947 consisted of only twenty-two assignments and, until the focus of English 2 changed in the late 1950s, concerned what students were learning in only the two subject areas of history and laboratory science.

Assignment sequences were never repeated for either English 1 or English 2. A new one was devised each semester. Baird told me that "this was my way of escaping boredom—never doing it twice the same way, never feeling 'I know how to do this,' always facing a new problem, and a problem that you didn't know how to solve. That way you never felt you were just a damned section man, or whatever, teaching a required course. You thought, 'This is making all the demands on me that can be made.' I don't know how many felt that way."

But although sequences were always new, they did conform to certain patterns. They generally began, for example, with several assignments designed to demonstrate the inadequacy of theme writing. A new block of assignments on the use of the library was used every fall. From semester to semester and year to year, students were faced with assignments inviting them to make lists of key words, to define terms "by context," to make judgments about paired texts, to revise a certain key paper "in the light of" what they had learned since first writing it, and at several junctures to take stock of their learning. The final assignment in a sequence generally called for such stocktaking. Baird did not always serve as the principal author of the assignments. His younger colleagues frequently spelled him at this task.

CHAPTER FOUR

No One Knows
the Answers

During the twenty years from 1947 when the "New Curriculum" was implemented until 1966 when it was overturned, English 1–2 was required of all freshmen and so carefully orchestrated that, in any given semester, every student in every class section addressed the same assignments. During this same period, only a few of the most senior members of Amherst's English department, such as George Whicher, escaped from having to lead sections of the course. Planning and leading the course—and responding to student papers—required a huge expenditure of time and labor on the part of its staff. Few instructors had time left over for research projects of their own. Few of them, moreover, could expect to stay at Amherst for more than a short time. Most of them labored under what Walker Gibson calls a "three-years-and-out-you-go rule" (1985, 139). The only compensation that Baird could offer these men was the opportunity to learn something. Baird says, "This was the dream that I had, that maybe English teachers, or maybe teachers, could teach one another. Maybe they could learn from one another. And how successful this dream was, I do not know finally" (1978b, 23).

In his article on "Theodore Baird," Gibson has explained that "the course was team-taught," but that in the context of English 1–2, team teaching did

> not mean that a group of people met a few times and went their several ways, nor that they participated directly in one another's classrooms. In English 1–2, teamwork meant something else and something fairly rigorous. (1985, 138)

Gibson told me that Baird never sat in on one of his classes. Nor did Gibson ever observe a class of Baird's. Gibson speculated that "maybe it was felt that it would be frightening to people, and it would have been; it would have been threatening." The collaborative exchanges which did occur, Gibson says, "took place at staff meetings." He describes the staff meetings as "semi-religious gatherings" and says that "you were there without fail." Armour Craig says, "I will never forget the day when Professor Baird said during a staff meeting, 'What do you need to fix a motorcycle?' You need a language. You need words. Here's all this funny looking metal, but how do you know it's a motorcycle? How do you know it's a motor? Why isn't it a radiator? What you need is terms with which to distinguish features of this blur." Craig added that the staff meetings were "a wonderful experience. It was the only place, the only place certainly in the Amherst English department, in which people would risk real differences, real misunderstandings, then try to get them straight." Baird said, "I don't think there was any other department [at Amherst College] where there was that kind of exchange."

According to Baird, "We had a meeting once a week, and it would last for an hour and a half, an hour sometimes. And at the beginning of each term, a teacher was given a complete set of assignments, so that he could sit down and work them out for himself in his own mind—what was the direction this writing would take? And he had this opportunity for reflection. Then, each week he came in to a meeting with this complete set of assignments and we would discuss the phrasing, the appropriateness, the intention, and the likelihood of any success in the next three assignments for the next week." Baird added that often assignments "were rephrased, they were even rewritten, or they were even rejected" (1978b, 23–24). On another occasion he told me, "We'd argue about how an assignment should be phrased. Somebody was always adding a comma somewhere." Instructors sometimes brought in sample student papers. According to Baird, "Another thing we did at these meetings was to say, 'Now this is a paper I have just read and I am going to use it, it is mimeographed, and I'm going to use it in my next class,' or 'I used it in my last class, and this is how I handled it.'" Baird has claimed that from this kind of exchange it was possible to "learn something, and you would go away and say, 'Yes, I can see how he did that and that's worth doing'" (23).

The English 1–2 staff in 1951–52. Seated, from left: *G. Armour Craig, Cesar L. Barber, Newton F. McKeon Jr., Theodore Baird.* Standing, from left: *Benjamin H. DeMott, Robert Ross Staley, Richard L. Waidelich, W. Walker Gibson.*

When I asked Baird if he remembered specific exchanges with younger staff members, he said, "It was fun just to hear someone tell how he had a good class. You got a view of somebody like Bill Gibson.[1] He was a wonderful teacher and very ingenious."

The fall of 1946 was Gibson's first semester of teaching at Amherst College. He had graduated from Yale in 1940, and unlike the only slightly older Craig, who had remained in civilian ranks thanks to his employment in the "sheltered occupation" of college teaching, Gibson spent the war years in the military. He was a poet, and he told me that "magazines at that time were crying for someone in uniform who was reasonably literate. Early on, *The New Republic* ran a soldier's verse contest, where it was perfectly clear that the writers and the subjects were going to be military, and I won." This distinction and a fair list of published poems enabled Gibson, immediately after he was demobilized in the fall of 1945, to qualify for a small graduate fellowship at the Iowa Writers Workshop. He spent a year working on his master's degree at Iowa, then because he and his wife already had two children and because "the prospect of going on for a doctorate was

W. Walker Gibson about 1950.

not only forbidding, but almost impossible," he began writing job inquiry letters. He told me that in the postwar climate, the job market was such that "I could have had six jobs by just writing an appropriate letter, and clearly the most attractive one was the one at Amherst." In April of 1946, he was invited to Amherst to interview for a job that would pay him $3,000 a year.

Gibson says he thought of Amherst as "a prestigious, rich boys' school, and I was not far wrong." He says, "I certainly knew nothing about English 1 whatever; I had never heard of Baird." He met Baird when he arrived for his interview and remembers that Baird "tried his best, though he must have done this a million times to a million candidates over the years, to communicate to me what was up. But I'm sure I didn't get it; I didn't get it at all. In fact from my point of view I was being hired to teach juniors and seniors something about the writing of poetry and fiction. That was my center, and if they insisted, I would teach a section of freshmen because that was what apparently they expected me to do and that would be part of the deal. It probably took me a couple of years to realize that I had the cart before the horse, that the real center of excitement here was in that freshman course."

Baird, Craig, and Gibson all remember the course very positively. Baird said that "the heart of the course was in the assignments" (letter to R. Varnum, March 16, 1991). He told me that "the questions were difficult. You could catch glimpses of real thinking sometimes. That's what kept me going. That's what kept me alive as a teacher. My chief motive in running the course was I was trying to keep from being bored." Gibson suggests that the aim of English 1–2 was for students to recognize both that "the world they live in is the world they express in words" and that "control of that world and of themselves depends considerably on their control of their own words" (1985, 146). Craig told me that "we kept insisting, all the time, at least I certainly did, on getting them to hitch control of their words to the control of their actions, where they know what they are doing."

Craig told me that "what we would do in the first semester was work out an approach to putting the world of experience into a world of words, and we would do this in lots of different ways. We would, for instance, work out a little vocabulary, starting with 'map,' or 'skyline,' or something like that. These would be examples of discovering and understanding a key term. Then in the second semester, we would say to these freshmen in effect, 'All right, while we have been working out this way of talking about writing and reading, you have been taking a lot of other courses.' (Because they all did take other courses, and we knew what they were and what they were doing.) 'All right, you've been doing this and that. Can you tell me what you do when you do history? What are some key terms? Where do you find a key term? How do you find it?'" Craig added, "There was obviously an autobiographical dimension to this because they were writing about 'what I do when I do,' and as one very bright student said in a piece that he wrote in, I suppose, the late 1950s, 'What you are really asking us in this course is: What do you know? How do you know you know it? How do you say it?' He was right."

Students' papers were published in class and used as examples of successful and unsuccessful writing. The papers which were published were selected by the instructors rather than volunteered by the students. Craig remembers that he often started discussions of the papers he had chosen to publish in his class by asking his students: "Does anything go wrong here? Is this a passage in which he [the student author] takes a turn? Is this a passage in which he discovers something?" Craig told me that "what mattered was the performance, and that is what the students were judging." Gibson sometimes had his students rewrite a sample paper. He described this classroom procedure in a November 2, 1946 letter to Baird. Gibson reported he had asked his students to rewrite, in class, "a mimeographed example of a particularly bad paper—bad in a certain useful way, that is." The example was a paper on a technique for teaching swimming. When the students had finished their revisions, Gibson

> had several of the boys read their versions aloud. They all wanted to expand the original, but since I didn't let them, and in fact limited them to the actual material of the original, they were forced to see that the story was incomplete. Those few who claimed to know what was being talked about, I made act out the stroke. The conflicts were delicious.[2]

One of the functions of the first few assignments each fall was to demonstrate to students that they did not know as much as they may have thought. Walker Gibson has observed that in the first several assignments of any English 1 sequence, students generally

> floundered and fell all over themselves. Such floundering in the early stages was expected and indeed necessary. (If the students had been able to answer such questions wisely during the first week of the course, there would be no need to continue.) (1985, 141)

Armour Craig explained that students "came to us with very strange and very harmful presuppositions about language. What we tried to direct their attention towards was language as that which controls your experience." He recalled that many students had been of the sort who "don't want to know anything. They want a finishing school. They want to be given the manners and the verbal behavior that will convince the prospective employer that they are from the highest eighth of the country."

When I asked Craig how he had dealt with such students, he said, "I gave them Cs and Ds." He said that many students had thought it necessary "to talk pretty about metaphor." They used to ask, "What do you want, Sir? Do you want me to talk about metaphor?" Craig said that in fact "the papers that we praised, the writing that we praised, was a real passage in the sense that the 'I,' the agent, moved from one place to another in his or her terminology."

One member of the staff would have spent his summer drafting a set of assignments for the coming fall. When the term began, he would find himself at staff meetings in the position of having to explain and defend his thinking. Gibson says of the experience of writing the assignments, "One did that with the sense that someone was looking over his shoulder." Baird says, "Making a sequence was hard. You start somewhere with a question: what is a machine, what is a mask, what is history, what is a game, etc. etc. Then you work it out with what examples you can think of, for 25 or 30 assignments. This is hard work and you have to face a staff of eight or ten people who will tell you they don't see what you 'mean,' that you don't know how to punctu- ate, that they don't see where this leads or how it follows. There you are, and your assignment may be quite altered at the end of the hour and you have to accept that. This was not always pleasant to your ego" (letter to R. Varnum, May 4, 1991).

Baird says, "I always hoped that others would make these assign- ments, and this was from my point-of-view, less successful. There was always the problem of getting them to do them on time" (1978b, 25). In a June 18, 1948 letter to Gibson, Baird complained, "From my point-of-view I have done much more than I should do." Recalling one staff member's particularly dismal performance, he declared,

> I'll never forget the day we met, the day before classes began in
> the fall, to receive an outline of the first month's work, and we
> were told that this fellow had been too busy (quarreling with his
> wife) to get anything ready for us. There we were. There we sat.
> A common responsibility makes friction sometimes.[3]

Such problems aside, Baird's younger colleagues did share in the responsibility for writing the assignments. An instructor named Frank Poland wrote a series on machines for the fall of 1947. Craig wrote a series on apprenticeship for the fall of 1949. Indeed Craig, who thinks he may have written as many as fifteen or twenty series, wrote more assignments than anyone except Baird himself.

Some of the sequences Baird remembers writing personally are those on "what or who was your 'true self'?" "what is a conviction?" "what is good English?" and "what does it mean to learn?" (1978b, 25). His younger colleague, William Pritchard, told me that of the many sequences which were used for English 1–2, Baird's tended to be "the most inventive." Craig concurred, noting that "the most inventive pedagogical imagination that I certainly have ever encountered is that of Theodore Baird." Baird himself observed that "I don't think anybody ever took this course as seriously as I did. I took it seriously—ALL the time. I put my best mind, such as it was, to this simple thing" (1978b, 26).

Baird says he had a "formula" for making assignments. He says, "I would take a general proposition of some kind, or to put it more exactly, I would take a question. The great thing I learned from [Oxford philosopher R. G.] Collingwood was that you had to learn how to ask a question. And the question I asked was simply something like this: 'What is a conflict?' And then I would go on from there and say, 'Have you ever felt any conflict?' and 'What was it like when you felt conflict?' Or I would say, 'What were you arguing about?,' 'What was the issue?,' 'How did you address yourself?,' 'How did you feel?,' and so on." Baird adds that "we had a whole semester on conflict" and that "it was very interesting because there were students in my class who said, 'I have never known conflict.' Now I would like to have somebody tell me what a teacher does when a student says something like that" (1978b, 24).

Craig says that a typical assignment instruction was to "do thus and so about X; describe as thoroughly and carefully as you can what you did when you did something about X." Craig adds, "We would always at the end say, 'Now define X.'" He remembers that "we frequently had assignments that asked one way or another, 'You are in a situation where you're at a loss. What does it feel like? How do you know you're at a loss?' Or in a situation in which you don't understand something that somebody says to you, what is the experience of not understanding? What is the experience of being at an impasse? How does this differ from the experience in which you were stuck, but you got out of it? How did you get out of it?" Craig says he always told students, "I am not going to ask you to talk about your sexual or religious experiences; all I am asking you to talk about is your experience as a student, as somebody who is trying to know."

Gibson agrees that the staff did not mean for students to write about "How I Hated My Father." According to Gibson, the assignments did mean "you had to go back to your experience and analyze it in a way that you never had before. Sports, of course, are great for this because we get so that we can excel at a sport or at least do it

Armour Craig in his classroom about 1960.

competently. We can be competent at a sport and utterly unconscious of what we're doing." Gibson speculated that "it would be very difficult to get [tennis star Andre] Agassi to say what he does when he serves, because it's just a routine for him."

Gibson contributed assignments from time to time and remembers "the kind of imagination and excitement that we young guys would be stirred up to, so that we would write some additional assignments." In the spring of 1947, during his second semester teaching the course, he wrote several questions for the English 2 mini-series on English. In one of these assignments, which was of the paired-text type that Baird had been using since at least 1938, Gibson asked students to

> Read two mimeographed passages. Both are printed in prose form, but actually one is a poem. Decide which is the poem, . . . How did you decide?[4]

The assignment appears on a March 28 memorandum of Baird's together with the observation, which may be Baird's or may be Gibson's, that

> With proper secrecy, and ambiguous passages, two-thirds of the boys ought to get this wrong. What is a poem anyway?

Years later, when I asked Gibson about this observation, he didn't remember ever having written such a thing, but he conceded, "That sounds like an English 1 instruction." He then suggested sarcastically that it might be used as a "little frontispiece remark for your whole thesis:'With any luck two-thirds of them will get it wrong.' If two-thirds of them got it right," he added, "we would have to give up."

Gibson wrote a series of science assignments for the spring of 1954 on wind and the use of a wind anemometer.[5] The first three tasks Gibson gave students in this series were to "Look out the window and make an observation about direction and force of the wind," to "Describe everything you looked at in order to make this observation," and to "Define observation." Later he asked students to go "to the weather shelter in front of the Biology Building and read wind direction and velocity from the instruments there." He asked them to contrast the language they used in reporting on this activity to what they used in reporting the earlier observations they had made from their windows. In the sixth assignment in his series, Gibson asked students to

> Build your own anemometer. Use paper clips, cardboard, thumb tacks, pencil stubs, or anything your ingenuity can devise. (You must bring your anemometer to class.) Write a careful account of just what your plan of building was, how you proceeded, and what your difficulties were.

Next, Gibson asked them to

> Run a series of tests with your anemometer in which you invent and use a Scale of Measurement. Explain carefully the terms of your scale, and describe some readings.

He also asked them to explain what it was that their scales measured and to say whether or not they thought their activities had been scientific. Then, after informing them that a scientist "doesn't just make observations; he makes sentences, with subjects and verbs," Gibson asked them how they might go about making their activities scientific.

When I asked Gibson about these assignments, he said, "I remember I interviewed Arnold Arons a couple of times to do that. I think it was maybe ten or twelve assignments in which the big moment was the manufacture of your own anemometer. And then of course you make your own system for it, and the only difference between the system that the kids make and miles per hour is a communications matter. The kids' systems were private, that's all."[6]

Arnold Arons, whom Gibson interviewed in order to write the anemometer assignments, had come to Amherst College in 1952 to teach physics and to reorganize Science 1–2, the two-semester course in science mandated by the New Curriculum for all freshmen. In a 1955 article, Arons described Science 1–2 as a staff-taught course involving "all the members of the mathematics and physics departments as well as one man from chemistry and one from astronomy" (76). He noted that "one of our principal objectives is to make the student explicitly aware of the process of acquiring knowledge in any field" (77). Baird has said that English 1–2 "received a great deal of support when Arnold Arons came here and taught Science 1. I think this must have been one of the very few colleges in the United States where the English course for freshmen was not hostile and was, you might say, in harmony with a science course" (1978b, 26). The two courses were not only in harmony, they reinforced one another structurally, and together they constituted every freshman's orientation to Amherst College. No student could escape from either course. Arons acknowledged that he and his Science 1–2 staff were "dealing with a captive audience," and he noted that "our approach is practicable in a small, homogeneous college, but we have serious reservations about its practicability in a broader context" (1955, 113). Baird told me that he and Arons "got on well together, and I would always give him our set of assignments." Arons himself, in an account of Science 1–2 he wrote for Gail Kennedy's Review Committee on the New Program, said that

> every opportunity is taken to show them [students] how the growth and use of language in science is a special application of the general concepts which are concurrently being developed in the freshman English course. The student is required (in parallel with the English department) to formulate statements entirely on his own in precise words which will make sense to other individuals. The English course is frequently referred to during our classes, and mention of the science course arises with increasing frequency in the English section meetings. This carry

over has produced clearly visible effects in student morale and attitude toward both courses and is proving to be a powerful educational force. (Kennedy 1955, 211–212)

In a 1987 letter he wrote from Seattle to the editor of the Amherst alumni magazine, Arons included himself among "those who were significantly influenced by Baird and English 1–2" (26). He said that, upon his arrival in Amherst in September 1952, one of the first things he did was to call Baird and ask for information about English 1–2. Baird responded by inviting Arons to his home. According to Arons, "We sat down in that beautiful living room, with its outlook on the surrounding trees, and he [Baird] cordially and considerately tried to tell me about the enterprise" (26). Arons recalled Baird's saying "that I would recognize the English 1–2 approach as essentially operational." Baird mentioned Bridgman and, perhaps, Korzybski as well. Arons added that "from that point on, for the remainder of my sixteen years at Amherst, he [Baird] regularly and conscientiously sent me draft copies of the planned English 1–2 assignments for each semester" (26). Arons acknowledged that

> From the English assignments, I learned a great deal about the teaching of my own course. I learned how to ask better questions leading the students into confrontation with operational definition. I improved the questions intended to lead them into explaining steps of reasoning and interpretation. I learned how to write fruitful term paper assignments. (I had previously tended to fall into the common trap of leaving such assignments far too open and general so that the students had no focus and merely floundered around. I began to see how it was possible to structure an assignment in such a way as to provide a framework for serious thought yet still allow diversity of approach and insight.) Most significantly, however, I learned from those end-of-course assignments how fruitful it was to invite students to reflect on their own intellectual experience. (27)

With respect to Bridgman, operational definitions, and Baird's methods for teaching students to define terms operationally, Walker Gibson told me a version of a story I heard from several individuals. Gibson said that Baird "taught by the force of his personality." He

explained that Baird "enjoyed circus tricks. He would take a wastebasket, turn it upside down, sit on it, and then he would say, 'What's that?'
And the kids of course would say, 'That's a wastebasket, Sir.' And of
course he was trying to get them to give an operational definition.
'This isn't a wastebasket; it's a bench.'" If you put flowers in a wastebasket, it becomes a vase. Sometimes Baird pulled the stunt of entering
his classroom through a window. Gibson explained, "The idea, of
course, was that the window was a door."

When I asked Gibson to tell me about his own experiences
teaching English 1–2, he said, "It was a terrific struggle to begin with,
not only for me but for other young people. It was very difficult to see
through what we were getting at, the distinction for instance between
a dictionary definition and an operational definition, and without
using fancy vocabulary like that, how to dramatize that difference for
students. I remember that first year early on, finally stumbling on some
revelation about what an operational definition could do, and that was
a kind of breakthrough for me. I guess I could say I was learning with
the kids."

I told Gibson I had been reading about operational definitions in
Julienne Ford's *Paradigms and Fairy Tales,* and I mentioned her example
of the frightened rabbits that were seen to be "emitting more fecal
boluses per hour than is normal for rabbits" (1975, vol. 1, 149). Gibson
assured me that the English 1–2 staff had simply wanted to know what
observations underlay any statement. "When you say, 'those rabbits are
afraid,' what are you looking at? How are you measuring afraidness?
It's a devastating technique, really." He admitted that he had found the
operational approach "congenial" and that it "taught me to be more
suspicious of my own pretension, not just my students' pretension, but
my own. If we're saying that your meaning depends upon what you
are doing, the way you are using a particular word, then that leads to a
consciousness of self and the operations that the self is going through
as it tries to make language, and that leads to more scrutiny of the
speaking voice." Gibson discovered it was useful to ask: "What kind of
voice do you want to come on with? If you come on with a voice that
is making just a little fun of its own language, then you are in a more
amiable position toward your subject and toward your audience and
maybe in an easier position to maintain, if you are careful, than if you
are solving the world's problems with every statement you make. For
me, voices are all creative acts. English 1–2 embodied a whole attitude

toward language, with the underlying assumption that we live in the world we make in language, and if that is true, then it is our responsibility to think a little about how we are expressing ourselves."

Baird made a similar point to me about responsible and irresponsible uses of language. In the course of an interview session I had with him, he also offered me several operational definitions, demonstrated something of his pedagogical style, revealed a good measure of the playfulness that underlies his verbal thrusting and parrying, and challenged me to define myself as a historian. He and I were sitting in the living room of his Frank Lloyd Wright house on a May afternoon, looking out at Mount Norwottuck in the Holyoke Range to the south. I asked him about a series of English 1 assignments in which students were asked to look at the Holyoke Range and explain what they saw. "As I understand it," I said, "your point about looking at the mountains is that whatever you see defines you. If you see Triassic Age arkose, you define yourself as a geologist."

"That's right," he replied.

I said I had gone hiking on Mount Norwottuck the previous Sunday. The weather had been beautiful, and along the trail I had seen lady's-slippers and honeysuckle azaleas in full bloom. "When I look at Mount Norwottuck and see flowers," I asked, "am I defining myself as a hiker?"

"No, you are defining yourself as a botanist or a horticulturist or something. You seem to think that being a hiker is a definite operation," he growled. "Well it is, but hikers don't see flowers; hikers hike."

"Can't they also see flowers?"

"Of course they can do both," he conceded, "but then they are using different language. You are a multiple personality depending on your use of language."

I asked him if using operational definitions meant you had to strip terms down to their bare essentials. Was that what he was saying when he defined a hiker as one who hikes?

"A hiker can also be a landscape painter, or whatever, but when he's a hiker, he hikes. What I have been hoping you would see was that in this course we had a definite view of language. This is what we were getting at with all our assignments. You use language to place yourself in the world. 'Where am I?'—that is the question."

"Are you saying language is the means of running orders through chaos?"

"Yes, yes exactly!" he beamed. "Various orders are run by various languages. This view of language was not accepted by all our students of course."

Emboldened by having scored a point, I asked, "Could a hiker have weak knees as I do? I can tell you that when I hike, I am aware of my knees. But that's not part of what it means to be a hiker, is it?"

"Of course a hiker can have weak knees. He can even wear spectacles," he said, adjusting his own. "The richer your vocabulary, the richer the hike. A hiker can be an immortal soul for all I know. I don't know why anyone would want to define himself as a hiker for very long."

"I could define myself as a seeker then, or as someone open to the experience of wonder."

"That's better," he approved. "Or be an immortal soul. Aren't you an immortal soul?" Then, almost as though I were a member of the club, he confided, "The problem is, when you face a class of freshmen, you find they are not used to playing with language. They don't have that sense of play. I would say the purpose of our course was to make their lives richer."

In the immediacy of the moment, I was happy simply to have acquitted myself as well as I had. But later, as I was driving home, I had time to reflect on the way my life and sense of profession were growing richer through my contacts with this grand and fierce old master. A question he had asked in the context of a 1968 assignment series rang in my ears: "In order to see anything at all you will have to define yourself to yourself. Who is this that is doing the looking?"[7] Knowing that I was looking at more than Mount Norwottuck, I felt the question as a personal challenge. I acknowledged being bothered, as a woman and as a writing teacher who had always done her best to nurture student writing, by the aggressiveness of the posture I felt sure Baird had maintained before students. But at the same moment I also acknowledged my envy of his intellectual and pedagogical authority. I was envious of his ability to provoke others to engage with him in a game of wits.

The present afternoon's exchange was not the first in which Baird had given me a taste of the phenomena I was trying to describe. He seemed to want me to learn by doing. He had repeatedly urged me to try writing a sequence of assignments, but I found a series of excuses for not doing so. Then, in a letter I have reproduced in Appendix C, he tried giving me an assignment. He told me to go to the Emily Dickinson house in downtown Amherst and to

> Look at it. What do you see? Define "Looking at a poet's residence." (Letter to R. Varnum, December 6, 1990)

I went to the house and wrote him a three-page account of my visit, carefully distinguishing between those things I had seen with my own eyes, things which had been told to me by my guide, and things I had inferred through my knowledge of Dickinson's poetry and temporal period. I tried also to indicate my operating principles as a historian. I said I believed that "empathy" must characterize the historian's relation to a human subject (letter to T. Baird, December 13, 1990; see Appendix C). Baird's response to my description of the house was that "the person who saw this building and the things in it on one floor after another did not know what he was looking at or did not know how to see what was there to be seen." He said, "You use the word *empathy,* as if that could, that word, possibly lead you to the poet." He also said of my report that "if, speaking as an English 1 teacher I say to you, it is entirely unsatisfactory you will understand why students felt frustrated, disgusted, angry with me. So that is something to learn." I was indeed frustrated and angry. I thought he had failed to see that my rhetorical purpose had not so much been to describe a house as to establish a relationship with Theodore Baird. But after calming down, I had to concede that I truly didn't know what I meant by "empathy." Baird had said in his letter, "The plain fact is the person who looks at a poet's residence is really not able to express much of what he feels. That was (as I see it) the point of the assignment. And the point of many assignments we made, to bring the writer to an awareness of the inexpressible"[8] (letter to R. Varnum, December 17, 1990).

I could easily have written Baird off as an ogre. And I might have done it except that he had made me aware of my limitations and caused me to reexamine my responsibility as a language user and historian. Later, the process which he had begun in me was heated up when he wrote me that "I have enough pride, among other emotions, in this teaching to want you to take the course seriously" (letter to R. Varnum, April 27, 1991). It would not do, I discovered, to hold myself as a detached or sardonic observer. If I was to continue my study of

English 1–2, I would have to acknowledge my personal stake in my enterprise. I would have to defend the course against those who thought it undeserving of historical attention. I would have to try to characterize the intellectual excitement I felt sure it had generated. At the same time, I would have to register my distaste for the way its staff undertook to disorient students or trip them up. I would have to confess I was both repelled and attracted by the authoritarian structure of the course.

There was a great deal I was prepared to say in praise of English 1–2. I wanted to praise its staff for their enormous energy and ingenuity, for their collaborativeness, and for the sophisticated way they had framed assignments and provided students with opportunities for revision and self-reflection. I wanted to praise the staff for focusing on the making of meaning and on the question of how one knows whatever he (or she) claims to know. I wanted to praise the course for elevating student writing to center stage. I admired Baird for attempting to promote a wider exercise of human agency. I admired the way he and his staff had pushed students, as he had pushed me, to acknowledge their responsibility for whatever they said or wrote. I found it easy to suppose that English 1–2 changed the way many students thought about themselves. When it worked as it was designed to work, it helped them discover voices they had not known they could command. Baird once told me, "I felt that nothing is more interesting for a teacher than making it possible—by setting a trap—for a student to talk himself into something he had not been taught, had not known, could now make an English sentence about" (letter to R. Varnum, March 16, 1991).

The notion of setting traps, however, bothered me. So did Baird's refusal to reveal his objectives to students. He had expected them to find their bearings on their own. Many students must have had trouble addressing the English 1–2 assignments. Baird reported in his 1952 article on "The Freshman English Course" that he and his colleagues always had students "who never recover from the shock of discovering that we are not like the usual Freshman English course, and they tell us with perfect regularity two or three times a week throughout the year that they do not understand" (196). In a memorandum he issued on July 19, 1960, Baird observed that "no one I know has anything more than a tentative answer to any of our questions." He also declared: "We take for granted that at Amherst College we can say boldly to everyone interested that no one knows how to teach writing."[9]

Students must sometimes have felt they were groping for answers in the dark. In the introductory "Description of English 1–2,"[10] which I have reproduced in Appendix A, students were warned they might "feel at times that you are not being taught what you ought to be taught, that your teacher does not seem to give you the answers you seek, but you actually are in a situation where no one knows the answers" (2). In this document, which was written in the mid–1950s and subsequently read aloud by every instructor in every class section every fall on the second day of class, instructors not only denied having answers, they also defined their relations to both their students and their subject and stipulated what a student's relations to his teacher and his education ought to be. They informed students that

> The subject, the content, or however you want to describe it, of this course is writing. Writing is an action. It is something you do. It is not something you know about. (1)

"Every year," the instructors told their students, "this teaching staff makes a new sequence of assignments, dealing with a new and different problem, so that for all concerned, teacher and student, this is a new course, a fresh progression in thought and expression, a gradual building up of a common vocabulary, a more precise definition of terms" (3). They added that there was "nothing perfunctory" about these assignments and that students were "deceived if they look easy" (3).

From the course description, students learned they were responsible for their own education. Each student was also responsible for supplying the subject material for his writing:

> At Amherst you will find that the burden of knowledge usually falls on the student. Thus in English 1–2 you supply for your writing your own information, material, whatever you want to call it. After all, you have received an expensive education, you have probably been taught well, you have held various jobs and have played games, and you have had your own thoughts and feelings for eighteen years, more or less. This is your "experience," and from this seemingly shapeless, yet entirely individual source, you will derive whatever it is you have to say. If on first looking at an assignment you do not immediately recognize how you should proceed, you need not be unduly alarmed, for

this is normal, expected, intended. Upon reflection, however, you ought to be able to find something in your own past experience to talk about. If you wait for your teacher to tell you, you will be disappointed. (2–3, see note 10)

Students would not only have to make sense of their past experience, they would also have to make sense of their English course. They would have to put this and that together and make connections, but here again, they would receive little help from their teachers. They were told, "Whatever continuity you construct from one paper to another, from one class discussion to the next, will be your continuity, and yours alone" (3, see note 10).

The teacher's function, according to the "Description of English 1–2," was to ask questions and phrase assignments, not to give answers (4, see note 10). The teacher would keep records and, although he would not grade a student's papers, he would grade his semester performance. The teacher would

attempt to control the direction the discussion takes in the classroom. He will also read your papers. Specimen papers will be mimeographed and brought to class to be scrutinized. Your teacher will correct your papers, commenting on them in general, and at the same time pointing out those mechanical errors and careless faults which you alone can remove. Much of our conversation in class will be about ideas, techniques, meanings, but it should be said emphatically that your teacher is intent upon cleaning up your writing wherever it needs it. (4, see note 10)

The matter of grades is one source of the tension I see in the "Description of English 1–2." I see it as an authoritarian document which masks its own authoritarianism. On the one hand, English 1–2 instructors seemed to invite students to assume the authority of authorship and to view themselves as makers of meaning. On the other hand, the "Description" served notice to students that their writing would be corrected, commented upon, brought to class to be scrutinized by other students, and ultimately graded. On the one hand, instructors claimed not to know the answers, but on the other, they claimed the right to ask the questions. It must be clear to any student in almost any academic situation, and especially so in a required course or when the instructor attempts at the outset to define the terms and conditions for learning, that real authority does not lie with the student. And it may have been clear to at least some of the Amherst freshmen who listened as the "Description of English 1–2" was read aloud to them that real authority did not lie with their individual instructor either. It lay with some shadowy body standing behind him and identified most clearly in the "Description" as "this teaching staff."

Many students must have been mystified. Baird acknowledges as much when he tries to account for student opposition to English 1–2. He says students "found it puzzling. They thought that there was a mystery." He says students "were always saying, 'What is it you want?' And if you said, 'I want nothing,' then they were frustrated and they complained, and I don't blame them. If after assignment after assignment they felt that they were not getting on to something, they felt naturally enough that they were frustrated. And they were. But we all were, in a sense. This was the essence of it, that if we hadn't been frustrated, it would have been just a series of directions about how to write, such as: 'Be clear, be coherent, and be unified'" (1978b, 28).

Although they accounted for it differently, most of the faculty members I spoke with acknowledged that the course had generated a mystique. Armour Craig told me, "There was always a funny mystique about this course that there was a secret to it and that some people were in on it. It was the fact that it was in an academic environment that led people to believe there must be some secret. But there wasn't." Roger Sale said, "Students thought there was something in the assignments or sequence of assignments they should catch on to. Non-English faculty thought so as well." William Pritchard said, "At the best moments, and there were such moments, you felt as if you were exploring and as if you were thinking about very important matters, that is the relationship of words to reality, silence to speech, order to chaos, and all those oppositions that provided so much of the rhetoric here. And that is why people thought there must be a philosophy behind this, there must be a secret, if you could only find out the secret." John Cameron said, "In a very important sense, English 1, using the student as his own subject, had the effect of investing in the student a sense of authority over his own writing. Nonetheless in practice, the way in which that message or that orientation pedagogically was accomplished was paradoxically authoritative; that is to say, it mystified the process of teaching writing." Cameron then recited "The Secret Sits" by Robert Frost:

> We dance round in a ring and suppose,
> But the Secret sits in the middle and knows.

Cameron said Frost's couplet had been used in an assignment series during one of the early years in his Amherst career and subsequently was repeated and remembered in connection with English 1–2. He explained, "Those of us who were junior people, including myself, felt that 'The Secret Sits' captured a sense of the situation created by the course."[11]

Cameron, Sale, and Pritchard all belonged to a cohort of young instructors who arrived at Amherst College in the late 1950s or early 1960s and who were known collectively as the "seven dwarfs." Another member of this cohort, incidentally, was William E. Coles Jr., who has done more subsequently than perhaps any other individual to promote the use of frequent, sequenced writing assignments. Roger Sale, acknowledging he had been one of the dwarfs, explained, "It was the non-English faculty who used the phrase. I don't think there was ever a time, however, when there were seven such people together in the English department. The phrase must have been applied to a number of people over the years. I understood it to mean the seven slaves or the seven imitators."[12]

Sale came to Amherst College in the fall of 1957. Pritchard and Cameron arrived the following year. Before even Sale arrived, however, Gibson had left Amherst to direct the teaching of freshman composition at the Washington Square College of New York University. Gibson told me, "I think in the eleven years I was at Amherst, I probably learned what I had to learn, and it was time for me professionally to move on." He said, "When I left Amherst, I had a sudden burst of creative energy; I wrote a number of critical articles during the first few months that I was out from the wing of Amherst College, which is suggestive, isn't it? I was probably glad to be free." He added, "Any course that's as highly disciplined as this one was and that demands such unanimity of purpose from its contributors is bound to have a kind of confining effect too."

Roger Sale in 1958.

Despite these last remarks, the single most important point which Gibson stressed in all his conversations with me was that English 1–2 had been an exciting course to teach. Once I said to him that what attracted me, as a researcher, to the course was my sense that it must have been exciting for both teachers and students. He said, "I can believe that that is a very hard thing for you to believe. It's wonderful you said that, and it's crucial for you to try to have a sense that that indeed was our mood at that time."

The several faculty members younger than Gibson whom I spoke with all testified as well to the aura of excitement surrounding English 1–2. But in addition to that, they all spoke candidly about the dynamics of the course and about its mystique. Unlike Baird, Craig, and Gibson, who have all retired, Pritchard, Cameron, and Sale are all, as of 1994–95, still teaching. Pritchard and Cameron both now hold the rank of professor at Amherst College. Sale is a professor of English at the University of Washington.

I should take note again of the fact that Sale has been my own teacher. In 1974, I was his student in an introductory, graduate-level survey of twentieth century English literature at the University of Washington. I remember him as a dramatic and compelling performer, standing before us in his stockinged feet, guzzling water from the plastic tankard he kept on the podium, and with water droplets glistening from his beard, expostulating that the two roads which diverged in Frost's yellow wood really had been worn "about the same." He called us all by our surnames and threw chalk explosively at the blackboard or at the floor whenever one of us was so green as, for example, to claim to hear a self-satisfied voice rather than a self-mocking one in the final line of "The Road Not Taken."

One of the first things Sale told me when he agreed to let me interview him about English 1–2 was to "keep in mind that I was very young when I was at Amherst. I was not yet thirty. In fact, I was not much older than my students." He came to Amherst after graduating from Swarthmore and completing a doctorate at Cornell. His years at Amherst were 1957 to 1962. He told me that before he arrived at the college, the set of assignments for the coming fall was sent to him. He said, "I didn't have a clue as to what I was supposed to make of them or how I was supposed to go about teaching them. During my first two years it happened a lot that I didn't know what I was doing with an assignment until I got my students' papers back." The assignments for the fall of 1957 had been written by Benjamin DeMott and addressed the question: "What happens at a moment of education?" Sale said, "I thought this was a wonderful subject; I had never thought about it before in my life." He said, "I really felt just like a student when I arrived at Amherst, but I gradually got better at what I did. My students took English 1–2 for a year, but I took the course for five years."

Sale believes that the mystique which the course seemed to generate was in fact the product of ignorance or inexperience. He explained, "When you start out teaching, you feel a little bit like an outsider. I think so much of the mystique about the course was created not by people who were involved in it, but by people who were observing it. I don't think that DeMott or Baird hid anything to create the class, or that I was a fool for not getting it. It was simply that they did know what they were doing, at least better than I did, and they had been through this. And I could see [after] having done it a year or two, why this happened. It was a lot easier to handle after I had been through it, after I had seen what you do. For instance, I could see after maybe two years that in the first ten assignments, you were just waiting around. I remember saying that to a class, 'I'm just waiting around for you people; you're going to do something sooner or later.'"

Sale remembers that "the excitement for me was in looking at the students' papers in class. I found that thrilling. I never had to worry about making a class go; they went. If once or twice you ask students to discuss one another's papers in class, the student whose paper is discussed feels attacked, but if you follow that procedure every day, no one takes it too personally. Of course, I always handled the students' papers anonymously. One of the main things I learned from teaching English 1 was how to read papers fast." Sale also learned that "one great advantage of asking students to write a lot is that they stop regarding any one assignment as a command performance."

Especially during his first couple of years at Amherst, Sale had to spend a lot of time reading papers. He told me that "early on in my first semester, Ted said, 'I got down to doing a set in two hours.' I was taking about six, and I had two sections. I didn't understand this. I didn't see how you could possibly do a set of papers in two hours. But at one point, maybe in my third or fourth year, I did a set in two hours. I didn't even realize I was doing it. But I could now partly say why—because what happens during the course of reading so many papers by each student is that you get to know the student." He explained that as a semester wore on it became possible to write nothing more than brief comments on papers, but in order to get to that point "I have to have done some quite extensive commenting on earlier papers." He also explained that "early in a term, when a lot of the papers are very much like each other, instead of making the same comment on fifteen papers, you can in effect teach one of those fifteen papers and have all fifteen commented on."

Sale found that staff meetings were not particularly helpful. He said that staff meetings "were not exciting. Every now and again we would have a good conversation, but I know that one of the things that disappointed Ted about English 1 over the years was that the staff meetings didn't generate the kind of rich conversation I think he would have liked to have had." Sale said that the agenda for each meeting was to "review the next three assignments that were coming up. Oftentimes it was half an hour, forty minutes at most. And I could feel Ted and Armour and maybe DeMott begin to get restless when they would realize that not much was going to happen here—'Let's get home.' And the thing that I think we never did talk about, and perhaps it was not an appropriate place to talk about it, was the fear or the confusion of the less experienced teachers. It seemed a place for those who knew what they were doing."

Sale seems to have adopted the tricky English 1–2 stance of claiming not to know answers and yet to judge the answers which students gave. He said, "We always insisted that no one knows more than anyone else. We didn't necessarily know any more than our students did." He said he learned "that you could in the course of a month or six weeks just find ways of getting people to say, 'I don't know where I am; tell me.'" His response was always, "No, I'm not going to tell you," and if the student begged again, "Tell me," he would reply, "No, you find out." The result was that "often they would; often they would." Sale recalled that if a student attempted to account for "What happens in a moment of education?" by claiming, "Then I learned," the next step was for the instructor to ask, "What happened just before you learned? Tell me a story." He said that "an awful lot of what we were doing with them was, 'Tell me a story,' so that you could describe this, and then just indicating that you were not going to be satisfied with plump answers to these questions."

Sale felt reasonably comfortable with the course by the time he began his second year at Amherst. During his second year, Cameron and Pritchard joined the English 1–2 staff as new instructors. Sale remembers going for lunch with Pritchard and asking him, "Have you had a good class yet?" Sale says, "That probably was a very intimidating question because it implied, 'Oh, you may think you've had a good class, but I know better than that; you couldn't have had a good class yet, or you might have had *one*.' And I'm sure in that sense I was [doing] something like mimicking something that one of the older people had said. I too was trying to imply that—I'd been here just a year longer than Pritchard—but that year had been long enough for me to be able to say, 'Have you had a good class?' We might have been doing assignment ten by that point. Pritchard might have assumed that all kinds of good things had happened, but I was sitting back and playing Cheshire Cat."

William Pritchard had been well groomed for teaching at Amherst College. I see him as very much an Amherst man, thoroughly imbued in the traditions of the college. He graduated from Amherst in 1953 and is the only one of the fourteen men I spoke with who experienced English 1–2 from both sides of the podium. He took the course as a freshman in 1949–50 and says in "Ear Training" that it provided "my introduction to serious intellectual inquiry" (1991, 127). He says that by the end of the first term, if not earlier, he and his class-

William Pritchard in his office, speaking to students, about 1960.

mates "began to suspect that language was something other than the mirror of reality; that—in a phrase of Joseph Conrad's I would come to later on—words are, among other things, 'the great foes of reality'; and that the way we went about marshaling our words into sentences, 'composing' reality, could be both a matter for despair and for hopefulness, but was nothing less than central to what we did every day" (128). Pritchard describes himself as having been "a small-town boy from upstate New York . . . full of excitement about uplifting my way out of provinciality" (1985, 240). His instructor for English 1–2 was Armour Craig, who was, as it happened, the principal author of the assignments Pritchard addressed in the fall of 1949. Pritchard remembers that these assignments were on the theme of apprenticeship and "had to do with seeing and knowing, agreeing, order, mistakes, etc." To Pritchard, they seemed "very insistent, harping on a few questions over and over." He told me that Craig "tended to be somewhat mystifying, I think as a strategy." Pritchard also said that "a good friend of mine hated the course. There was lots of game-playing, pretense, holding back. I found it bewildering, heady, exhilarating. Craig was always talking about things, and according to people he said this or that, but I never heard a word. I was swimming in deep water, but I began to enjoy it. I got accustomed to it, got a little praise eventually."

Pritchard characterizes Amherst College in the 1950s as having had primarily a teaching mission. He told me that of the senior professors on the staff of English 1–2, "with the exception of Brower, and even he not until he went to Harvard, nobody published. These were voices that were not known on the general scene. It was as if up in this little hideaway, people were able to be daring and even outrageous in ways that they couldn't be if they were to enter into the professional English scene and publish articles." Pritchard himself graduated from Amherst and went on to do graduate work at Columbia and at Harvard, where he taught sections of Reuben Brower's Hum 6. Pritchard acknowledges that he was one of a number of "old boys (back then it was very much an old-boy network) from Amherst" who taught Brower's course (1985, 243). According to Pritchard, "Most of us in the 'Amherst contingent' (we were sometimes referred to as such) didn't think of ourselves as scholars, or even as potential writers of books.[13] There was rather—and I think in contrast to many of our peers from other institutions—an eagerness to get into the classroom and instruct others about the kinds of literary discoveries we were making" (1991, 130–131).

Moving from Amherst to Harvard and back to Amherst, as Pritchard did and as Reuben Brower and Armour Craig had done before him, had been a common education and career path for members of the Amherst faculty for decades. Amherst historian Theodore P. Greene, who himself graduated from Amherst College before returning there in 1952 to teach, has shown that in the academic year of 1950–51

> among the faculty of ninety-three men, twenty-two members were Amherst graduates (24 percent or one out of every four). Over one third (36 percent) of the Amherst faculty had received their graduate training at Harvard, and over two-thirds (69 percent) had taken their advanced education at an Ivy League University. (1978, 303)

Greene describes the town of Amherst in the 1950s as a small, rural community or "a place apart from the larger world" (291). The town's population of 7,000 residents in 1945 outnumbered the student population at its two colleges by a factor of almost three to one (283, 288). Massachusetts State College became the University of Massachusetts at Amherst in 1947, but with only 3,900 students enrolled there in 1949, the institution was not yet the giant it would become (307–308).

In late 1957, although he would not complete his doctorate at Harvard until 1960, Pritchard was invited by Benjamin DeMott, who was then the chairman of the Amherst College English department, to interview for a teaching appointment for the following fall. Pritchard remembers that before he went in for his interview with Amherst President Charles W. Cole, Theodore Baird advised him to "Speak Up!" (1991, 131). Pritchard told me, "When I began teaching at Amherst, I was twenty-six years old. My students were seven or eight years younger. I started with two sections of English 1, with twenty to twenty-five students per section. I prepared for teaching the course by reading some ten sequences of assignments from earlier years. It was an intense course for teachers. As a beginning instructor, you were never really sure you knew what was going on." Apparently one of his sections met on a MWF and the other on a TTS schedule, for he has said, "I found teaching at Amherst a full-time activity, most of it focused in the two composition sections that met Monday through Saturday and presented me with a set of twenty or so papers to read each night for the next morning's class" (1985, 245).

When I asked him whether he had gained a different understanding of the course as a teacher from what he had had as a student, Pritchard said, "Of course a lot has changed when one is on the other side of the desk. Supposedly now I should know what I'm doing, and there was some anxiety when I didn't know what I was doing. But no, I think I felt a continuity. I welcomed the opportunity to teach here for a number of reasons, but partly because I wanted to get clearer about certain things that I had never fully understood, and I think I did." When I asked him if he had ever practiced "mystification as a strategy" in the way that he had suggested Armour Craig may have done, Pritchard said, "I certainly engaged in it. I think it had to do with keeping the course going, keeping the thing going from Monday to Wednesday to Friday with some sense of continuity, some promise held out that things, at least some things, would eventually be resolved. But at the worst, I think I resorted to mystification, or at least to asking questions that I not only didn't know the answer to, but didn't quite know what the implications of asking them were. I think the course did allow that sort of thing, and not only allowed it, as any course will allow it, but made it more likely to happen." He added, "You were thrown back on your resources, and you didn't always have adequate resources, and you had to keep going there, you had to get through the class."

When I asked Pritchard about the theoretical grounding of English 1–2, he said the course had owed more to Frost than to the New Criticism. Speaking particularly of "Ransom and Tate, and Brooks to an extent too," Pritchard said the New Critics "had ambitions to make pronouncements about the proper bounds of different disciplines' relations with the humanities. And Amherst English really avoided that. Amherst English was more radical-conservative in some ways, if you can put those together with a hyphen. They were conservative insofar as there wasn't any reforming attitude; they did not look for political or social change. They were satisfied with the structure of society and even the academy. And this again is like Frost—leave it the way it is so we can push against it, or so we can play off against it. Frost says, 'I don't want the world to be any better than it already is; leave it to stew in its own mess, as long as I can do it up in poetry.' And I think the vision of the 1950s that at least I was given was we were all very satirical about American society and culture and how awful it was."

John Cameron, like Pritchard, began teaching at Amherst in 1958. At the time, Cameron was working on a doctorate at Yale. He remembers that "Bill Pritchard had returned to Amherst via Columbia and Harvard; that was the traditional Amherst connection." Cameron speculates that Benjamin DeMott, who chaired the department that year, "must have said, 'We need to get somebody from outside.' So he went down to Yale (that was 'outside') and hired me." Cameron remembers that his advisor at Yale "said he thought I might find Amherst congenial, though he said, 'a lot of people don't.' He warned me about this curmudgeon of a senior professor up there who was doing some strange things with the writing course."

Once at Amherst, Cameron says he quickly discovered that "English 1 was the name of the game. You had to play that game or you were nowhere." The game proved both fascinating and disorienting. Cameron's initial teaching load included two sections of English 1 and a section of the sophomore literature course, English 21, that had replaced Reuben Brower's English 19. He says, "The very experience of joining a highly organized and integrated enterprise like first of all English 1–2, second of all the English department, and third of all

John Cameron, lecturing, about 1972.

Amherst College was completely new to me and very exciting. I was astonished to find that I could survive something like that. For all the stress involved, I enjoyed my first year here, and I enjoyed the positive productivity of the collaborative courses, English 1–2 and 21–22." On the other hand, he found that "English 1 introduced me to a mode of intellectual thought that completely disrupted whatever universe of thought I had before. When I arrived at Amherst, after graduate and undergraduate English at Yale, with a tour in the military and a year at Edinburgh in between, I felt uneasy about my education. I was not very confident about what I knew, especially in professional terms. Moreover, I had a theoretical turn of mind, and although Baird himself warned this could be a dangerous, or at least counterproductive practice, I kept trying to draw out the theoretical implications of English 1–2. At the same time, I was trying to write a dissertation on Sir Walter Scott. I had a hell of a time doing it and didn't finish my dissertation for up to three or four years after I got here. It was traumatic, and I was obviously experiencing writing problems already that would continue to plague me throughout my career." Cameron conjectured that one reason why he had difficulty with the dissertation was that "the kind of thinking that teaching English 1–2 involved interested me and seemed to promise an approach to language, to reading, and writing that was more focused and cogent and organized, and was in fact more institutionalized, than anything I had had in my earlier education. But these new ways of thinking about literature and about writing had a very disruptive effect on my thinking."

Cameron remembers that having to read large numbers of English 1 papers was a particular trial. He said, "It was awful for teachers, especially if you had two sections. I still have trouble reading papers; I think it's partly because of that experience." He explained that those who had two sections "had to read something on the order of 120 papers per week for English 1 alone. It meant you couldn't possibly take any one paper too seriously. Yet, you had also to read papers with an eye to making your next class out of them. I used to pray to find the one or two good papers that I had to have for my next class. Of course, you could make a class out of bad papers if you wanted to. I came to disapprove of that, but I did it sometimes."

Another trial was having to teach the regularly featured block of assignments on the use of the library. Cameron said, "I hated teaching that series. The first couple of years, I found it intriguing, tried to psych it out, but didn't succeed. I was not alone. The way in which, to me, it lingers in the memory is it was that set of assignments about which people who were in-the-know had enigmatic smiles. You always felt as if there was something to be understood there which you didn't understand. I felt that way, most of my colleagues did, and certainly the students did. As far as I was concerned, it was never a successful assignment. All the students seemed mystified, but that is probably because I was mystified myself. The assignment was always: 'Describe what you do in order to use the library system.' The point may have been to illumine the relationship between a symbolic system, in fact several symbolic systems both within and in addition to the Dewey Decimal System, and physical or architectural space, or more generally to demonstrate this was one of those crucial relationships between the sign and its referent. There may also have been other points Ted wanted to make—how the Dewey Decimal System classified knowledge itself, and how historically constructed that situation was. But that aspect rarely got a significant discussion because the students were baffled by how we could criticize their sentences about how they found a book and by our concern whether the sentences were adequate to their experience. Almost by definition, there is a mystery there, and that mystery just flourished as the assignments were repeated. If you will, it epitomized the way in which the course itself seemed to mystify experience and language."

Cameron contends that certain features of English 1–2, particularly the assigning of writing tasks based on autobiographical experience and the classroom discussion of student-generated texts, created troublesome issues of authority between teachers and students. He said, "One of the problems with assignments that draw on autobiography but are addressed to a conceptual issue is that they often tend to be anti-intellectual in the sense that they seem to center authority for the truth of a statement in its authenticity as an autobiographical statement rather than its validity as an intellectual argument." He added that "when you put a pedagogy that allows for abusiveness toward students together with a demand that they write from experience, you are on very dangerous grounds indeed. Moreover, autobiographical writing creates a heightened tension in a classroom. It produces anxiety about the limits of personal expression. It is difficult for students at that age to define the boundaries of appropriate personal expression. Here again was the mystique of English 1–2: you had to know the rules to play the game, but no one would tell you what they were. Thus one of my harshest criticisms of the course is ethical. Among male students and teachers, the question of boundaries can be handled to some degree within the conventions of mentoring. But, I remember several students who had emotional problems, whose personal lives were out of control, and who responded to the autobiographical emphasis of the course by making disclosures that exceeded acceptable limits. The course structure invited disclosure, so the potential for ethical transgression was always there. Personal exposure creates emotional intensity, so pedagogical relationships could become supercharged. Teachers were tempted to make autobiographical disclosures as well. Roger Sale, for example, was a great one for bringing anecdotes of his family life to class. But the problem is that he was not vulnerable, whereas the students were. Though the pedagogy of the course never intended that students be confessional, that in fact tended to happen. I thought there was something potentially problematic about encouraging students to express themselves and claim the authority of their own experience, and then grading them on what they wrote. The high pitch of emotional intensity in English 1–2 classrooms stemmed from the conjunction of autobiographical writing with the often abusive style of discipline we practiced."

Cameron argues that the elevation of student writing to focal position in classroom discussions also generated authority issues for English 1–2 instructors. He said, "There was a great deal of tension created for teachers by the fact that there was no nonpersonal context for the discussion of what constituted good or competent writing. All you had was student writing. There was nothing to serve as a third presence or outside authority in the classroom. There was no acknowledged critical vocabulary. As a teacher and critic of writing, you always felt in the position of having to wing it. It was even possible to get away with being intellectually irresponsible. There was a kind of bluff you were asked to maintain. A teacher feels tremendously exposed in the classroom. I felt compelled to bluff about my personal identity and my professional authority in English 1–2 in a way which was much more extreme than it was in the sophomore literature course, where I could pose simply as the expositor of a text."

Cameron says that "English 1 was, in my view, very much an authoritarian enterprise" and that it was so at both the staff and classroom levels. Within the classroom, he attributed the authoritarian dynamic to the way in which the course mystified the process of teaching writing. He said that "the course tended to bring out something that wasn't always admirable in a teacher, or in me, and in many teachers, because it encouraged you to speak from a position of rather heavy-handed but ill-defined authority, and it put you under considerable pressure. It contained a mystique about which you were yourself mystified."

At the staff level, Cameron attributed the authoritarian dynamic largely to the personality of Theodore Baird. Cameron observed that "a charismatic individual, like Ted, who always seems to know more than you do, generates a certain mystique. Amherst College was an all-male, patriarchally oriented institution, and Ted was classically the embodiment, I would say, of a tribal chief, a patriarch, a powerful father figure. What was particularly troublesome about Ted's conduct of this role was that he refused to take true responsibility for it and would resist being characterized by it. He would pretend we were simply peers reasoning together, and that was as much destructive as anything else. Yet he carried this enormous weight of authority which, by not acknowledging it straightforwardly, he was able to exercise with less public discipline than he would otherwise have had." Cameron remembered specifically that "the year I came, in 1958, there was a college committee appointed to reconsider the then so-called 'New' Curriculum—the Koester Committee. It proposed cutting English 1–2 to one term. The proposal was discussed with great scorn in our staff meetings, with Baird's personal tone of sarcasm freely expressed, so that we understood, in no uncertain terms, that 'we' were not going to accept the recommendation that English 1 be cut back to one term." Cameron noted that "although it was always known as Ted's course, he often did not write the exercises. Those who did write them were challenged by him vigorously, and no doubt sincerely, to write them in their own way. But he was all too disingenuous in not acknowledging the force of his own presence, the effect of his own mark on the pedagogical practices and assumptions within which the writer of the assignments was expected to operate. It was difficult to think or imagine freely within this situation, yet that is what the often untenured staff member was 'invited' to do."

Roger Sale, unlike Cameron, remembers having had a reasonable measure of autonomy within the English 1–2 hierarchy. He told me, "Ted never once said, 'This is what we are doing.' And I know that at least in some cases when he found out what somebody else was doing, he was appalled, but I don't think he ever said anything." Sale added, "It was a funny kind of community enterprise because it is based so much on having each teacher teach the way that he wants to do it. Armour must have said to me, 'Be your own man,' hundreds of times. 'Don't think of this as someplace where you're trying to stand in for somebody else, for me, or Ted, or the assignment maker; be your own man.' And they really meant it. I don't think anybody else believed that, but I did."

Pritchard, on the other hand, agrees with Cameron that an authoritarian dynamic operated within Amherst classrooms. Pritchard noted that "because they were all male, we adopted a certain tone with the students. The instructor acted as a bullying older brother. Class-room interchanges were often adversarial. I used to goad or badger or tease or chastise students in ways that I cannot imagine doing now that the college is coeducational." He added, "English 1 students often made an analogy between the course and boot camp."

Cameron made a similar analogy. He told me, "The political and social climate of the 1950s allowed for considerable abuse of students by teachers. Students were subjected to very aggressive criticism, or to something almost like basic training. But that is only one metaphor for an experience which could also be called 'initiation.' The attitude at Amherst then, emphasized by the philosophy and pedagogy of the required core curriculum, was to sharpen the difference between the experience of high school and that of college, and especially that of Amherst College, which aspired to produce not merely educated persons, but the leaders of society. Less explicitly, it knew itself to be acculturating its students as figures of a modern elite. Its commitment to a democratic meritocracy was genuine. It was genuine in its effort to say, 'We want the best students we can get hold of,' given the blinders they had at the time about class, race, sex, and all the other matters. The desire to get the best students possible was in the institution's own self-interest. But at the same time it also prided itself on instilling the mores and values of the traditional, elite social classes that Amherst did in fact historically represent. What the pedagogy designed for the freshman year at Amherst involved, and quintessentially the English 1 course, was an acculturation process which took students from their suburban, generally middle-class, high school environments and taught them how to be Amherst students, and implicitly taught them how to be the leaders of the future. One of my senior colleagues used to speak, with a certain perverse irony (and pleasure), of 'frisking' the entering student of his 'principles' (which latter he characterized as unthinking and, perhaps, vulgar). No one would dare speak that way now. Even if some still think that way to a degree, things have changed."

Pritchard and Sale agreed that part of the purpose of English 1–2 had been to challenge students to reexamine their values. Acknowledging the cliché, Pritchard said that the course had aimed to lead the student "to think for oneself." It had also aimed "to complicate the well-groomed high school mind, to puncture certain kinds of pieties and shibboleths. Ideally, it was an exercise to see if you can say something more strongly about what you really believe, what you really see, what you really think is knowledge."

The metaphor which Sale used was not "boot camp," or "initiation," but "knocking the student off his pins." He told me that when he began teaching at the college, he found himself "surrounded by bright and well-educated young men who imagined they had arrived just by being accepted at Amherst. English 1 was supposed to knock them out of place, to knock them out of wherever they were, but Ted Baird and the other senior professors did not tell me that. The function of the assignments was to dislodge whatever assumptions the students had brought with them." Sale explained, "If you take a group of bright, high-SAT-scoring, high school kids, and you give them an assignment, nine out of ten will write the same essay. Almost any question you ask, they will all just funnel into one particular spot, and then they will be there. They are really just waiting to find out what you are going to do, and what they do is to write something that they think is not going to get them into trouble. And then it did get them into trouble, and then you would say, 'Why did you write it like that for?'" He said, "The assumption of this thing was simply to knock them off of positions of comfort, and the easiest way to get at that would be via their writing. But it wasn't their writing perceived as language, it was their writing perceived as a means of self-expression. 'Who are you when you're talking like that? Who do you think I am when you're talking like that?'" Sale said that during the time he taught at Amherst, "What I was doing in class, by and large, was moving from whatever the writing was in the students' papers into some other context about something else. At some point in the first term, early, I tried to say to a class that ice cream was more important than friendship. That was simply a way of trying to say, 'Why are you talking so piously about friendship?' That's all they were doing, being pious about friendship, and so you had to find a way to get at that because talking piously about friendship was something they thought was going to get them from today to tomorrow."

Sale tried other classroom stunts. He told me, "I came in through the window, as Ted Baird had once done, and I did things with wastebaskets. I came in through the window because someone told me Ted had done it."[14]

Sale agreed with Cameron that the institutional ethos at Amherst in the late 1950s colored the relations between teachers and students. Sale compared the environment at Amherst to that at Swarthmore, where he had done his undergraduate work, and to that at the University of Washington, where he has taught since leaving Amherst. He told me that "Amherst was very much a monastery. Moreover, Amherst had a set curriculum for the first two years, with English 1 and Science 1 as its two major components, and students thought this made the college unique or somehow special." He observed that students "looked at us and they thought, 'You guys know something.' I had not encountered that type of attitude toward teachers when I was an undergraduate; Swarthmore was not such a teacher-centered place as Amherst was. It makes a difference that students are all of the same sex and that they sit around in the evenings, all discussing the same English 1 assignment." He explained that "on any given night, half the freshmen were doing this assignment, and the other half were going to do it the next night, and all that made it a kind of campuswide event. That meant that the students were really looking at the faculty for what was going to happen. And all that just is not plausible at a large university where people come and go off the campus, where students have jobs, they have cars, they have families, they are of different ages—there are all these things which make the University of Washington so different from Amherst. To get the kind of attention that we got from those students, they needed to have very few distractions." He said, "Kids go through the University of Washington and never get that sense of being involved, first of all in a collective enterprise (because they don't see it that way), and secondly in one that is almost piercingly personal and relevant, without being private, but still personal—'something is happening to me.'"

In 1962, thirty years before he spoke with me, Sale had given a group of graduating seniors an account of teacher-student relations at Amherst College. The occasion was a valedictory address which the class of 1962 had invited him to deliver at their final "Senior Chapel" assembly. The men in the class of 1962 had been freshmen in 1958, during Sale's second year at the college. Sale's address was his own valedictory, as well as theirs, because he had been denied tenure and knew he would be teaching in Seattle rather than at Amherst in the fall. He told the young men in his audience that while the mission of Amherst College was to "provide leaders for a democracy," the ethos of the institution "produced something I call the habit of obedience." He characterized the relationship between Amherst students and their teachers as

a relationship that seemed to exclude all other considerations, and what we speak of as the world outside really became, for many of you, outside and thus almost irrelevant. The teacher is not turned to, thus, because he knows something but because he understands, apparently, a great deal more than the student about the process in which they believe and are engaged. The teacher speaks, and you obey, not by believing what he believes or even by doing what he tells you to do, but in a far deeper way than this—you obey by listening to the sound of the voice and by trying to catch some accent beyond the simple meaning of the words. In five years I have been more peered at with glassy and slightly abstracted eyes than I hope to be for the rest of my life. ("The Senior Chapel Address 1962")

Sale said that his students' habit of obedience had affected his teaching and that

one day during my first term here, I said something outrageous. My freshman history teacher in college had spent a whole term demonstrating that the history of Christianity was a very strange business. Well, one day, in response to an earnest question, I said, in a very knowing way, "You know, don't you, that the history of Christianity was a very queer business?" The response was immediate. It was as though everyone in the class except me had been waiting for that moment. The silence was profound: so this was what it was to be educated, this was Amherst. I could have immediately apologized to the class for being outrageous, but of course I did not. I too was fascinated and caught. I had never been listened to in that way before; I quickly discovered that the more outrageous I was, the more obedient the students became, the better I was listened to. From that moment on, only a far different man from me could have broken the chain. So I talked one day about ice cream, another about the Giants, another about my son's drawings, every day seeing more and better ways to teach, every day more and more gleefully and excitedly digging my own grave. The way I could be a teacher at Amherst was by constantly finding new ways to express my response to the habit of obedience. The way I was to be eccentric was now clear; by the time you arrived the following year I was throwing chalk.

So it has been my eccentricity to be outrageous. The experience has been one of the most exhilarating I have known. I have discovered long hidden parts of myself, and my task has been to teach by being at Amherst. I cannot really speak here for my colleagues except to note that I do not think my experience was unique. ("The Senior Chapel Address 1962")

Sale concluded by warning the men in the class of 1962 against the habit of obedience and by contrasting the ethos of the college he and they were leaving with that of the state university to which he was going. He told the Amherst seniors that

> If you are to lead, you cannot be thus obedient; if Amherst has taught you the habit in order to fulfill the ancient and magnificent role it set itself, be rid of it nonetheless, and hurry.
>
> So, I say goodbye. You are off, I hope, in spite of all I have said, to lead. I am off to where the dream is not of a whole man but of a whole society. ("The Senior Chapel Address 1962")

In the fall of 1961, the beginning of his last year on campus, Sale had accepted what Cameron describes as "part of the challenge" and taken a turn at writing a series of assignments.[15] Sale remembers that he started with "a single intellectual construction which then gets chopped up into thirty different things." He recalls that "I had thought of something in the summer (perhaps I could have written it into a paragraph); I then made it into assignments. Not having done assignments before extensively, I didn't really see what students would do with the questions, and quite often I think in those first six or seven assignments, I was really quite startled at what they did, or quite startled at what somebody else teaching the class was saying." He added, "I had constructed a sequence which began with the question, 'Is everyone entitled to his personal opinion?' It mattered to me how the questions went together because I had a goal in mind and a definite agenda of items, including a Pater passage, I wanted students to read. At the beginning, I probably pushed my point too hard. The other teachers may have felt bewildered, but I was too nervous to ask. As it happened, we left the drawing board on assignment four. Toward the end of the semester, I began to have more fun. I had a group of assignments on pronouns which everybody loved. Unfortunately, the pronoun assignments coincided with the series of meetings at which I learned I wasn't going to be promoted. Even so, I remember that by that point in the semester, I was having fun."

When the decision regarding Sale's promotion was made public, John Cameron remembers that "I was scandalized by the denial of tenure because I admire Roger, and he was obviously worthy of tenure. He was an eccentric person, but in no sense was that eccentricity or off-beatness, however you want to put it—in no sense was it disabling or wrong, on the contrary. He approached things quite differently from other people. He was a passionate teacher, much admired, possibly even too much. So I think there was also probably—this is pure hypothesis, an intuition—there was probably some envy."

Sale acknowledges he learned a great deal from the experience of teaching English 1–2. He notes, "I have adapted a lot of what I learned at Amherst. I still do sequences of assignments, for example, but as distinct from Bill Coles, who is a great and good friend of mine, I don't construct sequences with a tight, step-by-step progression. Moreover, the antagonistic Amherst style, where the teacher effectively tells his students he is going to knock them off their pins, does not work at a large, urban university. At the University of Washington, if students get lost, they just wander away." Sale testifies that "the two things I would say I learned at Amherst were the importance of reading papers fast and of making student writing the center of a writing course. When I came to the University of Washington, these two things separated me from most of my colleagues there. Most of them hated reading papers and resented the hours they spent doing it. I could read papers quickly and get them back to students quickly. The main thing I would say I give students is, not love or handshakes, but the sense that I am paying attention to what they do." Sale adds, "It is still the case that most teachers, reading a paper, will not think that what they are doing is seeing a writer write. They are almost always beginning by trying to figure out what their final comment is going to look like—how good is this?—instead of trying to see the writing as a process that the writer has gone through, which is the real fun. How you learn to read papers fast is that you think of yourself as having a conversation—the writer is writing; I'm writing back to you."

At Amherst College teachers sometimes found themselves witnessing the marvel of a writer writing. Cameron told me, "You welcomed students who discovered they could use the papers to put on the teacher or the class, who would be deliberately outrageous, sometimes subtly deliberately outrageous, who would fictionalize. When they do that, they are actually learning something fairly important. That's really what Bill Gibson's notion is—create the persona, and you do it with verbal constructs. And when a student caught on to that in some way, without cynicism, or ideally without cynicism, they learned something."

In the spring of 1948, one student submitted an example of the kind of deliberate outrageousness, or in this case nose-thumbing at authority, which English 1–2 instructors welcomed. The student's name was Robert M. Cornish; he wrote a play entitled *Occupational Hazard*[16] in response to an assignment devised by Walker Gibson and William Taylor.[17] Gibson and Taylor had asked students to imagine five men on vacation at a resort hotel in the Rockies. The group, which included an American historian, a landscape painter, a commercial pilot, a geologist, and a brigadier general, was gathered on the terrace of the hotel, looking out at a prominent, snowcapped mountain. The task for the student was first to write five propositions about the mountain, one appropriate to each observer, then to "give a one-sentence definition of 'language' suggested by this exercise," and finally to define "mountain." In Cornish's play, the scene opens upon the group of men lounging on the cliffside terrace of their hotel. They are drinking to "the glorious spectacle of beautiful scenery, beautiful weather, and cool refreshments" (1, see note 16) when they are interrupted by a small, hysterical boy demanding a scooter. A character named Williams, who is apparently the boy's father, explains coolly to the youngster that he already has a scooter, that there are scooters all around him, and that any chair is in fact a scooter. He demonstrates by crouching with one knee on his own chair "and painstakingly pushing himself along the floor" (2). Unsatisfied, the child bangs his head against the flagstones. The adult men return to their drinks and to their discussion of the snowcapped peak in the distance. The general, whose name is Frome, sees it as "an excellent natural defense zone" in case of invasion from the Pacific. The pilot sees it as "a great obstacle to night weather flying," the painter as "a model far more challenging than the Last Supper," the geologist as a "magnificent specimen of stratified igneous material," and the historian as a symbol of the Great American Frontier (4). Williams, however, has the last word. Slowly and deliberately, he declares, "Gentlemen, that mountain is a nonentity" (5). When the hostile grunts of the others subside, he continues, "Gentlemen, we but project our points of view upon the blind flux which we call the universe." Then "in an evangelical, come renounce your sins before God tone," he observes, "That chair in which you are sitting, Frome, is a scooter, and as well a locomotive, an automobile, a parachute, what you will. Everything is everything else. That mountain is everything you have said it is, and yet it does not exist" (6). The others begin to advance slowly on Williams; he looks on with amused detachment. Suddenly they rush him. Grabbing his arms and legs and giving a mighty heave, they throw him over the ramparts.

In 1965, the Amherst faculty voted to throw the nineteen-year-old New Curriculum itself over the ramparts. English 1–2 and the other core courses fell with it. A quarter of a century later, John Cameron told me, "In one sense, a genuine sense, the course had a nonauthoritarian dimension in that it sought to instill within the student himself a sense of his own authority over language, and I don't in any sense denigrate that or want to back away from it. It was the strength of the course and the strength of our approach to teaching writing." He added, "There is a kind of sometimes smug, but sometimes very self-authenticating discourse that comes from people who have moved through Amherst College and this department. It is an important legacy."

CHAPTER FIVE

Boot Camp

John Carpenter Louis, who took English 1–2 in 1959–60, reported in his 1971 dissertation on the course that it "exercised a special fascination, and constituted a special challenge, for the majority of its students" (56). In 1955, a group of students from Amherst's Theta Xi Fraternity who had undertaken to evaluate the Amherst curriculum reported that English 1–2 "is apt to have a very strong influence on its students" and explained that the course "nearly alone among freshman courses, makes strong, unsettling, and almost inescapable demands for intellectual self-appraisal" (3). Twenty-five years after the course was canceled, I found that English 1–2 still represented a subject of fascination for its alumni. All of the alumni I spoke with had strong memories of the course. All had saved at least some of the papers they wrote as students in English 1–2. All except Geoffrey Shepherd told me that English 1–2 had had a significant influence on their professional lives and on their writing.

The purpose of English 1–2, according to the students from the Theta Xi Fraternity who evaluated the course in 1954–55, was "first, to get the student to say things on his own, and second, to jolt his thinking and destroy his notions that his own position is already entirely adequate, or that writing is easy, or that he can learn some sort of mechanical 'technique' for good writing" (4). This jolting was salutary, according to the men of Theta Xi, because "a valedictorian-ridden freshman class is full of young men who have generally too much intellectual complacence; self-conscious, perhaps, but sadly lacking in healthy self-awareness" (4). The Theta

Xi evaluators concluded that "catching on" or "not catching on" were the alternative forms a student's experience of English 1–2 could take and reported that

> Success in English 1–2 mainly involves, not the "solution" of the assignment questions or the production of "right" answers, but grasping with some awareness the problems themselves. Many people fail to see that the problem is the *discovery* of the problem, not primarily the deduction of a "right" answer. This is commonly known as "catching on," and unless a student "catches on," unless he grasps and feels some earnestness in the problem presented him in the assignment, the paper he produces will be confused or insignificant. (4)

Robert Bagg, an alumnus of English 1–2, told me that he eventually caught on to the course. He said that he and his classmates were asked "to study the actual intellectual operations we would go through to come to a conclusion. Probably the most important early discovery in the course was what we call 'operational definition.'" He said, "We would always be asked, how do *we* see the truth, how would we formulate this problem in a way that we could accept and live with? And that habit of taking responsibility for making judgments which would then be followed by others is an extremely valuable one." According to Bagg, the course focused so insistently "on strategy of arguments and on definitions, that knowledge gained from English 1 would influence any further writing of papers. Let me put it this way: if you were studying the steps by which you became convinced of the correctness of a definition or of the validity of an argument, you were studying self-persuasion, and if you understood how you were persuaded, that would give you a rhetorical advantage in constructing papers to persuade others."

Bagg also told me he thought the English 1–2 staff had aimed deliberately at disorienting students. Bagg, whose observations are consistent not only with the Theta Xi evaluation but also with what Roger Sale told me about knocking the student off his pins and with what William Pritchard told me about complicating the well-groomed high school mind, recalled that English 1–2 students "were dealing with a large mystery. But remember that the large mystery was a strategy to disorient the students who brought to the college and to this course a whole lot of easy misconceptions inculcated by parents, television, media, and high school teachers about how knowledge was acquired." Bagg, who studied classical Greek as well as English while at Amherst, likened the English 1–2 experience to initiation into the Eleusinian mysteries. He said, "What the course did was make everyone, in one sense, autonomous because we were not following a model; we had to solve every couple of days an intellectual puzzle, on our own. But it also established a community of people who were all trying to devine a central mystery. And eventually the mystery emerged in ways that we could talk about and share, and the central statement that we would come upon went something like this: 'I have used words to create my reality.' You could compare this to the Eleusinian mysteries. The initiates were enjoined, on penalty of death, from revealing what happened, and the box was opened in the temple, and each initiate was shown the secret of life that was contained in the box. No one knows what's in the box. The mystery was kept throughout all antiquity. There are some wild guesses as to what was in the box. [At Amherst] There was a conspiracy on the part of faculty to preserve the mystery."

Another alumnus, Thomas Looker, told me that "there was a high-priest quality about the instructors in the course. They had an aura. It resonated with something in me to think they knew something I didn't." He said, "One of the things about English 1 is that they didn't tell you, they didn't express any formulas. Now that's an approach; that's an idea about writing. You would somehow design the course to evoke an experience. The course has to be something that you go through, a process, an experience." He added, "The thing was, none of us knew what 'they' meant, and they wouldn't tell us. They obviously wanted something, and we didn't know what it was. They would say, 'We want you to find out what you want and to discover your own voice.' The result was complete confusion." Looker added, "Another way of looking at it is that we were being socialized at Amherst College into a community, into a men's club, a macho, WASPish power elite. English 1 contributed to that by its style. Part of the Amherst experience was to survive English 1–2."

The students who took English 1–2 were a bright group of young men. Amherst historian Theodore P. Greene, summarizing material published in the 1954 *Report of the Review Committee on the New Program* (see Kennedy 1955, 254–272), says that Amherst's postwar admissions policies brought together a brighter and geographically more diverse group of students than ever before:

> In 1953–54, almost five candidates applied for every place in the entering class. For the first time in decades, the class admitted that year included a majority (53 percent) who came directly from high schools instead of from private prep schools. Only 15 percent of that class were sons of Amherst alumni, and the earlier classification of "relatives" of Amherst alumni was no longer recorded. This class came from thirty-two different states or foreign countries instead of the sixteen areas represented in the class of 1941. Its official verbal aptitude had climbed to 583 from the 498 of the last prewar class, and its mathematical aptitude to 626 from the earlier 514. Professor Kennedy noted that "a real effort" had been made to recruit more Negro students, but in 1953–54 only eight students (averaging 2 per class or 7/10th of 1 percent of each class) were Negroes, a fact which he attributed simply to the lack of sufficient large scholarship grants. (Greene 1978, 302)

Robert Bagg was a member of the class admitted to Amherst College in 1953–54. He is one of six English 1–2 alumni I interviewed, or one of seven if you count William Pritchard, whom I have counted primarily as a faculty member. Pritchard, as already noted, took the course in 1949–50. W. Geoffrey Shepherd, like Bagg, took it in 1953–54. John Bookwalter took it in 1956–57, and Douglas Wilson in 1958–59. Both Thomas Looker and John Stifler took it in 1964–65, the penultimate year of the course. Both Pritchard and Stifler were in sections led by Armour Craig. Bookwalter's instructor was Theodore Baird. Both Bagg and Wilson studied with John F. Butler, Shepherd with Richard Waidelich, and Looker with William E. Coles Jr. Pritchard, Bagg, and Shepherd are now tenured academics; Looker and Stifler combine journalism with college-level teaching; Wilson is a college administrator; and Bookwalter is a surgeon. Pritchard, Wilson, and Looker are now employed by Amherst College. Bagg, Shepherd, and Stifler are employed by the University of Massachusetts at Amherst. Looker,

Top left to bottom right:
William Pritchard, class of 1953.
Robert Bagg, class of 1957.
W. Geoffrey Shepherd, class of 1957.
John Bookwalter, class of 1960.
Douglas Wilson, class of 1962.
John Stifler, class of 1968.
Thomas Looker, class of 1969.

like Bagg, told me he eventually caught on to English 1–2. Shepherd and Bookwalter both said they never quite did.

Bagg, who came to Amherst from Milburn High School in New Jersey, told me that although he had initially felt mystified by English 1–2, he had accepted his situation. He said, "I accepted it. I knew I didn't have it, but I thought that if I stayed with it, maybe I would eventually get it." Shepherd, who was Bagg's classmate, told me that "I'm still not sure I really ever understood what English 1–2 was after." He compared himself speculatively with other alumni I had spoken to and said, "I may be one of your people who most deeply was puzzled and disoriented by English 1–2, and still managed to keep going by simply recognizing that there was a puzzle I wasn't solving, but just nonetheless keeping going." Shepherd said the course staff had seemed to be "trying to jolt us from one direction or another and say, 'What you thought was reality, isn't reality, and now you have to rethink it.'" He said English 1–2 was a "disorienting course which was presented in this aura that it was tremendously important, that it was a critical element of your education in which self-doubt and self-reexamination were required, in fact so much of it, that you couldn't even quite figure it out."

Shepherd had never heard of English 1–2 before coming to Amherst in 1953, but he confronted it and Science 1–2 upon his arrival. He told me, "It was immediately apparent to me and to everyone that those two courses especially were meant to alter your sense of values and expression." He came to Amherst from Ames High School in Ames, Iowa, and he said he found the college to be "your classic New England college. In a way, it was just what I had expected: lots of good teachers, and small, and you got to know people." He said Amherst was "an all-round, balanced kind of small college. But it did have those two courses that hit hard. They were not just a chance to hone your skills at writing and thinking and seminar talk. They were out to pry you loose from something, and ajar. So that was less friendly than the general good humor of the place."

Thomas Looker, who came to Amherst seven years after Shepherd and Bagg had graduated, described the college as a "boot camp." He said that "there was a real brutal, boot-camp mentality to the freshman curriculum. I learned a hell of a lot in English 1, and I don't regret taking it. I do regret taking Science 1; that was a very harmful, hurtful course. But I don't think that English 1 had to be taught this way. It was, and for reasons that I'm not quite sure of. I didn't become an English major, and I might very well have in a different department or at a time when there was less feistiness around. I was intimidated as hell. There was a real brutalizing quality to it, and I'm sure that a lot of students, very justifiably so, couldn't get around it, because there's nothing that can be more damaging than people attacking your writing in this vicious way. I mean, I had that reaction, but it didn't prevent me from learning. But there are ways that you could be equally critical and yet still not be quite so nasty."

John Boe, who came to Amherst in 1961 and who has written about his experience, does not describe either the college or English 1–2 as "boot camp." His metaphor for the course is "Puritan English." In Puritan English, Boe says, "you learned to admit your sins, your ignorance, your worthlessness, and to pray for grace; in order to get it, you had to suffer" (1992, 6). Boe remembers the kinds of comments that English 1–2 instructors used to write in the margins of their students' papers. He says:

> A favorite was to place a mark after one or two sentences and write, "Read to here." This was cruel, of course, but it did teach us not to spend a lot of time "clearing our throats." Since I was a moderately good student, I didn't get the full brunt of the mean spirited criticism. But the really mean comments became legend in the dorms, like the time somebody's professor (was it William Coles?) handed back a set of essays and one student discovered that of the three paragraphs in his essay, the first two had been completely crossed out, and the third had been cut out with a scissors. The young man came up whimpering to the professor, holding out his paper. The professor explained succinctly: "The first two paragraphs were so bad I had no choice but to cross them out. Then the third paragraph was EVEN WORSE. What else could I do?" (6)

Like Thomas Looker, Robert Bagg used the metaphor of "boot camp" to describe the Amherst College he had known as a student. Bagg told me that in 1953 when he came to the college, it had seemed "more like a boot camp than a welcoming college, and the boot camp aspect was determined by the very restricted and set curriculum. We had no choice as to what courses we took, or very little choice, for our first four semesters." He said, "We were not allowed to have a normal social life. We had Saturday classes. We were not allowed to have women not only in our rooms, but in our dorms. So it was both monastic and militaristic. And the teachers were tough guys; most of them had been soldiers. This was back in early 1953, and the sixties hadn't happened. And we were not promised an education but a chance to get one. What we were told was this: we had been accepted at the college because the Admissions Office thought we were pretty good, but the faculty did not necessarily agree with that, and we would have to prove ourselves."

Some of the customs governing student life in the 1950s when Shepherd and Bagg attended Amherst and even in the early 1960s when Boe and Looker were students, especially those which subjected freshmen to hazing by upperclassmen, must have contributed to the "boot camp" atmosphere that Bagg and Looker told me about. According to the *Amherst College Student Handbook, 1953–54,* which is the volume of the *Handbook* that would have been given to Bagg and Shepherd, "Certain customs are traditional in the College and it is well for Freshmen to observe them in order to avoid embarrassment" (12). Among these customs were the following:

> Amherst men say "hello" when passing each other on the street or campus. Freshmen say "hello" first.
>
> Freshmen sit together as a class at all football games.
>
> After morning chapel all Freshmen must rise from their seats and remain standing until the Faculty and the other three classes have passed out of the Chapel.
>
> Freshmen are forbidden to wear preparatory school insignia; sweaters carrying such insignia may be worn inside out.
>
> Amherst men know the words and music of Amherst songs. (12)

College custom also dictated that first-semester freshmen wear beanies both on campus and off. According to the *Amherst College Student Handbook, 1953–54:*

> The length of time that the "beanies" must be worn shall depend upon the outcome of a freshman-sophomore hill dash to be held on campus October 11, 1953. If the Sophomores are victorious the "beanies" must be worn until Christmas recess. In the event of a freshman victory the "beanies" may be discarded immediately.

Freshmen must not walk on the grass or unpaved paths
until the "beanies" have been discarded. (12)

The custom requiring the wearing of freshman beanies was
observed at Amherst College until 1963–64.

Chapel attendance remained compulsory until 1967–68. In
1953–54 when Bagg and Shepherd were freshmen, every student
was required to attend two of four morning chapel services conducted in Johnson Chapel each week, and *The Amherst College Student Handbook, 1953–54* indicates that an attendance monitor
would enforce this requirement (16). As an upperclassman, Geoffrey Shepherd, who describes his time at Amherst as "the deep
middle 1950s in which everything was extremely quiet and orderly
and cheerful," organized what he thinks may have been "the first
sit-in, student sit-in, on any American campus." The issue was compulsory chapel. Shepherd and his friends had decided to protest this
"abridgment of human freedom" by remaining seated at one
chapel assembly during the "Doxology." Shepherd remembers that
"we all went up there, and they sat in the front row, and I sat off to
the side in the front row. I sat in the faculty section with all the faculty right behind me. And we came to that point, and the organ
broke out in the "Doxology," and they looked at me, and I looked
at them, and they all got up, and I stayed seated, with Dean Esty
breathing down my neck."

Shepherd and Bagg met each other when they were freshmen
in the fall of 1953 and have subsequently remained friendly. They
lived in the same freshman dorm, became fraternity brothers, and
played golf together. Although they were placed in different sections of English 1, they addressed the same series of assignments.
This was a series involving maps,[1] locating oneself on a map, and
defining what it means to be "on the spot." Bagg and Shepherd had
to look at a map and then at an aerial photograph of Amherst College and, in both cases, to explain what they did to recognize "the
spot you are now on." They also had to address a cluster of assignments having to do with Edward Hicks's lion in his painting of *The
Peaceable Kingdom,* a newspaper account of an escaped lion, and
what it might mean to see a lion on the loose.

Bagg told me that "being on the spot" in the context of the
assignments on the escaped lion had to do with being an "eyewit-

This aerial shot of the Amherst College campus was given to English 1 students in the fall of 1953 along with the following assignment: "Let us assume you are now within the area contained in the photograph and you recognize this as a photograph of the spot you are now on. What do you do to recognize this?"

ness," which term "is meant as a metaphor of authority. Eyewitnesses can't be wrong, whereas we all know that they can be." He said the course and the assignments "introduced a kind of skepticism about the ability of language to represent reality, but also a sense of admiration for how close excellent speech could come to mirroring our needs for understanding reality, if not reality itself. And what a map does, which was of course the central item discussed, is to deal with our needs for getting around, regardless of whether it's an accurate representation of the terrain." He said, "One of the centers of English 1 was an examination of metaphor and a training in how to rely on metaphor and how to retain the sense that metaphors do not describe reality but suggest it." He explained that "the metaphors that relate to the maps are spatial" and that "if an item appears, or a building appears in the lower half of a map, it is either in a southward direction—lower half of the paper equals south, left-hand equals west, top equals north, right equals east. So this is an establishing of spatial relationships in the larger world using a defined square of paper. If you're looking at a picture, what is drawn in the lower half of the picture is meant to be closer to you, and what is in the top part of the picture is meant to be far away. This is a metaphor which has been established as a convention. So that is an example of a kind of metaphor which we don't even think about, which is kind of assumed, and our world is full of accepted conventions of that sort that we don't even have to think about but simply accept. And English 1 wants to get us to understand that these are conventions so that we will never be at the mercy of conventions, and when a convention is the problem, we can say so and change it." According to Bagg, the difference between a map and a photograph is "different language, different visual language. One is composed of lines; the other is composed of shapes and shadings. And you look for a configuration of shapes and shadings which conforms to your sense of your knowledge of the building that you are in."

Bagg said that "at one point I tried out the formulation that all language is metaphor." As he recalls, his instructor answered "that it is and it isn't, which may not seem terribly helpful, but I think that I wouldn't have said that unless I had gone through, maybe in my mind or on paper, a whole lot of ordinary sentences, which did not seem at first blush to contain metaphors, and then unearthing the suppressed metaphor in each one." Bagg implied that no one could really understand how the course worked "unless you had been struggling with the actual effort to define reality using words. You wouldn't have experienced an extensive grappling with these problems unless you had taken the course for ten weeks or thirteen weeks." He kept all the papers he wrote for English 1–2 but was able to locate only one of them easily. That one is an essay he wrote for English 2 which, in 1954, won him Amherst College's annually awarded Armstrong Prize for best freshman essay.[2] Bagg told me that "if I could find my original answers, I could show you what I wrote, and then you could see how I was missing a point in the first few weeks of the course. But I could also show you what metaphor would mean in terms of those questions and those maps and diagrams. There was a picture, you may recall, of 'Goldie the Lioness,' and I believe it was a Douanier Rousseau picture [actually Edward Hicks], but I'm not quite remembering, of *The Peaceable Kingdom*. It was a whole lot of animals in the piece. 'Goldie the Lioness' is a name, but it is also a metaphor, and it is also a view of reality. It implies that what would normally be dangerous and hostile in a jungle world, a Darwinian world, has somehow been captured and controlled by a more benign sensibility: the lion lies down with the lamb. And one of the ways of signaling this transformation is through nomenclature—you give 'Goldie' the name of a movie actress or someone who is a friendly aunt."

Geoffrey Shepherd saw these same assignments as "a kind of puzzle" created for students by the English 1–2 staff. As a freshman, he asked himself, "What were they after? I know how to write pretty well, but I'm not sure what they want me to write." He said he knew the staff must have "set this up for some reason, and they are apparently angling for some kind of way of thinking about yourself and who you are and where you are. So it was hard immediately to distinguish this from some kind of philosophical deal of who you are and where you are." He said that the map assignments and those on the lion involved "using other fields, geography if you will, and painting, art, to get some kind of new view of oneself. So I guess we all were—not all, but many of us were respectful enough—so we thought, 'Aha, they must know what they are doing, and this must be an important thing to do, and I just wish I knew how to do it better.'" Shepherd said he never did figure out "what these people in English were after with their obscure targets, maps, lions, and things you see. And maybe I was just too practical-minded, but even at the end when you would have thought, 'all right, I've soldiered on through this course, what was it really about?' they didn't say then even. At least if they did, I didn't hear it."

By the time he was a senior, Shepherd said he had decided English 1–2 was a course in "semantics." During his senior year, he applied for a Fulbright fellowship, which he did not get, and he remembers going for an interview with a group of faculty members who would rule on his candidacy. Charles Cole, the president of Amherst College, was a member of this faculty group and, Shepherd said, "Over at the end was Professor Baird, whom I had heard so much about but never met. And so somehow this came up: 'What was English 1–2 about?' And so, not having thought about it for three years, I said, 'Well, the best I can make out, it seemed to be a course in semantics,' by which I guess I meant that it was trying to get at what language really is, and how you form it and use it."

Shepherd said, "That's precisely what I thought they had been getting at. 'How do you use words to formulate your location on a map?' 'What relation is there between your spatial existence and your verbal description of that?' And the same goes for interpreting a painting or a human-created image of some sort: 'What process lay behind the creation of that image?' 'What is the relation between that and any words that you use to describe it?' or 'Describe your relation to that image or to some other reality which that image might represent, namely an escaped lion, or real lion.' So sure, I'd still say that ["semantics"] is the best word I can think of, a single word for what those crusty guys were trying to get at. And I guess I was a little startled when Baird got all upset at that: 'Well, that's not what it really was!' And so it was a sticky point, and that's when Charley Cole burst into laughter, and I sort of got through the moment."

Shepherd's instructor for English 1–2 had been Richard Waidelich. Shepherd told me Waidelich was "very gutsy, good-humored, not aggressive. He was a very energetic teacher. He loved to sort of probe—and 'What do you think of this?'—and seemed to be unendingly cheerful and so probably a good teacher." Shepherd said, however, that at some point in his freshman year, "I began to realize that instead of a teacher in a high school class, that here I was dealing with a teacher, but also a department. And the department itself might have had groups within it that were part of the debate, or the department might be united on one side of a debate that was going on in the profession, so that was part of useful learning too, to begin to understand what controversies mean in a profession. But we were clearly just foot soldiers down in the trenches being hit by the artillery that was being shot off by other people for other reasons. And I survived it." He said, "English 1–2 wasn't just cheerful. It was serious and did want to disorient people and stir them up. On the other hand, you could say, seen from the students' point of view, this was just another effort by the college as a whole to mold them, to make them think in ways that they wouldn't have thought before, to jolt them, to lead them, to make them more humble. I guess that the last element of my view of the people doing the course was that they played it as authorities, they did not say, 'We are with you here. We know you are an inquirer. You have spent a lifetime, a short lifetime, but a lifetime thinking, and we have some alternative ways of developing your thought, and let's work on this together.' They hit you with this stuff, and they wouldn't explain it. They had a hidden agenda as we would now say. They wouldn't reveal it to you. They were very much like authorities in a prison, making you do certain things, or at least making you comply with certain new and hidden ways of thought. And so naturally, it was hard to just give in and say, 'I surrender. I will do whatever it is you want.' And as I said, many of us had a feeling that this was all being done for other reasons; it wasn't necessarily for our welfare. This was an expression of the battles going on in the English profession about how criticism should take place, which may have meant a lot to these people. But as a kind of side effect, I think they overdid it in taking a whole year of freshman English, with these puzzling, and offbeat, and unexplained things, perhaps with some good effect, but certainly in a way that established authority."

Robert Bagg's instructor for English 1–2 was John F. Butler. Bagg describes Butler as "quite a different personality from the Arnold Aronses, and the Armour Craigs, and the Theodore Bairds, and it may have been one reason why John didn't get tenure. He was a much more supportive and helpful person, and he was quite willing to talk to students for a few minutes, several times a week. I would go in virtually every week for encouragement, or to try out a new idea, or to go over a paper with him." Referring to Grosvenor House, which in the 1950s housed the English department, Bagg explained that "the way the course was run on a daily basis was through discussion of selected paragraphs from the previous assignment. And this is what made the course so difficult for the faculty. The first thing that John Butler or Bill Pritchard would have to do is read through twenty papers (some would be only a page long) very carefully, make quite elaborate comments, and then excerpt single sentences, whole paragraphs, sometimes the entire paper, and have them typed by the secretaries in Grosvenor House (this is before xerography), and run off, and distributed at the start of a fifty-minute class. And then we would discuss the pros and cons, the successes, the anomalies in each of these pieces of writing. It was an honor to be published there." Although he acknowledged that some instructors were sharply critical of their students' papers, Bagg found no fault with this. He said, "You would gain greater sophistication by being rebuked in the margin about dumb things or inadequate things that you were saying, so everything you did was subject to challenge. And I think it produces a willingness not to be alarmed at being told you're wrong." Bagg added that he and his friends "would get together, we would talk in our rooms late at night, and English 1 was a subject. Your fellow students were seen much more as rivals and competitors than in today's more mutually supportive environment, so there was a tension between disclosing how you had cracked a problem and wanting to check it out with your friends, and your desire not to give away something that would get your rival an A as well as you. But in general with your close friends, you exchanged papers, you developed a theory of what the comments by your teachers meant. Some teachers would be very sparing of the use of the word 'good,' and some teachers would be openly contemptuous if you wrote a bad paper, like: 'This is nonsense!' They would be quite brutal if you had missed an assignment. There was no formula handed to us. There was no text, as in say physics or history, which would enable us to, if we studied hard enough, do well. It was the textbook that was invisible, and this was, we realized, a large part of the point of the course, that we were expected to come up with answers."

Bagg is now a professor of English at the University of Massachusetts at Amherst, and Shepherd is a professor of economics at the same institution. Bagg is also a poet. Bagg says that Shepherd, as a freshman, was "a kind of rationalist who couldn't be satisfied by metaphoric answers. He wanted exact, almost scientific answers, and it's no accident that he became an economist." Shepherd says that Bagg got "English 1–2 deeply in his thinking." He says Bagg "internalized" the course and it "changed his life."

Bagg acknowledges that "there is less likelihood I would have chosen to be an English professor without this course," and he marvels at "the intellectual work that went into this. There is nothing like that now." He says that what English 1–2 "gave to people who did the course really well" was "a sense of command over language." He also says, "I think it's one of the most successful courses in the history of education because it institutionalizes for an entire class, without allowing anyone to sidestep, evade, not take the course, not undergo the experience, something which will be immensely valuable later." Bagg explains that the course "provided a methodology, and methodologies of this sort, when they are at least partially successful, always give their possessors a sense of omnipotence, and certainly English 1 did. Later on, of course, I discovered the limitations, and other ways of approaching language and reality. But during the first part of my career as an academic and as a poet, I just simply implicitly trusted what I had learned about how I would go about dealing with a problem."

When I asked Shepherd whether English 1–2 had changed his life, he said, "No. I was just puzzled by it." Comparing himself to Bagg, Shepherd said, "I'm probably much more typical of the students at that time in that I dealt with it more or less successfully, and then it just rolled off me." When I asked Shepherd how he had managed to survive English 1–2, he said, "If anything, I just compartmentalized. I recognized that I was supposed to go through some new vision, didn't get it, and well, that was too bad. But they weren't helping me, and so I couldn't help it. And then freshman year was over and that was that." One of the things that subsequently helped him gain a perspective on his English 1–2 experience was writing for the *Amherst Student* newspaper. During his junior year, Shepherd became "chairman," or editor-in-chief, of the *Amherst Student*. He told me that "writing for the newspaper, I think if anything, was a way to get back to normal, dealing with writing about reality."

In November of his junior year, when he was competing for the chairmanship of the *Amherst Student,* Shepherd published an editorial[3] which was critical of both English 1–2 and the literature course for sophomores. He expressed concern at the fact that only 2 percent of the Amherst student body was contributing to the *Amherst Literary Magazine* and speculated that one cause might be "the literary hypercriticism ingrained into each of us. Who of us, armed with the tools of analysis of English 1–2 and 21–22, can but be discouraged by our own first efforts to write a short story or poem?" He added, "If it does nothing else, English 1–2 teaches us that writing is a strenuous job, especially at first. This is perhaps the greatest deterrent to would-be spare time writers" (1955, 2). Commenting on this editorial, Shepherd told me that "English 1–2 made us extremely self-conscious, and sort of introspective about and defensive about expressing ourselves, because we were faced by these authorities who knew better than we did what language was for, and who made us crawl through a complicated series of obscure lessons, supposedly to find out what we were doing whenever we tried to sit down and write. And some of us, obviously me, came out still puzzled and somewhat shaken in our confidence about using words. And I picked on the poor *Literary Magazine* much too hard, I suppose, using it as a vehicle for saying this."

I asked Shepherd whether, after completing English 1–2, he had personally felt blocked in his writing. He said the course "made me more cautious about whether I know what I'm dealing with. I wouldn't say that it's blocked me though, in the sense of paralyzed. But again, that's partly because I quickly got into other kinds of writing, including making up editorials, which isn't exactly creative, but it's not just reporting what went on on campus last night. And so I could more easily pass on from English 1–2 with some confidence." Shepherd told me that in the course of his professional career he has "published, or edited, or revised twenty books or revisions of books, fifty or sixty articles, most of them relatively practically oriented, about real industries, about monopoly, and the need to resist monopoly, and things like that." He summarized his response to English 1–2 in this way: "'Was I unable to write later?'—no, I had no problem. But, 'Did I go on to write or to major in the subject [of English]'—no, I steered clear of it. 'Would I accept the premises of English 1–2 and the New Criticism?'—absolutely not!"

Shepherd says, "As an academic, my impression is that courses of such a resolute determination to do something in a very specific way, and not only to do it once, but to do it to a whole class over a long period, are extremely unusual. First of all, you don't get to do that sort of thing. You're not in a position to exercise that sort of authority, especially if you're doing something very controversial. And so you are dealing with a truly special phenomenon here. And I suppose it's a tribute to Baird's crusty, curmudgeonly nature that he was able to enforce this—on a par with Arnold Arons, who was an extremely difficult person. But in a sense, there's one thing that's really different about English from physics which you might find helpful, which is physics people got flunked mercilessly. I got a *D.* Bob Bagg got a *D.* We weren't flunked out of college, but there was absolutely no compassion. I don't know what Bob got in English 1–2 (of course that was where he was good), but I was somewhat better in English than I was at physics, and I don't think I got a *C;* I think I got a *B.* So there wasn't this kind of destructive side to it, where they were willing to sacrifice the victim for the sake of the experiment. So that's one reason that, if anything, probably the results were more benign. People were puzzled by English 1–2, but not deeply offended, or angered the way they were about Science 1–2. And so maybe that's one reason that Baird got to keep doing it. He was doing something that was pretty odd, but he wasn't hurting people."

The day after I interviewed Geoffrey Shepherd, he called me. His call gave me what I took as a dramatic indicator of the continuing fascination which English 1–2 holds for him. He said he had been regretting not having taken the opportunity to ask me, "the one person who probably knew," what the course had been about. I told him he was not the only Amherst alumnus I had spoken to who reported having had trouble catching on to English 1–2.

John Bookwalter, who came to Amherst in the fall of 1956, when Geoffrey Shepherd and Robert Bagg were beginning their senior year at the college, had the same difficulty Shepherd had had in catching on to the freshman English course. Bookwalter told me: "I never did really dope it out until quite a bit later." He said, "I was in a fog the whole time. I was treating this stuff very concretely." He said Arnold Arons's course was "also tough for me, but I felt like I was in the ballpark there. I could play that game a little better; I felt a little more competent. But it was the combination—the two guys [Baird and Arons] were coming at you with real-world stuff in a way that I was completely unprepared for." Bookwalter's instructor for English 1–2 was Theodore Baird, and Bookwalter said of Baird that "although I did not understand, he never told you. He never in his classes, or once, said: 'The key here is . . .' Nope, you had to find your own way there."

When I asked Bookwalter whether he had felt frustrated by English 1–2, he said, "I was pretty confident of myself in those days. One way to say this is that an intern has more confidence than somebody who has been around a long time." Bookwalter had come to Amherst from Columbiana High School in Columbiana, Ohio, near Youngstown, where Baird had grown up. Bookwalter describes Columbiana High School as "a fill-in-the-blanks, check one of five, true-false place." He was the son and grandson of physicians, and he expected to go into medicine himself. He was one of several premed students in Baird's section of English 1–2, and he remembers that Baird "bitched about it. He said, 'Another one of those premeds!' you know. He thought that was sort of a waste." Despite Baird's attitude toward premeds, Bookwalter believes Baird personally arranged for his assignment to his class. He believes Baird made this arrangement because Bookwalter's father was physician to two of Baird's cousins in Ohio. Bookwalter said Baird "probably wanted to see what happened if you went to Columbiana High School and came to Amherst along with the guys from Exeter and Andover." Bookwalter said Baird had "seemed like a pretty senior guy to me" and "I felt it was a real honor to have him for an instructor in that class. I knew it was his class. I thought that I had been singled out simply because of his relationship to my parents via his cousins, which I also thought was very kind of him. I always felt honored to be in his class."

Bookwalter said Baird "was a guy that sparked your interest just because you knew if you weren't thinking and he got you, he wouldn't let you go." He said Baird's class "was a no bullshit class. You didn't get away with a flip remark or something. He'd nail you. You were on your toes in his class, the same way you were in Arons's class, because he'd call on you. 'What do you think about that?' And he'd make fun of you if you didn't do it right. He had no hesitation about being derisive of your efforts. And yet you never felt that 'he's picking on me.' You always felt that you had come up short intellectually, not that you had some character defect. I don't think people, and I don't know how this was in the rest of his classes, but certainly we in that class never felt that he had a grudge against any one person. But he was tough. He was a tough guy." Bookwalter remembers that Baird "leaned over his desk and looked over the top of his glasses. He was always leaning forward over his desk. He wasn't leaning back, reclining away from anything. He was trying to get to you, I thought." Bookwalter added that Baird "was not a pompous man in any way. And he had a very lively sense of curiosity. It was wonderful once he'd get going on something. He was a very, very interesting man; you have to give him that."

Bookwalter thinks he had only twelve or fifteen classmates in Baird's section of English 1–2. He said, "I had the sense that we had a little bit smaller class than some of the others. I'm not sure, but I just had that sense. I don't know whether he [Baird] was privileged to have fewer [students]." Bookwalter told me that attendance at class meetings was always excellent and that, so far as he remembers, all his classmates were conscientious about keeping up with the assignments. He remembers talking about assignments with his classmates after class. He said, "We'd talk about it, and everybody would get some sort of an idea, and then our friends would do the same thing, and we'd see how we did from his [Baird's] comments." Bookwalter said that "I was never as organized in my life. I'd go in and do those things the night they came out, which was often dumb because then someone else would get a better idea, and I was already done." Although he told me that he never went back and revised a paper of his own after seeing what a classmate had written, Bookwalter said he learned a great deal from reading and discussing the excerpts from other students' papers that Baird mimeographed for the class. He said, "You'd see the excerpts that would get printed up and read and the example of the good or the not-so-good. It was very interesting. And I think you would kind of gauge yourself, in part you would gauge your efforts against the ones that you thought were good, and you'd say, 'Well gee, maybe this guy has got a better lock on reality than I do.'" Bookwalter told me about one specific paper of his own that Baird chose to publish to the class. He said, "It was something that I answered, a series of questions that I answered in a completely concrete way because I was so upset at the abstractions that we were always trying to get at. And he [Baird] laughed; it was pretty funny. It was almost a parody of what I thought he wanted."

Bookwalter said Baird "was kind of an acid commenter. There was no palsy-walsy in Ted Baird. He was just a very acid wit, very sharp, no compassion that I can remember. This was a straight intellectual endeavor, and you got ranked based on the quality of your intellectual contribution, period." I asked Bookwalter if he would mind telling me the grade he had received from Baird, and he said, "I probably got a 70 or 80. I think my average was 81 or 82 first year, and the college average was 80, so I was in the middle, maybe a notch above the middle, but partly there because of the relative poverty of my high school education." Bookwalter thought his lowest grade had been in either English or French. He said that although his English course had seemed difficult to him during his freshman year, he had come to believe that it had had a positive effect on both his reading and his writing.

Bookwalter is now a surgeon on the staff of the Brattleboro Memorial Hospital in Brattleboro, Vermont, and he said, "I read a tremendous amount in nonmedical fields, as much as any physician I know, and I'm a pretty good writer, and I attribute it to having to write three essays a week. And that was pretty intense. And I don't think you could beat it. The topics, 'What is blue?' or something like that that would seem like an idiot's topic to me at the time, were wonderful training." He said that English 1–2 "is probably the best thing that ever happened to me in terms of expressing my thoughts on paper." But when I asked him whether he had done much writing since leaving Amherst, he said he had only published one article, and that was an article about his invention, the Bookwalter retractor, which is a device for improving the exposure of a surgical field. He said, "I've often thought about writing more, but I haven't done it because there are other things that are easier to do. I've got a knack for these mechanical things that I do, and it's so easy for me, it's like just falling off a log." The Bookwalter retractor is manufactured by a surgical instruments company, and Bookwalter said, "The most passionate writing I've done in the last fifteen years has been to whatever product director I have at [the company] to find out why they're not making something right and to berate them." Bookwalter added, "I don't see how it can hurt somebody to take some courses in an area that they're not interested in." When I asked him whether he had been interested in English before coming to Amherst, he said, "No, but I became more interested in it through that course."

In the fall of 1958, during Bookwalter's junior year at Amherst College, Douglas Wilson entered Amherst as a freshman. Wilson told me that "some students found English 1–2 quite stimulating and really got into it, and others hated it, were exasperated by it, and felt that they never quite got the hang of it. I'm from the former group, probably aided by the glow of hindsight." Wilson said, "I don't imagine there was one seventeen- or eighteen-year-old who came to college that year who had ever been asked a question like 'What do you do when you pay attention?' or 'What do you mean when you say the word *mean*?' It was just a totally foreign experience. Some kids took to it with delight and enjoyed it; others saw no point in it. I can't say that I saw a point in it, not right away, but I enjoyed it."

Wilson told me he had come to Amherst College "for the subjective reason that I thought I would enjoy a place like Amherst that was small. I was interested in American history, and I knew that the college's reputation in that area was high." He had graduated from the University School in Bloomington, Indiana, which "was associated with Indiana University, and was a lab school for the education department, and tended to be the school in town where most faculty children went." Wilson told me his father was "a professor of English. He taught American literature and creative writing and was a novelist and writer himself. And so I think probably that background, and certainly that family background, made English 1 more of a stimulating experience and less of an intimidating one for me than it might have been." Wilson said, "I remember that when I came home at Christmas time, after the first semester, my father seemed puzzled and not at all persuaded about the value of what we were doing. It seemed bizarre to him." Wilson added that his father had thought English 1 "was gimmicky, a kind of new thinking that had come along and that English departments ought to watch out for." He added, "I suspect my father thought composition was to write about a topic, a subject, and then to have the teacher criticize the writing for its grammar, for its expression, for its style, for its rhetorical concerns, for its sequence, its order of presentation, that kind of thing. And I don't remember that we had any of that in English 1."

Wilson said, "I was a good student in English 1. I was not a good student in physics. I had had good preparation at University School, and on my own I had kept a journal as a teenager. This was not a high school requirement. I fell in love with Emerson around age fifteen and tried to adopt his style and voice. I made solid progress in English 1, but I didn't begin brilliantly. Even the most talented student writers began awkwardly in English 1. It took us all time to get our bearings." He added, "I can see now why many students were exasperated, because the questions were very repetitive. We had, I think, three assignments a week, and the first would ask, 'What do you do when you pay attention?' And the second would ask, 'What do you do when you pay attention, and how do you describe what you mean when you say you pay attention?' And the next would build on that. But there would be a lot of redundancy and repetition so that you felt you were being asked to do a set of push-ups over and over again by a drill sergeant." Wilson said that although "there would be a slightly new twist each time," with each new question, what struck him particularly was "the redundancy; it was like being asked by a drill sergeant to do yet one more chin-up."

In the fall of 1958, Wilson said, "The central questions were 'What does it mean to pay attention?' and 'What does it mean to say something means something?' We also had to consider: 'How much can a writer express?' 'What is inexpressible?' 'Why?' 'What can no writer do?' and 'What can a writer hope to do?' The course was enormously helpful in preparing me to write for other courses. It taught us concentration—how to pay attention. It taught us to focus on the question at hand." Wilson, who is at present the secretary for Public Affairs at Amherst College, went to the Amherst College Archives before speaking with me to review the assignments he had addressed as a freshman. He said, "I jotted down a few notes because I didn't so much remember specifically what the questions were as what, with hindsight, I think the value of it all was. 'What it means to say you pay attention.' 'Describe an occasion when you shifted your attention.' 'When you say, *I know what I mean,* what does *mean* mean?'—on and on, like that. It was quite baffling. According to the professors who taught it and who talk about the course now, many students thought it was a sort of riddle and there was a correct answer, and once they could figure it out, then they would ace the course. They were exasperated because it appeared to them to be a kind of riddle, and yet they couldn't find the answer because in truth it wasn't a riddle."

Wilson's instructor for English 1–2 was John F. Butler, who had been Robert Bagg's instructor in 1953–54. Wilson recalled that "someone told me, or I think I heard that Butler wrote the assignments the first semester of my freshman year,[4] so in that sense, we may have been right at the best spot, since he was the author of our agony, so to speak." Wilson remembers Butler as "a very lively, animated, youthful, and upbeat person" and as "very kind, like an older brother." He added that "John Butler was not macho; he was very sensitive." He said Butler "kept things lively. He was always in charge." When I asked Wilson whether he could remember any specific classroom discussions, he said, "Frankly, I'd be at a total loss to remember any particular thing either another student or the professor said in the class. The assignments themselves and the questions they would ask, and the discipline, agony, or whatever, of trying to address that, having to go through that, and go through it so often, was where the profit lay." He also said, "I didn't think of English 1 as a social event. My sophomore American Studies class was much more social, because my classmates and I would debate issues over lunch. We carried learning beyond the classroom. English 1 was more a private learning experience. The bulk of my learning occurred in the course of addressing the very challenging homework assignments." Wilson said, "I think that English 1—maybe this is partly because I was a shy freshman—I think the work done for English 1 was a more private thing. I think writing is a more private thing. I remember, or I think I remember people running up and down the corridors screaming that they can't understand the assignment—'What the hell does so-and-so want?'—it was all madness anyway. But I don't think there was discussion about the assignments per se. My freshman roommate was one of those who just had no affinity for the exercise at all. I think that was true of other students. Some came here and were basically good scientists and not particularly attuned to the humanities, and others were the other way around."

Wilson guessed he had spent about three hours writing each of his English 1–2 papers. He said, "You didn't have to do any research; you didn't have to go out and look things up or read a book. You had to sit down with a pencil and paper, or a typewriter, and create something." Wilson doesn't remember that Butler wrote extensive comments on his papers. He said that Butler's comments "were never nasty in the way, I gather, some English professors can be. His comments were never insulting. I think others had a very different style and would write devastating things on students' papers. Butler usually either wrote a question in the margin or a compliment." Wilson said that what had been difficult for him personally was having to read his writing aloud in class. He said, "I had a very severe problem in the course, which was that one of its methodologies was to mimeograph papers that the professor thought were worth discussing, and then the student who wrote the paper was called upon to read it."When I said I had understood that instructors hid the identities of the authors of the papers they chose to discuss in class, Wilson said, "Not in Butler's class. He actually had the author read it. And my problem, which was a severe phobia, was public speaking. I simply could not, literally could not, sustain any spoken voice in an oral presentation."When I asked him to describe the in-class publication process and to estimate the number of times his own papers were read, Wilson said, "As I recall, it wasn't the entire paper that would be read or distributed, but it would be an excerpt. Butler would take something that he thought was the nub of an issue. My memory is that they were maybe a paragraph or two. And mine maybe four times in the semester. He probably distributed two or three excerpts in the course of each class period." Wilson added, "I think the whole point of the discussions was always to push the students, including the one whose work was being discussed, to think a little more about the question, to be more precise in the description, to do more inner questioning, to be more explicit about the experience."

When I asked Wilson to explain what he thought the value of the course had been, he said, "Gradually the course made us aware of the link between writing and thinking, and of the value of precision." He said, "The course wasn't just about being a good writer. It was about what can be expressed, what is inexpressible. A rather glib label that I think about when I think about that course is that it was an exercise in the precise expression of meaning. It was very good for getting young people who had never really thought an idea through to do so in a very disciplined fashion, and to worry about the words that they used and how accurate they were in describing what they wanted to express. This may be happy hindsight, but I really think that the exercise had wonderful benefits for the rest of one's college career and for work after college. I went into the newspaper business."

Like Robert Bagg before him, Wilson wrote a paper for English 2 that won Amherst College's Armstrong Prize for best freshman essay of the year.[5] Like Geoffrey Shepherd, Wilson became chairman, or editor-in-chief, of the *Amherst Student* during his junior year at Amherst. After graduating from the college, Wilson earned a master's degree in international studies from Tufts and then joined the staff of *The Providence Journal* as a reporter. He served as both a correspondent and a bureau chief in Washington, D.C., before returning in 1975 to Amherst College to assume his present position in Public Affairs. Wilson told me that as an undergraduate "I discovered two things at Amherst in regard to my professional interests. One was I didn't want to be an academic, although I had thought I wanted to be a professor of American history. The other was that I loved journalism." Wilson said that while he was working as a reporter, he often thought that English 1–2 had "made me much more attentive to whether what I was writing actually reported what I heard or observed and whether it made sense." On the other hand, Wilson said, "I think English 1 may have made writing more of an agony for serious writers than it might be otherwise, because you really are looking a third and fourth time at word choice and things like that to make sure they represent not only as clearly but as economically as possible what you really intend to say."

John Stifler and Thomas Looker, both of whom came to Amherst in the fall of 1964, two years after Douglas Wilson had graduated, agreed with Wilson, and with Geoffrey Shepherd for that matter, in observing that English 1–2 had sometimes had the effect of making students more self-conscious about their writing. When I asked Stifler whether English 1–2 had influenced his decision to become a writer, he said that it "probably helped me to be one in some ways and probably interfered in some ways, because I'm a pretty self-conscious person already, and it certainly heightened my self-consciousness." Looker said, "Immediately after English 1, I was less satisfied with my writing because I was more sensitive to what I was doing wrong. Everyone after English 1 had this period where it was difficult to write. It has always been difficult for me to write, so it's hard to separate that, but it was particularly difficult [after English 1] because you had this fear that someone would tear it apart." Looker qualified his remarks by adding that "I left feeling that I might be able to learn how to write. I knew what I had to do." He said, "I feel in learning to write better, there is some corner you have to turn. It's not very complicated, but there is a corner you have to turn to get it, whatever it is. It is not something that immediately transforms your writing, but it gets you on the right track. I may be totally off base, but I know this is my experience. English 1 had me turn the corner. It got me around to some sense of how language worked."

Looker and Stifler are the two youngest alumni I spoke with. They both came to Amherst with good backgrounds in English and in writing. Looker said, "I was always interested in writing." He said that as a freshman, he was self-conscious about his "simple prose. I knew I could do journalism. I wanted to write fiction, but I wrestled with whether or not I was good enough." He had prepared for college at George School in Newton, Pennsylvania, which was a Quaker school and, according to Looker, "very internationally oriented." He told me he had come to Amherst planning to major in history and explained that "I had always loved history and got into African stuff because I figured there would be less competition. I was fascinated by non-Western things in general. I loved American stuff, but the field was so crowded." He said he came to Amherst "assuming that I was going to go into journalism. I loved the whole newspaper business, the drama of it. I had spent time at NBC News, and I walked around with an 'NBC' on my clipboard."

Before enrolling at Amherst College, Stifler had graduated as first in his class from Montgomery Bell Academy in Nashville, Tennessee, which was a competitive, private school for boys. His father was an Amherst alumnus, and his grandfather had taught physics at the college. John Stifler is the only alumnus I spoke with who not only saved all of his English 1–2 papers, but who made them all available to me. The large leather case in which he has always kept these papers still sports the identification card which he filled out as a freshman at Amherst College and which identifies him as: "John Stifler, 1600 Pennsylvania Ave., Washington D.C., State of Confusion."

Stifler had visited Amherst College during his sophomore year of high school and talked there with a couple of friends from Tennessee who were Amherst freshmen at the time. Stifler says his friends "talked about the papers that they were writing and how they had lots and lots of papers to write for this composition course, and they were difficult assignments." Stifler's friends "said they would get their papers back and in the margin would be written, 'What the hell are you talking about?' They thought it was pretty funny, in a way, because it was a system they couldn't beat, and I remember later in the conversation telling them that I honestly didn't imagine that I would have much difficulty with English composition in college. And they laughed, 'What the hell are you talking about?' They were lording about how the arrogance of someone who is pretty well educated at a good college preparatory high school can be deflated by freshman year at Amherst College." As soon as Stifler arrived at Amherst, he encountered the three required core courses: English 1–2, Science 1–2, and History 1–2. He came quickly to perceive that English 1–2 was not merely "a required course; it was a required ritual." He did not do well in History 1–2, "but the English and science courses, which are the courses that dominate the memories of most people who were students at Amherst then, I really did get something out of, and the English course most of all."

Stifler's instructor for English 1–2 was Armour Craig. Looker's was William E. Coles Jr. In the fall of 1964, both Stifler and Looker addressed a series of assignments for English 1 that had been written by Robert C. Townsend.[6] The themes for Townsend's assignments were masks, poses, and being oneself. The focal word for the semester, according to Stifler, was "sincere." Stifler said that as a freshman, addressing these assignments, "I was trying to be dutiful, and you read my papers and you see that they are very dutiful, very careful, and built block upon block. They were very sincere." The first assignment in Townsend's series employed a quotation from Oscar Wilde: "The first duty in life is to assume a pose; what the second is no one has yet found out." For this assignment, students had to answer four questions:

> What pose (if any) or poses have you been urged to assume? What poses do you know how to assume? Do you think a man's life should consist of assuming various poses? Do you see any alternative?[6]

The third assignment in the series was built on Polonius's advice to Laertes in *Hamlet:* "To thine own self be true."

At the fourth class meeting, Stifler handed in a response to this third assignment. At the fifth meeting, he was dismayed to find his response had been mimeographed as one of two sample essays for discussion. Stifler told me in 1990 that in anticipation of talking with me, he had reread this paper for the first time in twenty-six years. He said, "I was pretty embarrassed to read it, but what embarrassed me was that the style was so plodding." He said that in 1964, when he saw his paper listed anonymously on what he and his friends called the "shit sheet," he thought, "Oh well, okay, it's my turn to be raked." Stifler had written:

> I believe that being true to my self basically means abiding by standards that I have established through instinct and through the instruction of my parents from my earliest childhood. Specifically, I feel that lying, cheating, or misrepresenting myself, either to others or to myself, constitutes a violation of these standards of truth. To further this explanation, I recall a few instances when I have not been true to myself. When I was in the second grade I was told by the teacher that I must stay after school because I had been talking too much in class. Not wanting to suffer the disgrace of being reproached by my parents for having to stay after school for misbehavior, I inconspicuously sneaked out of the classroom when the rest of the class left, so as not to arouse my parents' suspicion by arriving home late. The plan succeeded completely; the teacher, trusting that I would do as he had requested, had forgotten to check on my obedience in this matter, so that I escaped with impunity. I paid for this deception many times over, however. For three days I lived in desperate fear that the teacher would loose all his fury against me for my disobedience; even when my fear had subsided, I nevertheless could not look that teacher squarely in the eye for the rest of the year, and even when our family moved to another town, the memory of my false deed continued to haunt me for four years. This incident may seem ridiculously trivial to a "mature" person, but it impressed its import upon my senses indelibly.[7]

Stifler recalled that "to my own surprise, I turned out to be an example of what to do, rather than what not to do." Aided by penciled notes he had made in 1964 on his copy of the "shit sheet," Stifler remembered that Craig had "said something like, 'All the points that are made in this paper rest on observations—you can't get into trouble when you do that.'"

Like Stifler, Looker used the term "shit sheet" to refer to the mimeographed collections of excerpts from student papers which English 1–2 instructors distributed for classroom discussion. Looker said, "I don't know where the term cropped up, but that's what it

was called, or that's what I've always called it. And that's what people who talk about it to me have always called it. And when I've
used it, no one who has ever taken the course has raised any eye-
brows about what it was."[8] Looker said, "I counted it up once, and
I was on the shit sheet four or five times." When I asked Looker
whether, in Coles's section, the excerpts on the shit sheet had been
listed anonymously, he said, "The authors weren't identified, but
sometimes you could tell who they were anyway." Looker then
told me about a time when one of his own papers had been listed
on the shit sheet. He had written about a production of *Hamlet* and
had been "up all night, as we always were, like until 2:00 or 3:00,
which in those days was all night. And I was struggling with this
paper in which I described psyching myself up as Laertes my senior
year at George School to get angry with Hamlet and have our
sword fight. And it was a difficult role, and I didn't really get into it,
and so I described how I tried to physically pump myself up in the
wings, and I was just describing what happened and then wrote
some conclusion. Well, Coles put this on the shit sheet, and as he
began reading it, the class began laughing, and he began laughing,
and it was a hysterical piece. He did a little bit of editing in it
which made it funnier. But essentially, I hadn't written it funny at
all, and yet it was funny, and so the experience was of thinking you
were writing one thing and yet something else was coming out.
And when I went to Coles afterwards, I said, 'You know, I didn't
really mean it.' He said, 'What do you mean you didn't mean it?'
And he read me some lines, and he said, 'What do you mean? That's
funny.' I said, 'Well yes. Yes, it is funny. Yes, you're right. But consciously I didn't realize that.'"

After explaining about the "shit sheet," Looker introduced me
to another bit of English 1 student jargon and told me about writing a paper that had finally "crossed the line" and won Coles's
praise. Looker said, "My essay was not the first essay to 'cross the
line'; it was the second, and that was typical. The first one was by a
guy who was the writer in the class. He wrote like a writer. He
obviously knew what he was doing. He was going to write novels
when he grew up. So he wrote the first thing that crossed the line.
And then I followed with the second one. It was actually the very
next essay; I mean I was sort of imitating him." Looker added, "I
have this image of suddenly this other guy's paper is being discussed

in class and beginning to get these glimmerings that Coles is not tearing this apart. Maybe this is it! Why does Coles like this? You would start trying to figure out what was going on. And I don't remember if I consciously tried to imitate, or if things had made sense. I would have to go through and study my chicken scratchings that I put on the day's paper. But the very next thing, mine crossed the line. But that was always the pattern: this other guy was the pathfinder, and I followed." Looker explained that at that point they were "about a month into the course. It was about the eighth or ninth assignment that finally crossed the line, so to speak." He added, "You hadn't arrived once you wrote one good paper. My very next paper after the good paper was half dumped on, and then the paper after that was totally dumped on. And so the whole semester proceeded with me; I mean you didn't suddenly learn how to write. It was a long, long process, and I stumbled along."

Looker told me that the first paper he ever wrote for English 1 was a paper about himself and his father. Speaking from memory, he recited what he thought Coles's comments had been: "'I can't believe it; are you kidding?' 'We call this student irony.' 'I seem to have heard this before.' 'This is a string of platitudes, one thumping cliché after another.' 'Who is the father? Who is the boy? Have you seen them anywhere before? The funny papers maybe?'" Looker said, "I remember that by heart—'the funny papers!' 'Where have you seen these people before, Mr. Looker? The funny papers maybe?'" Looker said that during the first month of the course student's papers "would just be torn apart in class. Coles was, I think, the most English 1 exponent of English 1. I don't know how Baird operated, but I imagine it just fit Coles perfectly. We used to talk about him as having a 'halfback approach' to English literature, I mean not even the quarterback, but the halfback—this tough little guy. He was actually a nice guy, but the persona that one got, the voice that one heard was this kind of—'Mister Looker'—in a sneering tone. He was feisty in the way that a lot of Amherst teachers were in those days. There was this—'We are tearing you down so that you will put yourself back together'—attitude. And so you were really torn. The sense was of being really torn apart on the shit sheet."

Looker remembered that on the fourth or fifth assignment of the fall series, Coles "spliced together an essay from sentences from all different essays and put it together as all about sincerity—'sincerity this; sincerity that'—and he just put some sentences together, and it made perfect sense. And he said, 'What does this mean if I can do this?'" Looker explained, "What it meant is that we were all writing in the same voice, all writing a bunch of thumping clichés that didn't mean anything." He added, "There's a quality of humiliation there, even if it's shared, or even if it's anonymous, and that is damaging. It's brutalizing, and the only time it works is if the culture at large supports this sort of stuff, and Amherst 'men' in those days were supposed to survive that. This was part of the macho-ethic business. These were the days where the mythical and perhaps apocryphal story of the introduction to Amherst (you know, in the opening welcome) is: 'Look to your left; look to your right; one of you (or maybe it was two of you) is not going to be here in four years.'"

Looker said Coles "was tough; I found him fair. He seemed to have a wonderful ear, and he was funny. He wasn't funny 'ha, ha'; he was sort of abrasive, but he was open essentially. You felt you could go and talk to him. He wasn't pompous. He was sort of the archetypal good Amherst teacher for me." Looker explained that "I heard a compassion in the sneer," and he remembered that "Coles used to say, 'If I circle something and I put *SP* in the margin, you're not going to pay any attention to that. If I circle it and I say *This is Fascism!* maybe you'll think about it.'" Looker said he recognized what Coles was doing "as a posture of someone who really cared and who was trying to get you to see what you were sounding like. The kicker was, he was sneering not at you, but at the voice on the page. When I wrote like a cartoon character, he said, 'This is a cartoon character; come on! You're a human being; don't write like a cartoon character.' And it was the fact that they were rooting for you. Ultimately, they did think you had something to say, and they were kicking you in the pants to make you realize that you were doing violence to yourself. Now that's the most positive slant you can put on this, and obviously there was a lot of crap and all that too."

John Stifler told me that a frequent device his instructor, Armour Craig, had used in marking student papers "was two exclamation points. And I once asked him, 'What does this mean?' He said, 'It means *Come on!*'" Stifler showed me sections of the papers he had saved from English 1–2 and some of the comments Craig had written in the margins. Stifler said, "You know, I look at this, and I think on one level, I still don't know what he [Craig] meant by any of that. But I think I got a lot indirectly out of comments like that." When I asked Stifler to tell me about the kinds of comments Craig had made in class, he said that at most class meetings in his section, Craig had led discussions of "one or two papers for that fifty-minute class period. We might spend half that time talking in specific detail about what the author seems to be trying to do in the paper or in some particular paragraph. 'What do you mean when you use a sentence like this?' or 'How can you come to a conclusion like this on the basis of what you've written?'" Stifler didn't recall that Craig had spent much time going over new assignments. Generalizing about the entire English 1–2 staff, Stifler said, "I think they felt that we would learn more if we just got it cold."

Stifler told me he had learned a lot from watching what his classmates did. He said that "every other night, or three nights a week, I can remember having a conversation with somebody in the class. It didn't even have to be somebody in the same section because half the freshman class at Amherst College on a given night was all trying to write the same paper at the same time. The other half would be doing it the other night because it was Tuesday-Thursday-Saturday. And the defenders of the system say that it was one of the wonderful things about the core curriculum. It did a lot to give people a sense of identity as freshmen at Amherst." Stifler specifically remembered "one very important piece of collaborative learning that happened around the end of October–beginning of November. A guy in the dorm was sitting in his room, reading aloud the paper written by another guy that I knew, who was in his class, not my class."

The assignment was the ninth in the series. Students had been directed to

> Describe a situation in which you felt another person was not being himself, not expressing himself sincerely. What was the occasion? What was said? What did that person say? Why did you think he was being insincere? What do you mean when you say, "He was being insincere"?[6]

Stifler said that the essay his dormmate was reading "read much more like a story than like the essays that I was trying to write in response to these questions. He described, he simply told the story of being in Spain, traveling. He had been on his own in Europe, traveling, that summer maybe, and he had lent some money to some guy who was Spanish or French or something, who owed him the money, and he'd been owing it to David for a while. David had written a letter finally to him, really pretty angry and needing the money himself, and feeling hurt that this guy hadn't paid him back. They were in two different cities, and the guy had written back, and David quoted the letter in his paper, saying, 'You know, I'm really, really hurt. Do you think that I would be so callous as not to pay you back? How could you? After all the things that we've been through in a friendship that we've shared together, how could you imagine that I'm not going to pay you? etc., etc., etc.'—a very poignant, long, thoughtful letter, which probably he [David] had with him and had just plugged into his paper. And he concludes the letter, and then there follows one more line in the paper: 'I never got the money.' And I learned—well, that was 1964; this is 1990—and I still remember that in some detail, and I sort of learned, I realized at that point that 'English 1: Composition' was writing in a pretty wide-open sense and that interesting stories could make the point about what constituted sincerity, for example." Stifler added, "I didn't immediately go write my next paper inspired to switch from a rather plodding, carefully constructed paragraph essay form to a more compelling kind of narrative. And I don't know that I got to that point during that semester, or even ever while I was an undergraduate, but I've gotten to that point now."

Stifler then showed me the paper he had written in response to the twenty-eighth assignment in the fall 1964 series. Professor Townsend, who was the principal author of the assignments, had asked Stifler and the other members of the freshman class to

Return to a situation in which you knew what it was to be yourself, more specifically to one in which you moved from not being yourself to being yourself. Where were you? Who else was there? What was said? Where precisely do you locate this movement from not being yourself to being yourself?[6]

As Stifler read me his response to this assignment, he told me he thought it sounded "extremely self-conscious." He said, "There are a lot of ways that a freshman can be intimidated; there are a lot of ways that anybody can be intimidated by a question like that. There are a lot of ways in which a grown-up could respond to it, saying, 'Why am I spending any of my time writing about this?'" But in 1964, confronted by the need to say when he had not been himself, he had begun his paper by confessing that: "I have spent the last three and a half hours attempting to write about such a situation, but I have been unable, at least this far, to do so; indeed, I am beginning to think that there has never been an occasion when I have not been myself." Stifler tried to get at the assignment by analyzing three personal incidents. He described a time when he had "taken a girl for granted" in high school, then a time when he had pretended to faint in order to get out of Latin class, and finally a time when he went to a drinking party, each time concluding in effect that "Yes, I had worn a *mask,* but this mask was in fact a very real part of myself."[9]

In commenting on this paper, Professor Craig seems to have tried to draw Stifler's attention to the various poses he had taken on as its writer. When Stifler wrote, "I *knew* I was taking her for granted and dating her solely because of the material advantages offered, but I also knew that the person who did this was really *I,*" Craig replied, "'I' who? Are *you always* on the make?" When Stifler wrote, "I'd heard about such parties, and I wanted to see what one would be like," Craig replied, "'I' the Experimenter?" Toward the end of his paper, Stifler had written:

> I hoped that this time I had a good paper; then I read it over, and I discovered that it sounded contrived, which, in fact, it was. I pictured Prof. Craig reading it in class, and in my mind I heard him cut my work to pieces.[9]

Craig replied, "Come on! *This* 'I' is a scared Rabbit, and he's not Thee." Craig's final comment at the bottom of Stifler's paper was

> O dear, O dear. All these complaints and self-lacerations. All I want to know is: who pushed the typewriter keys to write this

Assignment? Yet *another* 'I'? I think he does pretty well. This is NOT a moral problem. This is a WRITING problem.

The final "Long Paper" assignment which Stifler and his classmates were given in December of 1964 was built on a quotation from W. B. Yeats's *Autobiographies.* Yeats had resolved "to write out my emotions exactly as they came to me in life, not changing them to make them more beautiful." Stifler observed that Yeats had been "a wonderful person to work with" because "he was a man of many masks himself, and here he is writing about how he's figured out that the secret is not to use any masks at all. And this is at the end of a semester that began with a quote from Oscar Wilde." Stifler then showed me the paper he had written in 1964 in response to this Long Paper assignment.[10] Toward the end of the paper, he had written, "I understand this matter of expressing oneself sincerely and naturally," and Professor Craig had commented in the margin, "You DO!?" At the very end of Stifler's paper, Craig wrote:

> There are two things to be wary of: 1) embellishing stories about exiles you have never seen, and 2) Comments that you confuse with oracular declarations. *Relax.* When you *do* write of yourself and WHAT YOU *KNOW,* you *are* a good writer.

Stifler said that, since leaving Amherst College, he has known times "when I felt as though I could hear Craig's voice in my ear often, when I was teaching and when I was reading. It's very valuable. And he is certainly one of the three or four teachers that I've had, that I had at college, who made the most impression on me." Stifler is now a freelance writer and a writing consultant. He leads writing workshops at a Florence, Massachusetts, bookstore, and he teaches writing, as an adjunct at UMass, to junior-year students in the department of economics. He writes two regular columns for the Northampton, Massachusetts-based *Daily Hampshire Gazette,* including "Time Out," which is a weekly arts column, and "On the Run," a biweekly column on running. Stifler said, "If I had the chance to take only one course out of all the courses that I took in four years, English 1–2 would by far be the one that was of most value to me. It is the one that I have continued to learn the most from. It is the one that has had the most direct application to how I teach, to how I read, especially to how I read my students' writing." He said, "Setting aside everything else, the fact of having to come to class three days a week with a paper was wonderful." He added, "I learned how to do them at the last minute; I learned how to sit at the typewriter, and just roll a piece of paper in, and go. And boy! when you work for a newspaper, that's a really useful skill to have."

Thomas Looker also went into journalism. He freelances for National Public Radio (NPR) and in 1983 produced a thirteen-part, Peabody Award-winning documentary series entitled *New England Almanac* for NPR. He has written a book about NPR, *The Sound and the Story: NPR and the Art of Radio,* which was published by Houghton Mifflin in February of 1995. He is also a visiting lecturer in American Studies at Amherst College. During each of the five summers from 1987 to 1992, he taught a three-week writing course at Amherst for students who planned to enter the college as freshmen in the fall. He told me that what he did in these summer courses was "to merge the skills of an editor with some ideas from English 1." When I asked him what features of English 1–2 he had carried over into his course, he said, "The business of trying to get them to write as much as possible." He also said he had experimented with sequenced assignments. As an illustration, he said, "I've used 'understanding'—'How do you understand something? Describe a situation when you were misunderstood. What do you mean by being misunderstood? Describe the process of moving from not understanding something to understanding something.'" He described his course as having "a focus on language, a focus on voice, and an approach which does not lay down the rules, but where you try to get the students to hear stuff on the page. I try to respond to voices on the page and demonstrate responsiveness. I try to get kids invested in learning to write better and to get them to see the connection between the voices they create in their writing and who they are."

Looker said that above all, what he derived from English 1 "was an obsession with voice." He said, "English 1 was about a lot of things, but one of the things English 1 was for me was developing the notion of a voice on the page. There was an absolute bloody-mindedness about saying, 'We don't know what the voice on the page is, or how it got there, or how to improve it, but we just know when we hear it,' and that the voice on the page was a mysterious process. There was something that finally was a mystery; it was there, but it was a mystery. And so the whole course was— How do you hear it, if I hear it and you don't?" Looker added, "It is metaphorically consistent, and probably more than that, that I would get into radio, which is totally a medium of voices." Looker added that "one of the underlying messages of English 1 was that learning to write better equals finding your own voice, equals developing your own identity. It's intensely personal—you have something to say. English 1 was all part of that, and that was the central foundation of it, and that's why they [the staff] could act like assholes. They were doing it because, on some level, the best of them believed that you were doing violence to yourself if you didn't write well. And that was communicated to me somehow."

Other veterans of English 1–2 have also testified to the value of the course. John Boe, who took the course in 1961–62 and who now teaches writing at the University of California at Davis and edits *Writing on the Edge,* wrote in his autobiographical piece on "Puritan English" that "more than anything else, it was my Freshman English course (and it was all fresh *men*) at Amherst College in 1961 that prepared me to spend most of my professional life as a teacher of writing" (1992, 5). Boe says he is "not as mean to my students as the Amherst professors were to us" (5), but he suggests that

> there are two kinds of teachers, those who teach out of love and those who teach out of fear. I, like the people in the field I most respect today, am clearly one of those who teaches out of love. Still, I can see the benefits of having survived the pedagogy of fear, a pedagogy where confusing, even terrorizing the student seemed a primary goal, not an accidental effect. (6–7)

Douglas Wilson, who as the secretary for Public Affairs at Amherst College is responsible for organizing an alumni reunion every June, told me, "It is tempting to romanticize the course in hindsight. Many things that happen when you are between the ages of eighteen and twenty-one are watershed events. It is during those years that you begin to discover your own resources. That is why college reunions are such a big draw." Speaking of the course, he said, "Alumni still talk about it. Every year when there's a major reunion, one of the reunion classes from that period usually schedules a panel discussion about English 1." Wilson added that Roger Sale and William Pritchard had led a session on English 1 in 1987 at the twenty-fifth reunion of Wilson's own class of 1962.[11] I later asked Sale about this, and he said, "The thing that most impressed me in 1987 is that, twenty-five years later, these men still wanted to talk about English 1."

Theodore Baird also marvels at this. Speaking to me of alumni, Baird said, "Now, at every reunion, they don't come back to drink; they come back and have sessions. A doctor will tell them how to live, and a class reunion will have lecturers; they'll have an astronaut or somebody. One of the things they have is a session on the curriculum, and that curriculum [the "New Curriculum"]. Fifty years even out of college, they'll say, 'Why don't we have a course like English 1?' It's the damnedest thing. I have to laugh. I still laugh. I think these people now look back, and they say, 'Well, something was expected of me.' And in all their Amherst education, very little was. (See, that's a secret; don't tell anybody I said that.) Very little was—except to go on doing what they had done to get into college, which was to do their lessons. Very little was expected. We just said, 'All right, it's up to you.' They remembered that, and then they liked the idea of work. They think they had to work, and so they say, 'Why can't the college make the students work the way we did?' That's an old man's talk."

Robert Bagg, who has distinguished himself as a poet since leaving Amherst College, returned to the college on "The Occasion of Amherst's Sesquicentennial Celebration of Its Poets" in 1981 to give a "Talk." Bagg began by explaining that because he had once been identified by Allen Ginsberg "as a misguided recruit to what he called the 'Academic, or Amherst School of Verse,'" he, Bagg, wanted to tell his audience "what Amherst had taught me, and taught all of us who might feel skewered by that *Amherst, or Academic,* thrust." He said, "For our generation, the composition course, English One, the invention of Theodore Baird, set the intellectual style of the Amherst English Department." Bagg said that

for any of us interested in writing poems, the course had a special value. The exact process by which we knew something, the irreducible steps, was its daily occupation. And pursuit of the exact steps and modes by which we come to know and feel things is the best possible training for a poet. At the heart of the course's painfully yielded secret doctrine was the news that each human being must create reality and even sanity for himself in the act of writing or speaking.[12]

Speaking as an English professor in his more private conversations with me, Bagg said that English 1–2 had anticipated professional developments in English which are not generally supposed to have occurred until recently. He said, "In the last fifteen or twenty years there's been a revolution in English theoretical studies, and there's been a rise in methodologies which examine the ontological status of language, which is a stuffy term, but it simply means whether there's a trustable relation between language and reality. English 1 introduced that theme to us when we were eighteen years old, so I was not at all surprised when deconstruction arose." Bagg also pointed to "the discoveries that came long after the end of English 1, pioneered by Mina Shaughnessy, also Peter Elbow, that you did not improve people's writing by making them aware of grammatical rules and correcting their punctuation, that these skills were ones that were acquired in a much less systematic way than schoolmarms tended to hope. And so the fact that there was very little emphasis on usage and style in English 1 was really a plus, a discovery of something of the truth before it had become generally acknowledged."

CHAPTER SIX

Be Your Own Man

*T*he final act of the drama of English 1–2 at Amherst College plays itself out like a Greek tragedy. The mythic patriarch is dethroned by his rebellious sons, his kingdom is divided, and his fate can be seen as no less than what he has invited in urging each of them, in effect, to "Be your own man."

A number of factors combined to bring about the downfall of English 1–2. As Theodore Baird notes, "The movement in the 1960s was toward less organized education." Baird told me that by the mid-1960s the Amherst faculty wanted a curriculum with "a lot fewer requirements." John Cameron agreed, remarking that just as Amherst's postwar "core curriculum was supported by history, by national history, so when the core curriculum came crashing down in the late 1960s, it was no accident historically. And the admission of women [in 1976] was no accident historically. We held out a little longer than some, but not as long as others." Roger Sale pointed out that "since they all went at about the same time—that is coeducation and the dropping of the set curriculum and Ted's retirement all happened within a few years of each other—it is a little hard to know which is more important than the other."[1] Sale added that the course "couldn't exist without Baird's wit."

Already by the early 1960s, the pressures for social change were beginning to be felt on the Amherst campus. When in October of 1963, in one of his last public acts before Dallas, John F. Kennedy came to Amherst College to dedicate its new Robert Frost Library, a "conservatively dressed, decorously silent group of some fifty faculty and students stood quietly in rows outside Amherst's Alumni Gymnasium to greet" the president "as he drove up from his helicopter landing on the playing fields. Their purpose—as their neatly lettered signs attested—was simply to urge the president to support more strongly his own civil rights bill which was bogged down in Congress" (Greene 1978, 326). Baird remembers that he wrote a set of assignments for the fall of 1963 on "What is good English?" He says, "This was a nice set of assignments because it really faced these boys who believed in social equality, who believed in an integrated society, and also believed that Amherst should teach them good English. And they had to consider what this meant socially, what this meant economically, what this meant in terms of jobs, and in marches—marches, when they were going down south to march, but they were going to use good English" (1978b, 25).

According to Lawrence Babb and the other members of Amherst's Select Committee on the Curriculum who published *Education at Amherst Reconsidered* in 1978, Amherst's "New Curriculum" of 1947 and the practice of requiring specific core courses may have been in keeping with the national mood during the 1940s and 1950s, but was "resented in an era of liberation movements" by students who "felt already coerced by a draft law that made college studies an alternative to military service" (15). During the nineteen years in which the New Curriculum was in force, it had undergone periodic faculty review. It was evaluated in 1954 by Gail Kennedy's Review Committee on the New Program and continued without important changes. It was evaluated again in 1958–59 by Theodore Koester's Curriculum Review Committee, but the faculty as a whole adopted few of this committee's recommendations. It was evaluated for a third time in 1963–64 by Joseph Epstein's Committee on Educational Policy and through the recommendations of this committee was finally overturned (Babb et al. 1978, 5–6, 9). Lawrence Babb and his co-authors concluded in 1978 that

> By most criteria, the "New Curriculum" launched in 1947 was a success. Its survival for two decades, however, probably owes a good deal to vested faculty interests in large required courses, the strong personalities of those who were permanent chairmen of the core courses, and the unattractiveness of the particular plan suggested in 1959. (31)

In its 1964 "Report on the Curriculum of Amherst College,"[2] Joseph Epstein's Committee on Educational Policy recommended replacing "all existing required courses," including English 1–2, by five new courses. The five would consist of four "Problems of Inquiry" or "PI" courses and an interdivisional and interdisciplinary colloquium. There was to be a PI course in each of the three curricular divisions of the humanities, the social sciences, and mathematics and the natural sciences. The fourth PI was to address the "Composition of Knowledge" (3). In the spring of 1965, the Amherst faculty accepted most of the recommendations of the Epstein Committee but did not approve the implementation of the fourth PI course. The other PIs were first offered in the fall of 1966.

Armour Craig was a member of the Epstein Committee. John Cameron, who first informed me of this, told me that "the irony of the situation was that Armour, who was the loyal first son of Baird, was one of the agents of getting rid of English 1–2. I don't have all the details, but I do know that Ted never forgave him for it." After I had heard this from Cameron, I called Craig to discuss his role on the Epstein Committee, and he told me he had been the principal author of its 1964 report. He said he had understood when he wrote it that its effect, if its recommendations were accepted, would be to jettison English 1–2. However, he had hoped that a version of English 1–2, which he had always seen as more a college course than an English department course, would continue to be offered in the guise of the proposed "Problems of Inquiry IV: Composition of Knowledge." Craig said he was very disappointed when the faculty chose not to approve "PI IV." He said he had known it was hopeless to keep the 1947 New Curriculum going. He had also known that the English department would not keep English 1–2 going. The new generation of English faculty members, according to Craig, did not want to have to read as many student papers as the structure of English 1–2 required them to read. Some of them, including William Pritchard, who was deeply involved in designing the PI in the humanities, wanted to teach more literature in the freshman course than was customary in English 1–2. Craig told me he had regretted the demise of the 1947 curriculum. He said, "I took it pretty hard, but not so hard as Professor Baird."

Baird expressed his own dismay in a June 6, 1966 letter to Amherst President Calvin H. Plimpton. Baird told Plimpton that

I can say, at sixty-five, that this freshman English course has been the center of my entire intellectual life, and more than that, for to it I have brought whatever I have learned as a human being. I have been proud to serve Amherst and I have sought excellence.

That the English department now resumes the shape of all English departments is the obvious fact. How this came about I do not understand. A possible explanation is through the force of inertia. My example was not enough finally. . . . I do know that I do not find very widely shared any awareness of the importance of Freshman English as a writing course. In that sense I am alone.[3]

Baird's sense of isolation has the ring of tragedy. Arnold Arons, whose situation following the discontinuation of Science 1–2 was analogous to Baird's, responded in 1968 by leaving Amherst College. Pritchard, who served from 1966 until 1968 as chairman of the new PI course in the humanities, said of the discontinuation of English 1–2 that "younger people on the staff were beginning to get somewhat restless about the obligation to teach one or two sections of the course each year." He added, "With hindsight one feels that it had run its course and that, as Baird's own retirement approached (in 1969), it was time to go off on something else, somehow" (letter to R. Varnum, August 15, 1991).

Baird says of his junior colleagues, "They all know how to teach books. They all know how to deal with them critically in ways that I don't." However, he says of staff dynamics in Amherst's current English department that "I don't think they even agree on the books they read, let alone on an exam. So it is back really to where I came in, where there was no agreement, no intellectual common ground, and no exchange of ideas." He told me, "The whole academic world has changed. Nobody can afford to put as much time and energy into a common course where his own distinction does not come to the attention of the president, or the dean, or whoever it is."

The implementation of the 1966 curriculum did not result, however, in the outright cancellation of English 1–2. The English department decided to rename the course English 11–12 and to continue it as a two-semester freshman elective. The *Amherst College Bulletin: 1966–67* describes English 11 as a course in "Writing" and English 12 as a course in "Reading." Pritchard describes English 11 as "a course in writing about reading, rather than a course in composition." Speaking in 1991, he noted that "although it is an elective, we still teach about 60 percent of all Amherst freshmen in that course." Craig, who chaired English 11 in the fall of 1966, told me that in that course students still wrote "an awful lot of papers, but we had texts." He said that the central question of the course was "What do you do when you read?" Benjamin DeMott chaired English 11–12 for the three semesters from the spring of 1967 through the spring of 1968. The only time Theodore Baird chaired English 11 was in the fall of 1968, his penultimate semester at Amherst College.

Baird wrote the assignments for the fall of 1968.[4] English 11 that fall seems to have been conducted in much the way that English 1 formerly had been. There were thirty-three assignments that semester on the nominal subject of "language and belief," and these assignments were used in common by the entire English 11 staff. In the very first assignment of the sequence, Baird informed students that

> The subject of our discourse is Language. We shall try to understand a little how we use words, how we define words and make sense. The assignments that follow are a means of starting a conversation and keeping it going. If you consider each paper that you write as something less than a pronouncement, you will be happier in this course. The assignments do not have final answers, and at best they make possible a movement or train of thought.[4]

By the twenty-sixth assignment of the same series, it was clear that Baird was interested not only in the way words are used to make sense of the world, but in the way words are used to create a voice on a page. In that assignment, Baird noted:

> Language also enables us to look around and see something new. It enables us, somehow, to seem to get outside ourselves and to assume positions we may or may not really believe in. Thus we are able to speak almost in someone else's voice, to be insincere, to be ironical, to be sarcastic, to be, even, objective (whatever that means).[4]

In order to illustrate differences in voices and ways of using language, Baird quoted passages from nineteenth century Amherst College documents. His decision to do so, and thereby to focus on the changing ethos of the college, must have been motivated in part by his awareness that his own forty-one-year career at Amherst was coming to a close. In one assignment for his fall 1968 series, he listed a selection of words taken from Amherst President Edward Hitchcock's 1863 autobiography. Baird's list included such terms as "reason," "the supernatural," "conviction," "mind and matter," "intellect and heart," "imagination and fancy," "strength of character," "redemption," "salvation," "the Triune God," "Providence," "godliness," "piety," "prayer," "temperance," "fidelity," "orthodoxy," and "duty." Baird asked students to look at the words on the list and to "express the world or universe behind them." In another assignment in the same series, Baird quoted Amherst President Julius Seelye, who had said in his 1889 *Report* to the Board of Trustees that "all the influences of the college should conspire first of all to make the student pure and upright." In Baird's assignment, which was the fifth in his 1968 series, he cautioned students that President Seelye "was a living being, like you. Do not patronize him." Baird then asked students:

> What do you suppose President Seelye meant? What has happened to "pure" and "upright" and similar words? Is this change or whatever it is a matter only of fashion?[4]

When I first read this question, nearly a quarter century after Baird had written it, I wondered how he would have accounted in 1968 for changing fashions in education. How would he have explained the movement in a mere thirty years' time from talk of running orders through chaos and freedom of mind to talk of relevance and diversity as educational ideals? I suspect that by 1968, Baird must have felt that the tide of fashion had turned against him.

On October 1, 1968, Baird issued a staff memorandum commenting on his fifth assignment of the fall 1968 series. He said:

> My students when asked to move from Seelye's words to his belief simply said, he believed in purity. Then they began to talk as historians. This is boring.

I proposed in thinking about these assignments a metaphor, moving behind a man's statement to something, called belief. The process is surely one we go through all the time when we listen to others, though how we do it is not at all easy to express. It was the difficulty that made me think here was something worth trying to do.[5]

Baird then referred to a political editorial which had recently appeared in the *Amherst Student* newspaper, and he asked:

What does it mean to say we can move behind words to belief? It means we can see and express possible relationships in whatever statement is given us. The vocabulary of the editorial comes out for me in some sort of tension between good and bad where the opposites are by no means clear. The committee can be described as good and as bad, as if one could talk this way about the Triune God! The editorial's key word, as I read it, is politics. Here, too, there is good (mine) and bad (yours). Some words are clearly good, some clearly bad. How do I know this? I know because I know. It is this area that we have been moving toward, where we can say, I know because I know. Once we have reached here, rock bottom, we can then confront the problem of how one person with his beliefs faces the incredible behavior of the rest of humanity.[5]

The point Baird describes as "rock bottom" is the point, I take it, at which the student finds himself confronting his own will. It is at this point, as Baird explained to me in his letter about the inexpressible, that "we fade off in each one's belief. And will. I used to try to say, finally, *I exert my WILL*" (letter to R. Varnum, December 6, 1990; see Appendix C). It is also at this point, as he explained in his 1952 article on "The Freshman English Course," that the student finds himself saying "Why, I know what I am talking about" (196). At rock bottom, the student defines the relationship between his physical or verbal situation on the one hand and his beliefs and will on the other. Only beyond that point, does his action assume a purpose.

In the hope of moving students toward the rock bottom point, Baird asked them in the eleventh assignment of his fall 1968 series to contrast the ways they used language with the ways Amherst President Seelye had done so. Baird explained:

When President Seelye uses the adjectives "upright" and "pure" he believes that certain ways of living are better than others, and he calls those ways by these adjectives.

The same proposition about meaning is true of the language we use today. When we speak of "commitment" and "relevance" and "confrontation" we, too, are speaking from some private, inexpressible area of our being where, we say, we believe.[4]

Baird asked students, "Are we to suppose that President Seelye and his contemporaries differ from us only in vocabulary, in using words like 'upright' instead of 'relevant,' and we all of us are the same in striving for some good, however named?" The phrasing of this eleventh assignment seems to invite students to assume a position of tolerance, but in subsequent assignments, Baird would problematize the tolerant stance.

First, however, in his twelfth assignment, Baird instructed students to consider their own beliefs:

Reflect upon yourself as a believing being. What do you believe? Write out your credo. This is rock bottom.[4]

In his twenty-first assignment, Baird asked students to address the matter of conflict between different systems of belief:

Why do other people have to die as martyrs to gross absurdities? How do you live in any kind of peace with your fellows while they insist on believing what they do?

This paper is an invitation to write with abandoned self-admiration of your own capacities of tolerance. Or is it indifference?[4]

One anonymous student whose response to this assignment was mimeographed for classroom discussion and then preserved in the Amherst College Archives, wrote that

This question you have asked is a very underhanded one, for you force me to evaluate my mode of living. This evaluation is kind of depressing for I find that I am indifferent. Perhaps a better way of saying this is that I am divorced from reality.[6]

Another student, responding to assignment #12, wrote:

Credo. Existo. Man is alone within himself in the universe. Other men are there—I don't understand their existence, however, I believe in a personal God (not omni-present, -potent, or -scient) that exists. There is something beyond my physical body that exists; it is called the world. I believe that men cannot understand one another's beliefs, desires, therefore, I believe that men cannot tell other men how to believe. I believe that war begins when a man tries to dictate to another how to believe.[6]

Still another student, addressing assignment #21, explained that on the evening before he sat down to respond to the assignment, he had attended a campus event featuring Mark Rudd of the Students for a Democratic Society. This student, imitating what Baird had done in listing terms from Amherst President Hitchcock's autobiography, listed a selection of terms from Rudd's address. The terms on the student's list included "escalation," "moral protest movement," "educational confrontation," "year of resistance," "ruling class," "basic forms of capitalism," "free discourse," "ivory tower," "racism," "manipulation," "basically archaic," and "structural reform." The student concluded, along with Bob Dylan, that "the times, they are a changin'." He also concluded that "the status quo, here represented by the college's acting in loco parentis, is no longer applicable."[6]

On Baird's teaching staff for the first time in the fall of 1968 was Dale Peterson, a young graduate-student intern from Yale. Peterson, who is the youngest member of the Amherst English faculty I spoke with, told me he came to Amherst College in 1968 "as an anomaly. There had been people here who didn't have their degrees yet, but there had not been people who came as faculty interns." Peterson had a master's degree in Russian studies from Yale and was working toward a Ph.D. in American studies but had not yet completed his dissertation. He told me he was "interested in pursuing a comparison between Russian and American literature. I was really trying to define for myself a comparative literary field. This opportunity though was very attractive to me because I had not had much experience in the classroom, and I was very anxious and nervous about it." Amherst offered him the opportunity to teach Russian literature in translation and two sections of the freshman writing course. He said, "It was my

Dale Peterson in 1968.

clear understanding at that time that if I agreed to come to Amherst for two years, that I would be 'mentored,' and I would have some class-room experience working with senior people."

When I asked Peterson what it had been like, as a young faculty intern, to teach on Theodore Baird's staff, he said, "It was a terrifying experience." He said, "The course from the very first day, made a great deal out of the fact that there was only the subject of writing as an activity. In a radical sense, it was contentless. And therefore the sorts of writing that the students would be doing would not be pitched at get-ting right, or getting straight, or getting sophisticated responses to objects in the world, or texts, but instead they were to continually generate from their own experience ways of saying things, and then look at the ways that they said things." When I asked him what he had anticipated, he said, "I would not have been shocked to go into an introductory course in composition that was asking the student to learn what it might mean to pay very close attention to the ways in which a poem or short story had been constructed. Well, I found myself receiving, as the students did, except I got a little black binder (they had to go out and buy a little black binder), but I received, as an incoming instructor, free, gratis, a little black binder with the whole set of the semester's writing assignments, prepackaged, already there. Of course this particular semester, it had come, full-sprung, from Theodore Baird." As soon as Peterson received his assignment package, he said, "I looked at it, and indeed there were no texts as such. The students were always asked to say something about something that either came from their own experience or to say something about some proposition, some way of carrying on, from usually a Victorian gentleman. They were faced with oddly stodgy language. But for me, of course, this was totally unexpected. I don't think my shock was any different from the students'." Peterson says it was "a situation that made me immediately empathetic to my students. That is that, just as they were mystified, I was equally mystified; just as they were somewhat anxious starting out their college careers, I was an advanced graduate student reduced to rubble. And I was expected to submit graded evaluations of the compositions of these students."

Peterson said the 1968 assignments were "typically written in a way which is Robert Frost-like, cunning, witty, but also hard-edged; it's a very masculine witticism. The course assumed that language was rhetoric, all language was rhetoric. Some was dull, some was unimaginative, and some, [though] not necessarily true, not necessarily authentic or sincere, simply was more engaging. I do think Baird comes out of American pragmatism at some philosophical level, which is to say that the course was really a course in composition and writing, but what really mattered was what works. Try this, try that, try something else. What works? And what did 'work' mean? Work meant 'successful.' What did 'successful' mean? It gets across. It doesn't mean it's sincere. It doesn't mean you can really tell whether behind the words there is truth or lying. But it is strategic language. And this too, I think could be argued, is masculine." Peterson explained that the turns of Baird's "exercises, the rhetorical turns, had the characteristic implication that you and I know that nobody is sentimental or dumb enough to really believe this. In other words, you feel as if you have got to be hardnosed, tough-minded, and unsentimental to understand that things are strategies." Peterson added, "I think it was characteristic of English 1 to get students early on to write a credo of some sort, to write their beliefs down, and if you said you believed something about something, what do you sound like? The exercise was trying to get the writers to face the fact that every time you write, you are positioning yourself."

I asked Peterson about the use of the word "relevance" in the assignment series that fall. I had been a freshman myself in the fall of 1968, and I remembered "relevance" had been a buzzword on campuses all across the country. Peterson said, "That word was beaten upon very heavily, by none more forcefully than Theodore Baird himself. I eventually got to see some part of the demonstrations, the moratorium, which was a memorable time in the college's life, staged in the chapel, and Baird did come in, sat in the very back. I can't remember his exact words, but they were something to the effect that 'What do you ever expect to be relevant? Do you think your lives are relevant? Relevant to what?'"

Later, I asked Baird if he had ever stood up in chapel and interrupted a speech on the "relevance" of education. Had he ever asked, "Relevant to what?" Baird replied, "I'll tell you what I said. Some guy got up and said the faculty didn't treat the students as 'humans.' That was another good word that year, 'human.' I said, 'I am not human; I am a professor.' When I was hired, they asked if I could teach literature, not if I was human. Nowadays, they try to run a college on love. Students want to be loved. In 1968, I asked my students, 'If you are not upright and pure, in Seelye's terms, what are you?' A good answer might have been, 'I am human.'"

William Pritchard was on leave in 1968–69, but he remembers that "by that time, many people in the English department were in fact making strong efforts to be relevant." Although he was in England, Pritchard was aware that in Amherst "there was a strike in the spring of 1969, or 'moratorium' I guess they called it, big campus meeting. That was sort of spearheaded by a course that a couple of my colleagues were giving in literary criticism, but they had gotten off on certain ultimate questions—'What are we doing reading Keats?' and so on. 'What's the relation between reading Keats and the war?'" Pritchard said that until Baird retired, as he did effectually in the fall of 1969, "there had been at least the appearance of unity among those of us who taught the course. But without his iron hand, things fell into chaos and confusion. People were promoting different pedagogies and competing for power. Remember too that 1969 was troubled times. We were in the middle of a major curricular debate on this campus."

Dale Peterson conjectured that the troubled times were not the only reason why the course Baird had directed for thirty years did not outlive his tenure at Amherst College. Peterson said, "It's true it was the sixties, but the psychological dynamic surely would have crushed it." He adds, "I caught on to this by having come in at the very end of it, and then I watched the rapid shift that took place after. What seems to me plausible is that a lot of faculty five to ten years older than I had basically learned to play this game. They were the ones who had to deal with the situation that there was no way of succeeding to the permanent college community unless you could prove that you were an effective teacher of composition. So the logic tells me that people who were just crucially enough older than I had, thank you, learned how to play this game, and there must have been, underneath it all, a deal of resentment. They had seen, also, people in their own cohort who did not get tenure, didn't learn somehow how to play this game. Some of those, surely, were among their best friends. So I think there had to be a lot of psychological heavy weather here."

I asked Peterson to describe the atmosphere of the staff meetings in the fall of 1968. He said, "As a matter of fact, one of the things that makes me very uncomfortable to this day, and perhaps others similarly, is that I was virtually speechless. I had the culture shock of coming into this thing, and trying to figure out what this thing was, and then sitting around at those meetings. I had no particular authorization of my own, but as a graduate student, I was used to expressing myself. That's what I mean by this sense here that until you were initiated, the best thing to do was not to make a fool of yourself, particularly because it was clear that one of the things that happened among those who were talking at the meetings, again, was this play of often dismissive wit. In staff meetings it was clear that one of the things you would regularly expect of this course was to clean the dirt out of the carburetor. In other words, what the course would do was to get the students to speak whatever it was that they had been rewarded for speaking in high school, or to speak their hearts out, and then they would be made to make a turning. So there was a kind of entrapment. You would go into the staff meetings and one of the things that seemed to be clear was that if you taught this course, you could expect to be a part of getting students to get past certain things that they had learned. And not only should they get past it, but if they had any wit or intelligence at all, they were the ones who would get past it quickest."

Peterson employed the metaphor for the course that I had heard from several of the men I had spoken with earlier. He said, "People older than I who have not had good experiences with the course, either male faculty or I have met alumni, those who won't testify in praise of the course, often describe the course by analogy to boot camp or marine training. And somehow I really do think that males lend themselves to boot camp and marine training. Part of it has to do with the notion of wising up, catching on, the given competitiveness of all that. As I tried to describe, my own experience as an instructor— I was called the instructor; they were called my pupils—my own experience along with them was trying to scramble to catch up with what it was that I was supposed to be catching on to. Clearly, there was something I should be catching on to." He said the course "was very directed, but as I say, it never explained what the direction was. So that sets up a competitive atmosphere, where it's your own responsibility to be bright enough to outguess the system."

Peterson said that "one of the great successes of Theodore Baird's imagination is that it probably took young faculty five to ten years to be able to explain to themselves what the agenda was. You had the sense that this man knew what he was doing, but would never let on quite what he was doing." Peterson added, "My first year at the college, when I taught the composition course, I had very good relations with my students because it was probably transparently clear that we were actively about some rather strange process together, and that has its positive sides. But when I look back upon it, I must say that I have primarily feelings of distrust about the entire project. In retrospect, I see it as an exercise in liberal authoritarianism. That is to say that both I as a young instructor and the students received a clear signal on the opening day of the class that the instructor was in the room only to ask questions, but the students should not look to him for any answers whatsoever, the signal here being, in a way, deceptive. They were being in one respect told that they were the authors of their own compositions and that they could look to their own experience, that was where all communications and expression came from anyway. And so they were made to feel that they didn't have to pay attention to the otherness of things coming from strange cultures and so forth. The main business was to pay attention to what it was you dragged up out of yourself. That sounds very flexible, very inviting, but in fact I would argue that since I had a black binder in my hand, it was a highly elaborate sequence of some thirty assignments constantly asking questions, and not random questions—so the overt message seemed to be very, very self-authorizing for students, seemed to encourage the notion that they were all Emersonian selves (that was the overt message), but the structure of the course was highly authoritarian, and ultimately by coming at the same fundamental questions from multiple perspectives, relentlessly, it drove the bright students toward mind-playing."

Peterson said that because he arrived during the last semester of the course, "I didn't have to worry my young mind about articulating what really was the agenda. I'm smart enough to know that this course was always headed someplace. And I'm grateful in that respect that I came late enough along so that I didn't have to live with that sort of pressure. It was an exercise in cunning. The bright students were constantly being teased to come up with what it was all about. In the process, they probably wrote more experimentally. The bad part was, I didn't like the pressure, the insidious pressure that nothing was ever open. Everything was always covert, under the mask of only working from people's experience and the words they bring to it. So in that respect, and way in the advance of deconstruction, this particular course at Amherst College had invented Mystification 1."

Peterson said, "This course never, ever gave students the advantage of having some help with what it is that the project is. This course insisted upon not—again it was driven by liberal authoritarianism; I suppose it could pride itself on being Socratic—on never giving answers. The illusion here was that everybody was responsible for his own learning. We don't educate ourselves. It doesn't mean that we're spoon-fed. In my own teaching, I have no use for spoon-feeding. You don't give people the answers. But I really resented teaching a course in which I had to keep a secret. Well, I certainly had no choice because it was a secret from me as well! But it was clear that people more initiated than I, who knew the secret, were also very, very careful never to reveal that there was a secret to be kept, that there was, in fact, an educational agenda here."

According to Peterson, "One of the characteristic results of taking freshmen at Amherst College and putting them through the original composition course was that more than half of the students as a result of this would feel that they hadn't gotten it. They just hadn't gotten something. Whatever confidence they had coming in had been challenged, of course, but it was demolished, and demolished in a particularly insidious way because this was a course which begins basically saying: you are what we are interested in, you are the content of this course, your instructor is just there to ask questions, not to give answers, your instructor is just there to look at whatever it is you can say for yourself. It starts off with this inviting, self-authorizing gesture, but usually by the end, more than half the people who had been trying to write papers that were satisfactory somehow for a whole semester would feel devalued. And the smaller percentage who had begun to be rebellious, or experimental, or whatever, had begun to write interestingly. The simplest way to put it is: what a way around the barn to get there!"

Despite what Peterson says about student reactions to the freshman writing course Baird had organized, there were students at Amherst College in 1968–69 who were sorry to see Baird retire. I found evidence of this in student course reviews published in *Scrutiny: A Review of Courses Given First Semester 1968–69.* Of English 31, Baird's Shakespeare course, one student wrote:

> The tragedy of English 31 is that Professor Baird, one of the "grand old men" of Amherst is retiring. An extremely perceptive man, he is capable of slapstick humor and subtle sarcasm, of sincere interest in students untinged by an often genuine distaste for their comments. He is unafraid to reveal his own inabilities as a reader, and anxious for his students to reveal and discuss theirs. His love is language, and the process by which readers and authors can use language. ("Review of English 31" 1969, 18)

This same student noted of Baird's Shakespeare course that "the most general complaint was about the large number of *C*'s given in the course" (18). Another student reviewer described the staff-taught freshman writing course, English 11, as

> an unusual course. Three papers each week for eleven weeks; conventional, bizarre, challenging, tedious assignments; freedom, discipline, obscurity, direction. Most students, at the end of the course, considered it to have been a unique, valuable, and fascinating educational experience. . . . The course was directed by the progression of the assignments, yet was often obscure in that questions were rarely clear. It was disciplined—a paper for each class—yet there was considerable freedom in choosing approaches to the various problems. ("Review of English 11" 1969, 17)

Theodore Baird on the day of his retirement in 1970.

Baird told me, "I was not a popular person, and when I left, I always said I could hear the community sigh in relief. And certainly the English department was delighted to see the end of me." With respect to the effect of his retirement on the course, Baird said, "I kept this thing going. There was lots of opposition. There was sabotage. We had one man who used to go in with his assignments, then have them write something on his own. I knew this. What could I do? We had another guy who couldn't get to class because it meant getting out of bed in the morning." Baird said, "I maintained this [course] because finally, if you want to know the truth, I think I scared them. I scared them. They weren't quite brave enough to say, 'We are through with this.' If they had said that, what could I have done? I had no authority, just my presence." Baird said of those teaching at Amherst now, "Their minds tell them that the only way they're going to get ahead is to cultivate their own garden and produce something that will impress the president, so they'll go up." He said, "Nobody wants to do the kind of heavy work that we did at reading papers. The minute I got through, they dropped it. Why did they drop it? Not because intellectually they had moved on. It was because they didn't want to read three papers a week. That was admitted."

Dale Peterson, however, observed that American intellectual culture has changed considerably since the era of English 1–2. He said, "Contextualization is highly important nowadays in our whole intellectual atmosphere. And this is a course which even goes one step backward from New Criticism. Imagine trying to recreate New Criticism now! How far could it possibly go? And this was even one step backward from that because at least New Criticism acknowledges the organic otherness of something you're looking at. You couldn't get a quorum of trained Ph.D.s in English, at least, who would be sympathetic to a course that takes as its fundamental proposition that language is pure, that language is a kind of infinitely playable, value-neutral thing, as if it exists in an unconstrained way, only constrained by imagination. The odd thing about this, of course, is that directed as it was, what I think it saw itself as trying to bring into being is a notion among bright people that their imaginations could eventually, ultimately be almost endless. I think we're too skeptical now; we understand that imagination itself is a cultural construct. What would it mean to have a free imagination?"

John Cameron agrees that academia has changed. He said that at Amherst "we no longer see ourselves as providing students with a cultural identity so that they come out with 'Amherst College' stamped on their foreheads." He noted that the college has experienced a change "in the demography of the student body from the basically white, middle-class men that were admitted in the 1950s, when this course thrived, to the infinitely more diverse, though obviously still not totally diverse, population that are admitted now. And in any case, there is a strong ideological resistance now to having the cultural values taken away from them by anything like the likes of Amherst College. And so any course that was implicitly—and this isn't necessarily the case of English 1, but in practice it is—that was implicitly out to undermine the values, the cultural identities of students, would nowadays not go down, I don't think."

The one member of the Amherst faculty I interviewed whom I have not yet introduced and need to introduce now is Jan Dizard. He spoke to me at length about changes that have occurred at Amherst College since the time when English 1–2 was canceled. Dizard never taught English 1–2; in fact, he never taught English. He is a sociologist. He came to Amherst to teach sociology in the fall of 1969, a year after Peterson came to the college, and a semester after Baird had

Jan Dizard about 1990.

effectually retired. Although Dizard missed Baird, he witnessed much of the social ferment on the Amherst campus in the late 1960s and early 1970s and the transition to coeducation in 1976. A group of black Amherst students occupied a college building in the spring of 1969, shortly before Dizard came to Amherst, and as a result, Dizard was called upon that fall to help organize and teach the first course in black studies ever offered at the college.

The Amherst College which Dizard first encountered in 1969 was a larger and more affluent institution than it had been a decade before. And because two interstate highways were constructed in the late 1960s to serve western Massachusetts, when Dizard came to Amherst, neither the town nor the college was isolated. During the 1960s, however, Amherst College was outstripped in several important respects by the University of Massachusetts at Amherst. During the 1960–1971 administration of Amherst College President Calvin Plimpton, eight major new buildings were added to the physical plant and nearly $40 million to its capital assets (Greene 1978, 318). But during the 1960–1970 administration of University of Massachusetts President John Lederle, seventy new buildings were erected on the UMass campus, faculty salaries were doubled, and student enrollments grew from 6,500 in 1960 to 21,000 in 1970 (317). Amherst College was far more selective of its undergraduates than UMass, but the university was well on its way to becoming a major research institution. Meanwhile, a third institution of higher education in the town of Amherst, Hampshire College, was under construction and would admit its first class in 1971 (319).

Before coming to Amherst, Dizard had taught sociology at the University of California at Berkeley. He had a doctorate from the University of Chicago and an undergraduate degree from the University of Minnesota. With respect to his degrees, he was different from most of those who had been hired at Amherst in the decades before he was hired. Amherst College historian Theodore Greene reports that by 1972–73, the proportion of Amherst faculty members who were Amherst alumni had shrunk to 9 percent and the proportion of the faculty who had graduate degrees from Harvard had shrunk to 23 percent (1978, 330), but Dizard told me that "when I first arrived here, you could really mark from those who came in the late 1960s and those who had come earlier that of those who had come earlier, you would look in vain and there were one or two people at Amherst College who didn't have ivy in some place or other. Everyone else had either gone to Amherst or to some Ivy League school." He said, "It's not until the mid-1960s that you begin to see at the assistant professor level: Chicago, Michigan, Berkeley, and state universities. There still might be a Harvard or a Princeton or a Yale, but now you find that people come from all over. And of course you find a more diverse faculty as regards race, and of course you find a more diverse faculty as regards gender. All of that, it seems to me, has resulted in a declining appetite for the locker room mentality or for the drill instructor mentality."

Change in the character of the Amherst faculty was one of three broad areas of change Dizard discussed with me. He also discussed changes in the Amherst student body and changes in the ethos of the college. Dizard used "boot camp" as his metaphor for the college in the 1940s and 1950s. He said, "The Amherst faculty in the 1940s and 1950s saw itself as presiding over a boot camp and took some delight and satisfaction in terrorizing students."

Dizard said that before World War II, Amherst College had func-
tioned more like "a gentleman's club." He said that before the war "the
only kids who went to college, residential college anyway, were cultur-
ally certified candidates for the upper class. It didn't really matter; they
didn't have to go to college; they would have found some other institution to put the Good Housekeeping seal of approval on their foreheads." After the war, he implied, having the right connections was no
longer enough, and certification by Amherst College or an equivalent
institution of higher education became a more necessary precondition
of employment in prestigious occupations.

In a 1991 article on social stratification through education, Dizard
argued that "in a liberal society like ours which proclaims equality as a
goal but nonetheless is predicated upon institutions that produce a
remarkably constant hierarchy," one of the functions of an institution
like Amherst College is to enable elites "to base their standing on
claims of having earned it" (155–156). Dizard explained that

> Much of the stressful work associated with colleges like Amherst
> has less to do with learning (and may in fact get in the way of
> learning) than it has to do with maintaining the cultural expec-
> tations of sacrifice and of being tested. Only if one has been sub-
> jected to repeated stress and apparent uncertainty of outcome
> can one confidently assume a leadership role. (156)

Dizard told me that, after World War II, Amherst College began to
operate "as a kind of pressure cooker or meritocratic sieve, if you will,
testing the metal of the future leaders." He said that, in the 1940s and
1950s, the Amherst faculty "threw the fear of God into kids in the way
that fraternity hazing or boot camp throws the fear of God into them.
There was a meanness and a lot of badgering and a lot of public
humiliation in the classroom. Stupid writing was read aloud in class."
He added that "in those days, 300 plus words might be scratched out
or not read, or a big line is marked through, and it's due by 12:00
o'clock and if it comes in at 12:01, it's not acceptable. There are a few
people like that around here now, but not many. And those kinds of
terroristic practices used to be routine; they are what it was about."
The point, Dizard explained, was not to flunk students out of the college but to allow them to prove they could take it. He said, "The boot
camp analogy, it seems to me, is apt here. Not many people flunk out

of boot camp either. The point of boot camp is not to screen; it is to mold. And it doesn't matter if at the end of boot camp you, as a member of a platoon or whatever the unit is, are the slowest on the obstacle course or have the most difficulty climbing the rope or whatever, just as it doesn't really matter whether at the end of all this you wound up barely passing Arons's course by the skin of your teeth. They may have gotten D minuses or something like that, but they probably didn't flunk."

One of the positive effects of the boot camp atmosphere, Dizard said, was the creation of a group loyalty among students. He said, "That kind of badgering and humiliation and ritual denunciation and all that, along with the humiliating rituals of having to go to chapel every bloody day and the parietals, create a whole set of adult rules that bright and active and energetic kids can conspire amongst themselves to ridicule and circumvent and subvert, and by virtue of doing that, create all sorts of solidaristic bonds amongst themselves in the form of secrets and malicious, hilarious, caricatures of the buffoons that are terrorizing them. It's simultaneously austere and humiliating, and yet nurturing and supportive. I mean it sounds paradoxical, and perhaps it is, but there it is." He added, "There's no question but that the way the institution functions now, it does not produce the same intensities of solidarity amongst the students." He said that "one of the interesting things to follow in the decades to come (not years because it takes longer) is whether the kinder, gentler, if you will, ethos that now prevails here—although I don't think it's either kind or gentle, but as compared to boot camp, it is—whether it induces the same level and degree of alumni loyalty."

Dizard compared the collegiate experience that Amherst students had in the 1940s and 1950s to what their counterparts have today. He said, "Nowadays, the experience has got much more to do with personal anxiety about one's own adequacy, and that's in a context in which there is much more ambiguity. There is very little of the demeaning (you couldn't get away with the demeaning stuff; you'd be up on harassment charges)." He said, "The anxieties and the drivenness that one senses in the institution [now] come from the general perception, not terribly inaccurate, at least phenomenologically not inaccurate, that it's a profoundly competitive world out there, and how well you ultimately do in it is by no means clear at any moment in time. You can be getting good grades and doing well, and that still is no guarantee in the way that it once was. The performance anxieties here are not so much anxieties driven by the desire to avoid being publicly excoriated by an imperious professor as they are anxieties about whether you'll have a life to lead. They derive from the demands the culture is making upon students, not the professors." He added that "students no longer assume that getting in here and doing well means that you've got it made for life."

Dizard said that the "notion about higher ed being the historical American dream factory, that's really not very historical at all. That's quite recent. That's our lifetimes—yours and mine. So it wasn't until the 1960s, and even really the 1970s, when admissions departments get professionalized, and SAT scores become commonplace, and then with affirmative action coming in in the late 1960s and early 1970s, and a vastly expanded middle class that is committed ideologically and in principle to sending their kids to the best schools they can possibly get into, then you've got all of a sudden an enormous competition to get into places like Amherst College, and Amherst becomes selective in a way that it never had to be and never was before." He said that even the weakest members of Amherst's current student body "are better prepared, smarter, more hardworking, more focused, and function better than [their counterparts] at state schools and community colleges."

Dizard said that, at Amherst currently, "somewhere around a third of the student body are students of color."[7] He said that, with respect to social class, the composition of the student body "probably hasn't changed much at all. If anything, the student body has probably tilted more in the direction of affluence, in part reflecting what's happened in the national economy and the pressure on the middle class and the way that coincides with increases throughout the 1980s in college tuition."[8] He said the admission of women in 1976 did not have much impact on the class composition of the student body. He said, "All it meant in some sense was that we now admit the daughters as well as the sons of the upper middle class." He added that "levels of expectation that faculty have of how students should perform in class changed scarcely at all with the admission of women."

Dizard said, however, that current members of the faculty differ from Baird and his contemporaries in their conceptions of what a professor's role should be. He said that "the same kinds of competitive pressures that are producing steadily rising admissions standards are also affecting tenure decisions. You cannot get tenure at Amherst College after 1970 unless you have published something of note. It doesn't have to be the world's greatest book or the world's longest book or anything like that; it doesn't even have to necessarily be a book, although now it does, but unless you show active research and publications, you cannot get tenure after 1970 at Amherst College. Look backward in time, before 1970, and there are literally dozens of distinguished members of this faculty, whose names need not be mentioned, who didn't publish a line, or scarcely did." Dizard said that Amherst College has "become more and more like a university in terms of how faculty think of themselves and their commitments and their priorities. There are lots of people, myself included, who think twice before routinely assigning pages and pages of student writing during a semester when we've got our own God-damned writing to do. There's only so many hours in a day and so many days in a week. There may in fact be shadings and shadings in that. I mean, one of the things that goes along with being a boot camp is that teachers have to demand a lot, which means that they have very little time and energy left over for their own work. There's a declining appetite for that sort of stuff (just for the ritual of it at any rate) on the part of the faculty because they've got their own work to do, and if they don't do their own work, they're not going to get tenure or promoted. So I think there's a whole shift of ethos." Dizard said that the Amherst faculty has also become "more compartmentalized—more Balkanized, if I can use that term. And that's partly a function, I think, of the shift in professional emphasis and ethos away from the professional generalist or liberal arts teacher to the ethos of the professional scholar."

Dizard said that "to try to characterize the ethos of the faculty now, you would have one hell of a time. You wouldn't find unanimity, at least on the surface, amongst the faculty as to how they ought to go about teaching, or whether there ought to be a common curriculum. You can get clusters of agreement but no broadly shared consensus." He said the faculty have had several recent opportunities "to study the curriculum and see if there isn't something we can come up with. There have been a number of proposals—at least three since 1978, or at least two, some grander than others—but you can't get agreement, can't get it voted." He said, "There's no center—which I think is a good thing because I think the old center stank. There are some who would like to go back to that. They're not all old. There are some who would like more rigor, more of this, more of that. And there are people like myself who think that things are fine more or less the way they are. The function of at least a minimal gen ed requirement is as much for the faculty as for the students and is at least a modest kind of way of working against increasing specialization and atomization. There's nothing about which all of these various contending preferences can agree, and there's absolutely no shared sense of what ought to be done. I don't think that characterizes most departments; I think it does, to a degree anyway, characterize English."

Theodore Baird also spoke to me about the current lack of consensus at Amherst College. He said, "The college was all broken into. Now there is no sense of the college that I can detect, except in the sentiment of students. They think that it's a college, but it isn't really. It could be absorbed by the university [UMass] tomorrow, and called their liberal arts establishment, and nothing would change. There's no intellectual coherence. There's no sense of belonging to a common purpose. The poor old president is sitting up there wishing there were. He knows if he tried to bring into it a little order, he'd be immediately out. In a university you have such diversity, but in a college like this, you have the diversity and you have no one. The great word now is 'diversity.' We are unanimous in favor of diversity." Baird added, with a subtle reference to Emily Dickinson, that "I heard someone bragging the other day that he was this and he was that. He concluded by saying, 'I'm diverse.' I had to laugh. How can you use that language in the first person? 'I'm diverse; who are you?'"

The lack of consensus that both Baird and Dizard have observed may have had something to do with the cancellation of English 11–12 in 1992. English 11–12 had been offered for twenty-six years when it was finally canceled, and when I interviewed Dale Peterson in 1991, it was still viable. Peterson told me that in 1991 the influence of English 1–2 upon English 11–12 was still perceptible. He said, "I think what persists over time is the way in which, although we're now very much text oriented, what we try to get students to do is to observe what it is that texts seem to be inviting them to do, and also to watch what it is that they bring to the experience of reading a particular text." He said, "What remains constant, I think, is the notion that the writing we want to see from freshmen is writing which tries to express what the actual process of beholding and interpreting is like, knowing that compositions out there in the world have designs on us." He concluded, "So I think there is a continuum and that the first [English] course at the college still characteristically asks people to write overtly about what the fundamental process of reading really does involve. Now Baird's version wasn't interested in reading, but in what is the process of articulating experience. So I think there is that continuity. There's a strong predisposition to get away from the notion of a five-page paper and to have very succinct, one-, one-and-a-half-, two-page papers being written for almost the whole semester."

Peterson told me that in 1991 the staff of English 11–12 was not requiring assignments as frequently as the earlier English 1–2 staff had done but that sixteen or seventeen assignments per semester had become typical. He said the staff attempted "to assign things frequently enough so that students get the message that they are allowed to fall on their face occasionally, they are allowed to experiment." He said the staff still gathered for regular staff meetings. He noted, "In that respect I do have a good memory of what the shifts in time were. The inherited model when I came here was one member of the English faculty would be expected to spend the summer designing the whole course, the whole series of questions that were relentlessly about the same fundamental question. And then the next change was that every person conducting a section of the course was expected to volunteer to come up with an interesting exercise about that particular week's reading, and then the whole staff criticized that. We all had to agree before we left the room what the perfect wording was for that staff assignment, so that everybody had the same exercise to hand out. One person on the staff had originally brought it forward, but that person had been pretty badly criticized, or things were really shifted around, before we reached a committee consensus." Peterson said that in the third phase of the course, which was the phase that was current in 1991, the staff continued to employ a common reading list, but individual instructors devised the assignments for their particular sections. He said, "What we try to do is agree what we have that would be an interesting sequence of things to read, and we agree to get together once a week to talk about our experience, reading about, thinking about, and asking questions about this odd series of different texts. And that's worth doing. A lot of us feel that's really worth doing. We don't have to try to bludgeon people into giving the exercises we want, but we talk about what we're doing individually. That's where we are right now, which is quite a distance from all teaching an identical series of exercises." Peterson added that a fourth stage might soon come, and that John Cameron was pushing for it, where the staff would dispense with teaching even a common reading list.

For the three years prior to 1991, Cameron had refused on principle to teach English 11. He told me that he questioned "whether it is possible to operate collaboratively without the consensual assumptions that collaborative teaching seems to presuppose. I think that in part it has become, to my eye, self-evident that we don't share, at least to the same degree or in the same way, assumptions about pedagogy, or literary study, or even about the nature of the institution or the profession that we used to, or were compelled to share in the past."

A few months after my conversations with Cameron and Peterson, Theodore Baird sent me a clipping from the January 29, 1992, issue of the *Amherst Student* newspaper announcing the cancellation of English 11–12. William Heath, who at that time was chairman of the English department, was quoted as saying the department's new "plan calls for the introduction of several different courses, each with its own description, from which potential English majors could choose." According to Heath, the new courses, to be numbered English 1 through English 10, would continue to be writing courses. According to English Professor Robert C. Townsend, who was also quoted in the article, "It became evident that we couldn't operate as a unified department teaching a staff course" (Kim 1992, 1, 3). Baird's comment, in a note to me, was: "Here is the end of the story of the March of Mind at Amherst College. Freshman English is to return to what it was in 1927 when I appeared on the scene" (letter to R. Varnum, January 31, 1992).

But even if Baird is correct in thinking he has seen the end of the story of English 1–2 at Amherst College, which I doubt, elements of the course have been transported to other campuses. Ann Berthoff, as I said before, has referred to Amherst alumni and Amherst-trained faculty as an "Amherst Mafia," which is now dispersed across the country (1985, 72). I asked William Pritchard to give me the names of teachers and alumni he thought had been most influenced by Theodore Baird, and Pritchard listed himself, William E. Coles Jr., Roger Sale, Walker Gibson, Benjamin DeMott, William R. Taylor, Jonathan Bishop, John Butler, Richard Poirier, and Armour Craig (letter to R. Varnum, March 17, 1992). Pritchard did not include Reuben Brower, but that surely was an oversight. Brower took Amherst methods with him to

Harvard and passed them on to those who undertook his Hum 6 course there. Two other campuses where English 1–2 has had especial influence are Rutgers and the University of Pittsburgh.

In his 1985 article on "Theodore Baird," Walker Gibson noted that the English department at Rutgers "is well stocked with Amherst-trained professors," and he listed Richard Poirier, T. R. Edwards, and James Guetti, who are all Amherst graduates, and Julian Moynahan, who taught at Amherst in the 1950s (147). William E. Coles Jr., who taught at Amherst in the 1960s, now teaches English at the University of Pittsburgh. David Bartholomae, who also teaches English at the University of Pittsburgh, did his graduate work at Rutgers under Poirier and Moynahan. A third member of Pittsburgh's current English department, Joseph Harris, did his graduate work at New York University under Gordon Pradl, who had taken English 1–2 at Amherst with Coles. Bartholomae and still another colleague, Anthony Petrosky, have organized a course at Pittsburgh that employs such Amherst features as collaborative teaching, sequences of assignments, and class discussions of sample student papers.

Bartholomae and Petrosky describe this course in their 1986 *Facts, Artifacts, and Counterfacts.* Over the period of a semester, they report, their "students study a single problem, one easily located within the immediate experience and knowledge of beginning students," and they study it through a series of sequenced exercises, "using the basic methods of university inquiry: reading and writing, discussion and debate, research and inquiry, report and commentary" (30). The discussion at any class meeting, Bartholomae and Petrosky report, "generally centers around a piece of student writing," and the aim is not to discuss "the family," but "what X has said about families" (30). Sections of the Pittsburgh course are generally led by two instructors, and according to Bartholomae and Petrosky, these instructors do not "fill the silence with right answers or final explanations" (31). In one important respect, however, the Pittsburgh course is very different from its Amherst antecedent. The Pittsburgh course was designed to meet the needs of "basic writers," or as Bartholomae and Petrosky express it, "students whose performance when asked to use or produce written texts has placed them outside the conventional boundaries of the undergraduate curriculum" (preface).

In their preface to *Facts, Artifacts, and Counterfacts,* Bartholomae and Petrosky acknowledge that "whatever we have learned about writing assignments and using them to define a sequence of instruction began with the rich and compelling example of our colleague, William E. Coles Jr." In his 1985 essay, "Against the Grain," Bartholomae acknowledges Richard Poirier as "the first strong teacher of my academic life" (23) and William E. Coles Jr. as the colleague who "gave me a place to begin as a teacher and student of composition" (26). Bartholomae adds, however, that while he was writing his dissertation at Rutgers under Poirier, he experienced Poirier's example as a burden and had to struggle "to write myself free from his influence" (26). Bartholomae's reflections reminded me of what Baird had told me about being no one's disciple and about influence through "negative force." Bartholomae also gave me a way of understanding how Baird's influence may have worked on others.[9] I thought of Baird's example when Bartholomae spoke, in "Against the Grain," of teachers whose voices "cannot be ignored, whose speech we cannot help but imitate and whose presence becomes both an inspiration and a burden" (25). I thought of Bartholomae's essay when, in the course of my interviews with Walker Gibson and Roger Sale and of a phone conversation I had with William E. Coles Jr., all these men displayed what I took to be a desire to disabuse me of any notion I might have had that they were acolytes of Baird. Gibson went so far as to say that "the best thing that ever happened to me as a young teacher was to land a job at Amherst College in 1946, and the next best thing was to leave it when I did." Coles told me that Baird had made it impossible for others to imitate him. He said Baird always told junior colleagues they would have to construct their own courses for themselves. I have persisted, however, in being more interested in the ways Gibson, Sale, and Coles have been influenced by English 1–2 than in the ways they have distanced themselves from it.

Gibson, like Bartholomae and Petrosky at Pittsburgh and others, has experimented with transplanting English 1–2 methods from Amherst to other campuses. Gibson left Amherst College in 1957 to direct the teaching of writing at the Washington Square College of New York University. In 1967, he returned to Amherst to direct the writing program at the University of Massachusetts. Gibson told me that "the effect I had on the teaching of freshman English at Washington Square College was of course very, very much influenced by my own experience. And I had some followers there who were quite excited by all this, and here too, at the University of Massachusetts.

But I don't know how much you could make of that relation. If I could dig up, which I can't, assignments that we did in the late 1960s, let's say here at UMass, what relation would they have with the English 1 assignments? Well, they would have something, I'm sure, but nothing like the kind of day-by-day, rigorous, thirty-assignment affair that you see in English 1."

Robert Bagg, who also moved from Amherst College to the University of Massachusetts, told me there are spinoffs from English 1–2 in his teaching. He said he likes to devise such exercises as: "Here are ten propositions about the *Odyssey,* all of them false in larger or smaller degree. Find a quotation in the *Odyssey,* or several quotations which may be used to challenge these ten false statements. Go on to explain how your quotation bears on the false formulation. Finally, reformulate the idea in a way that fits the facts as you understand them." He says, "I don't think I ever would have come to that way of examining students if it hadn't been for English 1. The students all tell me that they love these kinds of questions."

Both Gibson and Bagg told me that John Carpenter Louis, who took English 1–2 at Amherst College in 1959–60 and filed a 1971 dissertation on the course, worked as an English instructor at UMass in the late 1960s and devised some sequenced assignments to use with UMass students. Gibson said, "Louis made the mistake, and he's not the only one, of trying to take English 1 techniques one hundred percent into new contexts, without trying to vary it, and to update it, and to put a little local situation into it." Bagg said, "Here's what John Louis did with Walker Gibson's encouragement. He established here at UMass a sequence for, I think, gifted students. And this is back in the late 1960s." Bagg said, "I taught in this course. And Louis based his assignments, which I admired—I thought they were great; I adapted them a bit after he left, and I taught similar courses—on an educational experience. 'Describe a time in class when you were a student in high school in which you learned something. What was it that you learned? How did you know that you had learned it? How did you confirm that you had learned something? Describe a situation in class in which you were uncomfortable. Were you learning something, or were you not learning something? What were the teacher's expectations?' I don't have this exactly right, but somewhere I have these assignments. It was about a twelve-assignment sequence, and it was very much on a model of what was done here [at Amherst College] but not quite so gloriously worked out." Bagg added, "Finally the student was asked to define learning, define education. And you can see the principles. It's all based on narratives of direct experience, on formulated narratives of direct experience, without recourse to dictionary definitions. I remember giving this sequence and getting some wonderful answers from students."

Roger Sale told me that when he moved to the University of Washington in 1962, he tried to do the kinds of things he had learned to do at Amherst. He said, "When I, in my earliest efforts at the University of Washington, went to try to do something similar to English 1, they didn't know what I was talking about, and I should have realized right away that of course they wouldn't, that I was asking questions that were just bewildering." He said, "So you just have to adapt. What I now like to do is, say, a sequence of assignments on a single work of literature, but it will be composition assignments. I just did a sequence this summer with some students who were going to become high school teachers of writing, and I gave them the first half of Frost's 'Home Burial,' and then the second half with very minimal sorts of statements about what I wanted them to write about. And then on the third assignment, I gave them a paragraph of Frost's about teaching here [at Amherst College], in which he said, in effect, 'When I sorted out with my students, who fancied themselves as thinkers, what they meant by thinking, what they really meant by thinking was voting, that is taking sides on an issue.'" Sale said of his own class and students that "it turned out when we looked at this matter, they had actually done some thinking, often without their knowing it. So I then say, 'Look back at your two previous papers on "Home Burial," and show me where you were voting and where maybe you were thinking.' And it was an eye-opener because the poem doesn't insist upon—but almost everybody who is taking an easy ride will side with one—either the husband or the wife, and turn the other into an awful person and this [one] into a victim." Sale added that his manner of interacting with students has changed considerably since he left Amherst. He said, "I find that I need ways now, not to flatter, but if I'm going to do some 'challenging' (let's use the buzz word), I also have to do lots and lots of encouraging." He said students "need to be told 'You can be smarter; you can be smarter! People get smarter; they also get stupider. I'm going to believe you're smart.'"

Some members of the "Amherst Mafia," including Sale, have written books which relate in different ways to English 1–2. Sale wrote *On Writing.* John Carpenter Louis wrote a 1971 dissertation on English 1–2. Walker Gibson wrote *Seeing and Writing; Tough, Sweet and Stuffy;* and *Persona.* William E. Coles Jr. wrote *The Plural I; Composing; Composing II;* and *Seeing through Writing.* Jonathan Bishop, who taught English 1–2 in the early 1950s, wrote *Something Else.* Bishop's wife, Alison Lurie, wrote a 1962 novel about the Amherst course.

Lurie's *Love and Friendship* is set in the 1950s at a fictional New England college that very much resembles Amherst. Several of the characters in her novel are involved in teaching a freshman writing course which, Lurie says,

> was really a course in semantics based on positivist and opera-tionalist principles; it should be said at once, however, that the use of words like "positivist" and "principles" was absolutely taboo. No textbooks were used; instead the students were sent out with pencil and paper to draw a picture of the view from College Hall, or with a tape measure to measure the length of their feet and their friends' feet. Then they would come back and write papers describing what they had done. After this, they would be asked to write more papers defining what they meant by the important words they had used in their papers, words like "observation," and "average," and "really there." (1962, 15–16)

The character who directs the course in Lurie's novel takes attendance at staff meetings, is "far more bear than man," and although named Oswald McBane, is known behind his back as "McBear" (25, 75).

Lurie and her husband, Jonathan Bishop, left Amherst in the 1950s. Bishop later taught at UCLA, and he is now at Cornell. In 1972, he published *Something Else,* which he describes as "one man's arrangement of some matters that have concerned him over a period of time" (x). In his foreword to this text, Bishop acknowledges Theodore Baird as "my most serious teacher, who is present as much in the contrary reactions to what I could learn from him as in the more positive echoes of his thinking" (xiii). In the opening chapter of *Something Else,* Bishop describes a course he taught at UCLA in advanced composition for science majors. He says he decided to ask his students to write about what they were learning in their science courses because he had learned at Amherst that

> Assignments could be contrived that would oblige the students to rehearse these and other activities slowly enough for the intellectual structure to emerge. Amherst had convinced me what that structure would prove to be in general. The mind knew nature by finding some language in terms of which to express it. To know how one knew was therefore to become aware of the particular language one was using, and its relation to other languages, not all of course verbal. (1972, 5)

Bishop added that the lesson he hoped to teach his UCLA students was that

> To "see" something was indeed to "say" it: the world was available for perception and comprehension in proportion to the number and relation of terms available. One could readily enough call these terms "metaphors" in the Amherst style; and work on to elicit an awareness of these. (6)

While Baird's influence on Bishop's UCLA course seems apparent enough, and while Bishop freely acknowledges it, my problem is to incorporate Bishop's remarks into a larger discussion of Baird's influence. What Bishop seems primarily to have carried away with him from English 1–2 are concerns with operational definition, the seeing-writing connection, and metaphor. Other members of the "Amherst Mafia" seem more concerned with voice, or the limits of language, or sequenced assignments, or not giving answers. Several of them, including Bishop, speak reverentially of *The Education of Henry Adams*. Others like to quote Robert Frost. Some members of the "Mafia" acknowledge Baird's influence in positive terms. Others, like Bishop or like Bartholomae with Poirier, speak of struggling against it. There seems to be no one essential element of English 1–2 that "Mafia" members carried away with them. The best I can do to sort out the relationships of various members of the "Mafia" to one another and to Theodore Baird is to invoke Ludwig Wittgenstein's discussion in *Philosophical Investigations* of the family resemblance of games. Wittgenstein observed that just as the members of a family do not all have the same eyes or the same nose, games such as football, bridge, chess, solitaire, and hide-and-go-seek have no one feature in common. With games and families, Wittgenstein observed, "we see a complicated network of similarities overlapping and criss-crossing: sometimes overall similarities, sometimes similarities of detail" (1958, 32ᵉ). It seems to me that each member of the Amherst "Mafia" resembles other members of the group in overlapping and criss-crossing ways. Each of them had to work out his own relation to English 1–2. The books that several of them wrote after leaving Amherst relate to English 1–2 in an equally complicated network of ways.

Some of the most widely known of the books that may be said to bear a relation to English 1–2 have been written by William E. Coles Jr. These include *The Plural I, Composing,* and *Seeing through Writing,* of which the first listed bears the closest relation to English 1–2. Coles taught at Amherst from the fall of 1960 through the spring of 1965. In a phone conversation I had with him in 1991, Coles told me he never wrote a series of assignments for English 1–2. He said that, even so, he had learned at Amherst that framing effective questions was the key to teaching and learning. He told me that working with Baird had changed the way he saw the world.

Coles's job at Amherst was his first full-time teaching job. Coles has written most fully about his Amherst experience in his 1981 article on "Teaching Writing, Teaching Literature." He says that before his first semester at Amherst began, he was handed a set of assignments and a memorandum explaining that "language using (in its broadest sense) is the means by which all of us run orders through chaos thereby giving ourselves the identities we have" (1981b, 14). He was dismayed to discover that, in the course he was supposed to teach, he would not have a textbook to rely on, or a handbook. He says, "There were only those damned assignments, the students' papers, and someone called a teacher who was supposed to make it all make sense" (14). Coles took his set of assignments and went to see the one person in Amherst's English department he knew, someone who had been at Amherst only a year. Coles says his friend quickly saw that what he wanted was a teacher's manual. The friend said there was no manual and explained that the course was designed to invite students "to see in how they use language a way of taking responsibility for the shapes of their lives" (15). Coles says that eventually the English 1–2 approach to the teaching of writing "enabled me to find myself as a teacher"

William E. Coles Jr. in 1965.

(15). When he left Amherst in 1965 for the Case Institute of Technology in Ohio, he found that having an approach to believe in gave him an advantage over his Case colleagues and provided him with "the best insulation there is against the besetting sin of a teacher: unacknowledged self-contempt" (1988a, 6).

For Coles, the most important aspects of the Amherst approach seem, judging from what he has written since leaving Amherst, to have been its concern to run orders through chaos, its concern with voice and self-definition, its impatience with "themewriting," its reliance on sequenced assignments, and its combative style of pedagogy. He has adapted assignments that were used at Amherst and acknowledges having done so in both *The Plural I* and *Composing*. He has adapted the course description that was used at Amherst, and versions of it appear in *The Plural I* (1988a, 10–14), *Composing* (1983, 1–5), and *Seeing through Writing* (1988b, 4–13). The version in *The Plural I* is the closest to the Amherst original, and in *The Plural I,* Coles acknowledges that it is "a modification of a statement developed originally by the teachers of English 1–2 at Amherst College" (14).

Although the version of the course description that appears in *The Plural I* contains several interpolations of Coles's own, much of it is quoted directly from the version of the English 1–2 course description that was current when Coles was teaching at Amherst (see my Appendix A). *The Plural I* version, like the Amherst version, warns students they will find themselves "in a situation where no one knows the answers" (1988a, 11) and that they are responsible both for supplying the material for discourse (12) and for their own learning (13). In one of his interpolations, Coles (or the instructor-narrator of his book) explains that while he is interested in helping each of his students to define a voice and a self, the self he is interested in is

> a stylistic self, the self construable from the way words fall on a page. The other self, the identity of a student, is something with which I as a teacher can have nothing to do. (12)

The version of the course description printed in *Seeing through Writing* represents a later phase of Coles's career than the one that appears in *The Plural I* and provides for course features, such as teacher-student conferences and out-of-class meetings among small groups of students, that were never attempted at Amherst. Even so, this version contains a lot of language Coles learned at Amherst. The following, for example, is a key passage:

> Though the assignments for this course are arranged, I want to say emphatically that they do not constitute an argument. Beyond assuming that language using (in its broadest sense) is the means by which all of us run orders through chaos thereby giving ourselves the identities we have, they contain no doctrine I am aware of, either individually or as a sequence. (1988b, 9)

For Coles, as for Baird, "running orders through chaos" seems to represent a writer's primary task and to entail a writer's defining himself (or herself) in relation to his experience, his language, his audience, and his writing problem.

After leaving Amherst, Coles moved from the Case Institute of Technology to Drexel University to the University of Pittsburgh. His *The Plural I* is an account of a class he taught at Case. Coles wrote his first draft of *The Plural I* in 1968, while he was at Case, but he did not publish the book until 1978.[10] He wrote *Composing* and its companion teaching manual, *Teaching Composing,* while he was at Drexel.[11] He wrote *Seeing through Writing* during the Pittsburgh phase of his career. All of these books, but especially *The Plural I,* show the influence of English 1–2 at Amherst College. All of them contain sequences of assignments. The sequences in *The Plural I* and *Composing,* like sequences at Amherst, contain thirty assignments each, but the sequence in the more recently authored *Seeing through Writing* has only twelve assignments. The sequences in all three of these books conclude, like sequences at Amherst, with an assignment that invites students to make sense of what they have spent a semester doing (1988a, 258–259; 1983, 119–120; 1988b, 213–214). The nominal subject of the sequence in *The Plural I* is professionalism and amateurism; in *Composing,* it is teaching and learning, and in *Seeing through Writing,* it is seeing and reseeing. Coles explains in each of the three books, however, that the nominal subject of his assignments is a metaphor for the real subject of his courses, which is language and the use of language (1988a, 6; 1983, 6; 1988b, 8).

The Plural I reads something like a novel, with characters and dialogue, and something like a case study of a writing class. The primary material for the book is a sequence of thirty assignments that Coles used in the late 1960s at the Case Institute of Technology and those samples of his students' responses that he duplicated for discussion in class. He says he reproduced these sample student essays "just as they were written" (1988a, 4). The remainder of his text is made up of his narrator's reflections on his teaching and of reconstructed class discussions. Coles, who notes both that he did not tape actual discussions and that he revised and re-revised his text over the course of ten years, says his reconstructed discussions have about the same relation to what went on in his classroom as "van Gogh's *Sunflowers* does to sunflowers" (4, 272). As for the relation between him and his instructor-narrator, Coles says that although his narrator is only a persona and "no better than the best I could do way back then," this figure is also "a good deal closer to me than a term like 'persona' can suggest" (273).

Coles says that when he arrived at the Case Institute of Technology in 1965, he received no guidelines for teaching its required freshman writing course, so he was free to teach his classes in his own way and to draw on what he had learned at Amherst (1988a, 5). He decided, as at Amherst, to collect a paper from every student at every class period (6). His students in the class section he represents in *The Plural I* were, as at Amherst, all male (2), and he seems to have interacted with them much as Tom Looker says he (Coles) interacted with students in Looker's section at Amherst. Coles's narrator in *The Plural I* says, for example, that he wanted to allow time at the beginning of the semester for "necessary streetcleaning" (16). He reports that he put together a portmanteau paper by pasting together sentences from papers that twelve of his students had written in response to one of his assignments (35). He says that he had no tolerance for "themewriting" (17) and that "I'd read a Theme no further than was obvious that that was all the paper was going to amount to; at that point I'd draw a slash line, write 'read to here' in the margin" (78). He reports that his students responded by pleading "it would help if you could tell us what you wanted" (34). Coles himself, in an essay on "Looking Back on *The Plural I*," which appears as a supplement to the 1988 edition of the text, recalls that at the time he taught the class he describes in *The Plural I*, "I'd never met a student I couldn't provoke into making an effort" (274). He says he tried to represent his classroom "as a place in which all of us *together* [he and his students] were involved in combat" (275).

Coles's purpose, like Baird's purpose at Amherst, seems to have been to take a student through a process that would enable him both to define his individual voice and to declare his independence of his teacher. Coles says that the concept of voice "can, after a time, become an appropriate metaphor for the life of writing—or for the lack of it" (1988a, 21). He says he tried to focus his students' attention "on language-using as a self-creating activity" (212). He says that "if, as seems to be the case, each of us with the languages or symbol systems he knows creates the worlds that make him who he is, then the more consciousness one has of himself as a creator with language and of the various ways in which language can make meaning, the more ready he will be to become the master of language rather than its slave" (181). Selfhood and voice are things that Coles seems to believe a writer has to earn. Yet there is a tension in his work, as there was in English 1–2 at Amherst, between his aim of encouraging self-authorization on the one hand and his students' dependence, on the other, on their social situation and on the central authority of their teacher. Coles concludes *The Plural I* by printing a student paper he recognizes "as a rejection of dependency, on the course and its procedures, on an earlier way of seeing, on me as a teacher" (270). And yet he tells the other students in his class that the student author of this paper could not have done what he did without the rest of us. The rejection in his paper, then, is made as it is made necessary, in the name of a re-creation of himself as an individual whose independence is conditioned by its new and free acknowledgment of its dependence—on both the self from which it came and on the rest of us as well. In the formation of that plural I, each one of us in that class has had a sharing. (270)

In the same way, and I think he would be the first to acknowledge this, Coles could neither have done what he has done without the example of Theodore Baird nor have contented himself merely to imitate his master.

Coles says that in the course of the ten years he spent revising *The Plural I* and thinking about what he was doing as a teacher and thinking about his presentation of what he was doing, he began to work "harder on transforming what I had simply lifted from other teachers into an approach of my own" (1988a, 276). He found himself, in other words, having to earn his independence in much the way that he was asking his students to earn theirs. The question of independence and dependence became even more complicated when he found he had to formulate a stance in his 1974 textbook, *Composing,*[11] and its companion *Teaching Composing* toward the teachers who would read and use these books. He chose, much as Baird had done, to disclaim his authority. Coles told his teacher audience that his comments in *Teaching Composing* on the assignments in *Composing* "are to be understood as representing only my notion of a procedure for myself" (1974, 4). He also invited his audience to adapt the assignments in *Composing* to fit their own calendars and needs (1974, 4).

Composing consists of a sequence of thirty writing assignments which Coles and three colleagues had field tested during an eleven-week term at Drexel University (1974, 1, 4). He had drafted the sequence before the term began, and he revised it with his colleagues at weekly staff meetings held throughout the term itself (2–3). In serving as principal author of a set of assignments, Coles was doing something he had not done at Amherst. In chairing a series of staff meetings, moreover, he was stepping into Baird's shoes in some symbolic way. But in publishing a sequence of assignments, he was doing what Baird had never done. And in writing *Teaching Composing,* he was supplying the teacher's manual that was never supplied at Amherst.

Although *Composing* is a textbook for a course modeled after English 1–2, the course is different from English 1–2 in some of its features and emphases. For one thing, Coles incorporates more extended literary passages into his assignments than was customary at Amherst. For another, he expects students to address only twelve or fourteen of his assignments, not all thirty of them (1974, 6). And in what I see as a philosophical shift, Coles acknowledges the mutuality of teaching and learning in a way that he is not likely to have done while he was at Amherst. He says that good teaching "is not simply something someone does; it is also something that is interpreted to mean good teaching by another someone who has thereby chosen to define himself as a learner" (84).

While Coles was writing *Composing* and *Teaching Composing,* he was also revising *The Plural I* and attempting to tone down what the publishers who had rejected early drafts of the book had called arrogance on the part of his instructor-narrator. He says he found that

> I had to create something to play against the all-consuming voice of my narrator. My students, in other words, had to get a hearing.
>
> And then I found I had to create my teacher as someone who could listen to them. (1988a, 275)

Coles gives students an even larger hearing in his 1988 *Seeing through Writing,* which, like *The Plural I,* is a fictionalized account of what happens in a writing classroom. While *The Plural I* is written from the point of view of a teacher, *Seeing through Writing* is a composite of the views of several students. The students receive a course description and a series of twelve assignments from their teacher, and these constitute an important part of the text of *Seeing through Writing,* but the bulk of the text consists of the internal reflections of individual students and of the conversations the students have with one another in the small group meetings their instructor has asked them to conduct outside class. The instructor is seen only through the eyes of his students, but what the students say indicates that each of them is engaged in a relation to the teacher. One student, for example, speaking to another, reports of the teacher: "If he thinks you can do better than you're doing, that you're just screwing off or something, he'll tear your head off" (1988b, 41). Another student, referring to the fact that she and her classmates call their teacher "the Gorgon" and to the fact that in Roman mythology the goddess Minerva wears the Gorgon's head on her shield, tells her classmates that they have misunderstood their teacher and that "he's really no more than an instrument of Wisdom (Minerva being the goddess of the same)" (95). Still another student reflects that

> It was the dittoed copy of her paper that had stopped her, or more exactly the notes she'd taken in the margins of it, that day, that ghastly day, on which for about half the period the class had worked over what she had written—she pretending all the while, and with every resource she could command, that it was just a lesson in writing she was receiving, that its point was to help her get better, to help all of them get better, and that in any case no one in class could know who had written the paper, or would ever have to know who had written the paper. She'd made it to the end of the period somehow, but she had cut her anthropology class. (102)

Coles's ability to represent the anguish of this last student indicates, I think, the degree to which he has succeeded in redefining himself since leaving Amherst College.

The tension between the influence of Amherst College on the one hand and the need on the other to develop an approach of one's own is evident in Roger Sale's 1970 *On Writing* in much the way that it is in Coles's work. In a personal anecdote concerning his Amherst experience that Sale includes in *On Writing,* he confesses that

> I sailed through graduate school, learning lots of things but not how to write, and took my first teaching job. One day, perhaps a month after the term began, I was carrying on to a colleague about something, undoubtedly being energetic but not very coherent. Slowly, I felt my listener lose attention, and he began staring out of the window. So I stopped, and he turned, and smiling very nicely said to me, "Why do you talk in that boring way?" I knew the statement was kindly meant, and was not crushed by his apparent rudeness. But I was dazed. I had been called brash and unclear and stubborn and rattle-brained, but no one had ever called me boring. It wasn't said about my writing,

but it was the only thing ever said to me that, to my knowledge, taught me something real about my writing. (54)

Sale goes on to say that his entire opening "chapter, in one sense, is my imitation of the man who asked me, 'Why do you talk in that boring way?'" Considered in another sense, Sale says, "[M]y imitation is my own, and the man who asked me why I was boring only began a process of change in me that continued long after I had ceased to imitate him" (56).

I was naturally interested in this anecdote and in the course of my conversations with Sale, I asked him to identify the colleague who had told him he was boring. He replied that, when he had taught English 1–2, "the three tenured members of the program staff were Ted Baird, Armour Craig, and Ben DeMott. None of them ever told me I was boring. I invented the story for the sake of my book. I think, however, that by look and body language, Baird, Craig, and DeMott all implied that I tended to go on in a boring way." Sale told me that *On Writing* "of course derived from English 1 but was written ten years later, and I was in a very different situation then." He said, "Ted didn't like *On Writing* at all. He thought that was a silly book; I don't think he even necessarily told me very much about why."

On Writing is a different kind of book from any of those Coles has written, but it reflects Sale's Amherst experience to much the same degree that Coles's books reflect his. *On Writing* contains no sequence of assignments. It is neither a textbook nor an account of the way Sale conducts his classes. He describes it as "a book about a particular kind of writing written all over America today: the English paper" (1970, 3), and in it he analyzes a number of specimen student papers. The general proposition with which he opens his book is that: "Writing can be learned, but it can't be taught" (10, 15). One of the propositions with which he concludes is that writing is a subject "that is not a subject at all but an action" (177). Forms of both these propositions, of course, may be found in the course description for English 1–2 that was current when Sale was teaching at Amherst (see Appendix A). The influence of English 1–2 upon Sale is also reflected in the impatience he expresses in *On Writing* with what he might have called "themewriting" but instead calls "canned" writing (33), in his attention to what he might have called "running orders through chaos" but instead calls establishing "relationships" (71), and in his concerns with metaphor and with the selfhood of a writer. Sale says that a key moment in the career of any writer is the moment when he (or she) discovers that "writing is a form of being himself" (52). He adds that such a moment came for him personally when he was asked, "Why do you talk in that boring way?" and found he could not "rest quietly in thinking that the rush, stutter, and confusion that was my expression should be my way of being me" (54–55). He recommends that students ask "themselves, sentence-by-sentence as they write, how *this* is related to *that*, how *that* fits into the *other thing*" (11). He explains that what a writer "knows is almost always a matter of the relationships he establishes, between example and generalization, between one part of a narrative and the next, between the idea and the counteridea that the writer sees is also relevant, between his experience and what he knows of the experience of others—in short, between any two parts of his knowledge" (71). Sale adds that because it is through metaphor that "we relate what we see to what we know," a student may acquire a sense of himself or herself as "a user of words" by paying attention to the way he or she uses metaphor (160).

Sale is not only concerned with the relations between words, however. He is also concerned with the relation between a student and his or her teacher and with the way that writing is taught and learned in American colleges and schools. Sale says that most writing courses are "disheartening" and that the work which many teachers and students do in these courses is "boring work, which most teachers and students know is boring" (1970, 44). He says that "the best way to establish and maintain truly open and respectful relationships between teachers and students is for the teacher to ask questions to which he does not really know the answer, questions to which there are no good simple answers but many good complex ones" (47). He says that the phrasing of assignments is important because a well-phrased assignment can "suggest to the student more ways in which he might say what is most on his mind about the subject" (46). Sale says that learning is an "action whereby a student learns who he is in relation to something outside himself" (55). He adds that although this balance is difficult to strike, a teacher should "be aggressive and forward enough to convince the student there is another mind out there intent upon him, yet quiet and withdrawn enough to give the student thinking room whenever it is needed" (56). Sale concludes that the best way to work toward improving the teaching and learning of writing is

> to ask about the relationship between teacher and student, and to insist that most of the writing that is done is bad because the relationship is mechanical or unreal to the student. When that relationship is one of power and acceptance of power, writing can be taught that is, at best, no better than the writing machines can do. When that relationship is one of real question, real answer, and real possibility, writing cannot be taught at all. But it can be learned. (58)

Near the end of *On Writing,* Sale describes English 1–2 at Amherst College:

> The great advantage of the course is that it keeps the emphasis so strongly on the papers that no student can fail to become more aware of himself as a writer, often by seeing how very well students can write without ever being self-conscious about style or learning. The great disadvantage of the course is that it requires an enormous amount of time and commitment from both teacher and student, more than most are seriously willing to give. (175)

Since leaving Amherst College, Sale had undoubtedly encountered teaching situations that were very different from the one he had known there. He speaks of "students who like to talk all the time, students who never talk, students who don't come to class more than once a week" (177) and of teachers who "get a minimal response from almost everyone and then scale their expectations down so that minimal response seems like a great deal" (29). Nevertheless, he concludes *On Writing* optimistically by asserting that the problems encountered by those who would teach writing and those who would learn to write "can be faced and understood and given a sense of direction that comes from believing the mind can make orders and sequences where none existed before" (177).

Walker Gibson, like Roger Sale, addressed himself after leaving Amherst College to the problem of making the teaching and learning of writing more engaging than it is for many teachers and students in many institutions. Of the books which Gibson has published since leaving Amherst College in 1957, the one which shows the strongest connection to his Amherst experience is his 1959 *Seeing and Writing: Fifteen Exercises in Composing Experience*. Gibson dedicates *Seeing and Writing* "to T.B." and as its epigraph he uses Baird's statement that "I think the students should entertain *me!*" In his preface to the book, Gibson states:

> Its assumption is that if young writers are encouraged to look hard at their own experience they will see something there and say something about it of interest to their teachers. It may be that teachers of college composition who are bored by their students' writing deserve what they get. This book proposes that students can be so directed to express themselves that they will inform, entertain, and instruct their instructors. (vii)

Seeing and Writing is a writing textbook, which, as its subtitle suggests, consists of fifteen exercises. Most of the exercises include both a short reading selection and the directions for a written "theme." Gibson explains in his preface that he had worked these exercises out with the staff and students of a writing course he was directing at the Washington Square College of New York University (1959, x–xi). Some of the exercises resemble ones he had worked out earlier at Amherst. His twelfth, for example, involves the building of an anemometer and is a version of an assignment he wrote for Amherst freshmen in the spring of 1954. Gibson arranges his fifteen exercises in pairs or clusters rather than in one long sequence and explains that the clustering is designed to "require reexaminations of experience in new terms" (viii). He follows the model that had been established for English 2 during the time he was teaching at Amherst College and frames various exercises in ways which invite students to speak either as scientists, or as historians, or as literary critics. His "Theme 4," for example, "asks for an account of a family conflict in the student's own life, while theme 5 demands a rewriting, or 'reseeing,' of this conflict in the terms of an anthropologist" (viii). Another cluster asks students to look at Chartres Cathedral from first Henry James's and then Henry Adams's point of view and then, in what Gibson told me was "an English one-ish kind of treatment," to describe the façade of some more familiar church "in language a historian might use" (106–107). Gibson told me that while

Seeing and Writing was quite obviously based on "something like" English 1–2, he had had, at Washington Square, to try "to adapt Amherst's attitude to a very different situation, where you couldn't get them to write everyday, for example, and where instead of making a relation among thirty assignments, I was making a relation among two or three." He said, "You don't at most institutions have the nerve to get kids to write for every single class, so that's why I modified it into a do-able weekly affair. The idea of providing reading matter which they could take off from was something that, on the whole, English 1 did not do, but it was a way of helping teachers. It was a way of making a program that somebody could read about and do without the kinds of hands-on supervision that Ted provided."

Where I see Gibson's Amherst experience most strongly in *Seeing and Writing* and in his subsequent work is in his concerns with voice and with what might be called either the inexpressible or the limits of language. There is a moral dimension to his concern with the limits of language, just as there is to Baird's. Gibson expresses it clearly in his preface to *Seeing and Writing,* where he explains that

> A liberally educated man is a talker and a writer, a composer of words. He is a man who can change his voice without losing track of himself: for him the terms of the historian and the scientist and the poet are all available ways of ordering a world, and their variety does not frighten him. In this book a systematic attempt is made to place the student in positions where he must see his experience from shifting points of view, and must change his terms and his tone of voice as he does so. . . . The liberally educated man, moreover, knows his limits. He knows, for example, that the words he uses are not identical with the things he sees, and he writes accordingly with modesty, good humor, and careful courage—in other words, with *style.* (1959, vii)

Gibson's term here is "style," but he might equally have said that the liberally educated individual writes with an awareness of his responsibility for his words. Gibson explains that both seeing and writing are acts of composing and that in order to do either

> You have to make a number of choices, both in the scene before your eyes and in the words you employ to your reader. In a very

real sense, when you look at something and talk about it, you are making it. You create the world before you by the choices you commit yourself to. (10)

Among the choices a writer must make is the choice of a voice. In his directions for his exercise on describing a church façade, Gibson asks students to consider the questions: "Who are you, who should you be, as you speak to a reader about the appearance of a church?" (86). He also tells students that "the state of our minds, as it really is at this moment, is inexpressible, and we can't 'convey' that state to anybody, not even to ourselves" (2).

Gibson published *The Limits of Language* in 1962, *Tough, Sweet and Stuffy* in 1966, and *Persona* in 1969. All three of these books bear some relation to English 1–2, but none so strongly as the 1959 *Seeing and Writing.* In the books he wrote in the 1960s, it seems to me, Gibson still was building upon an English 1–2 foundation, but he was constructing an edifice of his own. In *Persona,* for example, he employs the terminology of Aristotelian rhetoric even though Aristotelian (as well as Burkean) metalanguage had been avoided in English 1–2. And in both *Persona* and *Tough, Sweet and Stuffy,* he explicates literary passages in ways which, if they derive from Amherst at all, derive more closely from Brower's sophomore course than from the freshman course. *The Limits of Language* is an anthology of selections by twelve philosophers, scientists, and writers which all indicate in one way or another "that a good deal of life is inexpressible" (1962, x). The names of some of the philosophers and scientists whose writings Gibson features, such as William James, Alfred North Whitehead, and P. W. Bridgman, had been cited on the reading lists Baird had circulated at Amherst. Others, such as James B. Conant, Herbert J. Muller, and J. Robert Oppenheimer, had never (so far as I know) appeared on Baird's lists. Gibson concludes *The Limits of Language* with an essay of his own in which he addresses the matter of voice and asks: "What sort of speaking voice adopted by the writer, what mask, would be appropriate in a world where, as we have seen, the very nature of nature may be inexpressible?" (104).

Tough, Sweet and Stuffy and *Persona* are both extended essays on style. In *Tough, Sweet and Stuffy,* Gibson explains that "self-dramatizations in language are what I mean by style" (1966, x). He also says, in a statement that seems to echo similar statements of Theodore Baird's, that style "is partly a matter of sheer individual will" (24). In *Persona,* he says that all writing "implies a self-definition, and flexibility in such self-defining is a desirable quality" (1969, 51). He says that his purpose in writing *Persona,* very much like Baird's purpose in directing English 1–2, is to promote flexibility "so that we may widen our range of possibilities and make our way in the world with greater power" (52). Gibson says he hopes also to promote "greater sympathy for others, and more fun" (52). He says his purpose in *Tough, Sweet and Stuffy* is to describe "three extreme but familiar styles in modern American prose" (1966, ix). Of the three styles, or voices, Gibson seems to prefer the tough voice of a Hemingway narrator to the sweet voice of an ad writer or the stuffy voice of a government bureaucrat. I asked him about this, wondering if there were some connection to the masculine ethos of Amherst College, and he replied, "Twenty-five years ago, I didn't have the benefit of feminist criticism." He added, "If there's one thing that has changed our minds about an awful lot in reading and writing, it seems to me feminist criticism. And now I would have to look at that tough voice with its macho ego (I do at least say that it's 'I' oriented, capital 'I' oriented, as it certainly is), but I would be much more severe on it if I were to do it again, and the book would be then an exposition of three bad voices, three unattractive voices, and I suppose it would come out to a kind of warning that these are all voices in exaggerated form to be leery of."

I asked Gibson what he thought of James Berlin's treatment in *Rhetoric and Reality* of his (Gibson's) work. Berlin had identified both Gibson and William E. Coles Jr. as admirers "of Theodore Baird of Amherst" (1987, 153). Berlin had also identified them as two of the five leading exponents in the 1960s and 1970s of what he called "expressionistic" rhetoric (145–146). Gibson replied that his 1970 article, "Composing the World: The Writer as Map-Maker," in which Berlin had traced "expressionistic" ideas, was rooted as much in Viet Nam era "political outrage" as in any epistemological concern. Gibson added that "the expression 'expressivism' is one I never use, never have used." He said, "I would prefer not to suggest that there's a deep-down self in there waiting to be liberated. My metaphor would be: we're going to create a self." He said, "If you were a conscript of English 1, you would tend to look with suspicion on statements about having a deep-down soul. You would ask what every teacher of English 1 constantly asked, 'What is your evidence?' I think some people would be ready to say, 'Well, it's a feeling.' And there's nothing wrong with a feeling, but that's not what we said. What we said was: 'We would like to know why you say what you're saying. What is it you're looking at when you say what you say?'"

With respect to epistemology, paradoxically, English 1–2 could be said to have had either an "expressionistic" or a positivistic orientation. Its premise that writing can be learned but not taught places it, in Berlin's terms, in the "expressionistic" category. So does its premise that reality is constructed by the observer. So does its having called upon its students to write from experience and to develop their individual voices. On the other hand, the emphasis in English 1–2 on the operational definition, on the question "Where is your evidence?" and on explaining how you know what you know suggests that the orientation of the course was positivistic. In fact, in her 1985 article on the influence of I. A. Richards, Ann Berthoff categorizes English 1–2 as positivistic. She says that

> the Amherst course was underwritten, not by Peircean semiotics, but by a positivist operationalism. The guiding conception of language as a map for a territory of reality came not from *The Meaning of Meaning* but from General Semantics: it was Korzybski's vulgarization of Wittgenstein's early picture theory. (72)

I believe that English 1–2 had roots in both Ogden and Richards's *The Meaning of Meaning* (1923) and in Korzybski's *Science and Sanity* (1948), both of which feature prominently on the reading lists Baird circulated in April 1946 and May 1947.[12] Korzybski, in my opinion, however, is not a positivist. At least, he is not the sort of positivist who assumes an exact correspondence between words and things. One of the dictums for which Korzybski is most well known is that "a map is not the territory it represents" (1948, 58). The physicist P. W. Bridgman, who also had a strong influence upon English 1–2, is not in my opinion a positivist either. He had the perceptiveness to have observed that "it is impossible to transcend the human reference point" (quoted in Gibson 1959, 155).

Of the several historians who have written about English 1–2, I think that it is James Broderick, who observed that "English 1–2 is in many ways a typically American course" (1958, 57), rather than either Berlin or Berthoff, who comes closest to characterizing its motive spirit. But I would add that English 1–2 was a distinctly masculine course as well. In valorizing independent initiative, freedom of mind, self-authorization, and mastery, it was both American and masculine. In its intellectual orientation, it was both American and masculine. John Cameron told me that English 1–2, with its distrust of systems, metalanguages, and final pronouncements, was grounded in a "heritage of American, nonsystematic thought." Dale Peterson, who said that in English 1–2 "what really mattered was what works," told me the course was rooted in "American pragmatism." He said the style of the course was "cunning, witty, but also hard-edged" and marked by "a very masculine witticism." William Pritchard told me that in English 1–2 "there wasn't any reforming attitude." He said that those who ran the course "did not look for political or social change" but were content to "leave it the way it is so we can push against it, or so we can play off against it." Pritchard said that in the 1950s "we were all very satirical about American society and culture and how awful it was." The tough-mindedness he describes seems to me to reflect American intellectual culture in the 1950s. I believe that English 1–2 was rooted in its specific historical moment and agree with Cameron that its having flourished when it did was, as he said, "no accident historically."

Baird and his staff understood the connection between language and power, and it is no accident that English 1–2 flourished during the era of America's greatest economic and political power. During the fifteen or twenty years following World War II, Amherst students could aspire, and not unreasonably, to leading the free world. Baird conceived of writing as the means of fostering personal agency, and he worked to put students in the position where they could take control of their discourse and their lives. By contrast, the educational goal since the 1960s has not so much been to promote the freedom of the individual as it has been to promote the health of the community. By honoring diversity, teachers and administrators have hoped to forestall divisiveness. As Roger Sale said in his "Senior Chapel Address," although the dream at the Amherst he had known was of building a "whole man," the dream elsewhere in academia was already, by the 1962 date of his address, of building a "whole society." Since at least the 1970s, students have tended to identify themselves in terms of gender, ethnicity, sexual orientation, and other such factors, rather than to see themselves as free agents. English professors, as Dale Peterson told me, now tend to assume that the "imagination itself is a cultural construct." Professors in all departments, moreover, are likely now to express ambivalence about their relations to power. Currently, as Jan Dizard told me, the Amherst College faculty chooses to leave curricular decisions largely up to students. And currently, as both Dizard and Cameron told me, there is no consensus amongst the Amherst faculty as to what the mission of the college ought to be.

It would be too easy to dismiss English 1–2 as a course designed by white males for white males. There are, without question, aspects of the course which are distasteful by today's standards. It was elitist and authoritarian. It mystified many of its students, at least initially. Some students never caught on to what the course was about. Some faculty members found themselves having to bluff about their authority in the classroom. Some adopted bullying attitudes. Some alumni, immediately after completing the course, experienced an inhibiting self-consciousness in their writing. But despite all this, English 1–2 seems rarely to have been boring, either for students or teachers. It was a course in which teachers and students seem often to have engaged in real conversation. It was a course which seems to have enabled many students to claim authority over language and their lives. All in all, it was a course from which present-day teachers of composition could learn much that would be of value.

The combative pedagogical style of English 1–2 would probably not work in today's classrooms. Thirty-three assignments per semester would now probably be too many. It no longer seems desirable to try to centralize composition teaching under one strong authority. However, there are elements of English 1–2 which are still both practicable and exemplary. Collaborative teaching is one of these. The use of sequenced assignments to drive a process in which students become increasingly invested is another. The use of student writing as the subject material for classroom discussion is still another. I gave a talk on English 1–2 at a 1993 conference on the teaching of writing, and a teacher in my audience asked me to explain why anyone now would want to run such a course. I answered by saying, as Roger Sale had told me, that the course often succeeded in engaging students in something "piercingly personal and relevant, without being private." I explained that the course had pushed students first to perceive themselves as makers of meaning and then to assume responsibility for their discourse. I explained that, as Walker Gibson had told me, the fundamental premise of the course was that "we live in the world we make in language, and if that is true, then it is our responsibility to think a little about how we are expressing ourselves."

I will leave it to other historians to determine the extent to which English 1–2 was what Albert Kitzhaber termed it—"a maverick course"—and the extent to which it exemplified wider trends in the teaching of composition at its period. I will simply conclude by saying that I regard English 1–2 as a remarkable course, and all the more so in that it flourished at a period when "current-traditional" rhetoric is supposed to have governed the teaching of writing. The course antici-pated developments which are not supposed to have occurred in composition until the 1970s or 1980s. It employed in-class publica-tions well before such a practice is thought to have become common-place. It also made use of a kind of collaborative teaching at a relatively early date. It asked students to make sense of their experience and to explain how they knew what they knew. As Robert Bagg told me, English 1–2 raised the question of the "ontological status of language" decades before what he describes as the current "revolution in English theoretical studies." The course also focused on the making of mean-ing, which by many accounts is at the heart of contemporary compo-sition studies, and did so significantly before composition studies emerged as a recognizable specialty within American English depart-ments. Again and again, I have found myself marveling at the energy, imagination, and dedication of the men who taught the course.

Appendix A

A Description of English 1–2

*T*he relation of the student to his education, of the student to his teacher, of the teacher to his subject, must be defined at the outset of English 1–2, for until we can think clearly of what we are all doing, misunderstanding and dissatisfaction are inevitable. The subject, the content, or however you want to describe it, of this course is writing. Writing is an action. It is something you do. It is not something you know about, except in the same more or less ineffective way you know about health, or you know about the symphony. You do know, for example, that Good Writing should be Clear, Coherent, and somehow Pleasing to the reader. But how to make your writing clear, coherent, and pleasing is another matter altogether. Both you and your teacher know various rules, for the use of the comma, even perhaps for constructing a paragraph—as if it were made of building blocks.

Your teacher can tell you a little about where to begin, and he will do so by handing out carefully phrased assignments and commenting on them. It would be nice to add that he can finally tell you whether or not you succeed in what you have done when you hand in your paper. The fact is that writing remains an art, and about art no one knows how to teach another how to succeed, no one knows enough to pronounce finally that this or that example is a success. A teacher may praise something that a student has written. Another

This description, although not dated, was written in the late 1950s. The mimeographed document whose text I have here reproduced may be found in "Excerpts from description of English 1–2, usually read aloud on second day of class," in Box 1, English 1–2 Collection, Amherst College Archives.

teacher, conceivably, might make a different judgment. This may not seem fair, but such is the world once you leave childhood behind. Lawyers, no matter how clearly they present their cases, do not always win. Medical doctors sometimes make wrong diagnoses. As for literary judgments, there are critics who do not praise *The Faerie Queene* by Edmund Spenser (1552?–1599). There is a wide difference of opinion about Henry Miller, Samuel Beckett, and so on. These are the facts of your situation—of your teacher's situation—in English 1–2. Writing, even for freshmen in Amherst College, is an art. You may feel at times that you are not being taught what you ought to be taught, that your teacher does not seem to give you the answers you seek, but you actually are in a situation where no one knows the answers. This is only a pose, in practice. The best we can do is treat writing—and the writer—with respect and imagination, and in our conversations about writing and the writer hope to say something. In the classroom we shall have good moments and moments not so good. Do not expect too much. On the other hand, be sure you expect enough.

For instance, at certain levels of education the substance of knowledge, what we are to think about, is supplied by the teacher, and the term paper, the quiz and examination, serve to measure how much has been retained by the student of what has been transmitted to him. At Amherst you will find that the burden of knowledge usually falls on the student. Thus in English 1–2 you supply for your writing your own information, material, whatever you want to call it. After all, you have received an expensive education, you have probably been taught well, you have held various jobs and have played games, and you have had your own thoughts and feelings for eighteen years, more or less. This is your "experience," and from this seemingly shapeless, yet entirely individual source, you will derive whatever it is you have to say. If on first looking at an assignment you do not immediately recognize how you should proceed, you need not be unduly alarmed, for this is normal, expected, intended. Upon reflection, however, you ought to be able to find something in your own past experience to talk about. If you wait for your teacher to tell you, you will be disappointed.

You supply the material for your own discourse, while the assignments are contrived both to define a way of thinking and writing about something and to direct our general movement from day to day throughout the term. Obviously there is a discrepancy here. There is nothing perfunctory about them, and you are deceived if they look easy. Every year, this teaching staff makes a new sequence of assignments, dealing with a new and different problem, so that for all concerned, teacher and student, this is a new course, a fresh progression in thought and expression, a gradual building up of a common vocabulary, a more precise definition of terms. Whatever continuity you construct from one paper to another, from one class discussion to the next, will be your continuity, and yours alone. It can only be as good as you make it, no better, no worse. In the actual day by day conduct of the course, English 1–2 can become, at its best, a dramatic dialogue, where you and your teacher exchange remarks, you and your fellow students converse, with a certain amount of common understanding. This is enough to expect, and it is really a good deal. There will be no verbal formula to memorize, and although there is, as in all courses, a vocabulary to pick up and repeat, you will within a relatively short time, a few months, a year or two, be able to say only what you can say for yourself. Whatever you learn, you learn. This goes for all formal education, when looked at from any distance.

As for your teacher, he does not exist to give you the answers. His function is to ask questions, and if by inadvertence he should ever chance to tell you something, you should immediately turn the questioning on him. Whatever answers you reach in this course, they will be your own. You will do your own learning.

Of course your teacher will attempt to control the direction the discussion takes in the classroom. He will also read your papers. Specimen papers will be mimeographed and brought to class to be scrutinized. Your teacher will correct your papers, commenting on them in general, and at the same time pointing out those mechanical errors and careless faults which you alone can remove. Much of our conversation in class will be about ideas, techniques, meanings, but it should be said emphatically that your teacher is intent upon cleaning up your writing wherever it needs it. If you want to learn to write decently you will be able to do so.

Our regular policy is to invite the student to rewrite—as many times as he wants—any paper he is disappointed in. This is a standing invitation, and your teacher will read as many versions as you have energy to produce. When you hand in a rewritten paper include it with the original.

Your teacher will keep a record of your work, but grades are not placed on individual papers.

Finally some practical matters. Provide yourself with a snap-back binder. Put in it the mimeographed specimen papers, the assignments, your own papers, and bring it to class regularly. Use ink or typewriter, (dark ribbon, double space), write on one side of the paper, and leave a margin on the left hand side for possible comments.

APPENDIX B

English 1 Assignments for Fall 1946

1. a) Reflect on your resources for writing in English 1–2 and make a list of subjects—*from experiences outside the classroom*—you know you know.
   b) Select one in which you claim special expertness.
   c) Give reasons to support this claim.
   d) Write a paragraph, one page, in which you write out a) b) c) as an "English paper."

2. Write a paper, two pages, demonstrating or displaying this expertness which you claim.

3. a) Express again the subject of [the] paper just handed in.
   b) Redefine this subject so that it is manageable in this course.

4. a) Write a paper on an action you have repeatedly performed with distinction.
   b) Tell exactly how you performed this action on a particular occasion.

5. a) How did you learn this action?
   b) What did you do to learn?
   c) Define "learn" in this context.

The mimeographed documents from which I have taken these assignments are in two folders, "Eng 1–2 1946/47 Sec 1g [Baird] Assignments" and "Eng 1 1946/47 Sec E [Gibson]," in Box 1, English 1–2 Collection, Amherst College Archives.

6. a) Write a paper on an action you performed once and only once with distinction, an action you performed once but were unable to repeat.

   b) Tell exactly how you did it.

7. Rewrite assignment #4.

8. Contrast papers written for Assignments 6 and 7 (technique and fluke) and make a list of differences between a Technique and a Fluke.

9. Make a vocabulary (a list of keywords with definitions) for this course. Do not use [a] dictionary.

10. "One man's fluke is another man's technique." Take a new personal example and show how an accidental performance of one man might reasonably be a matter of conscious skill for another.

11. "One man's routine is another man's technique." Take an example and show how routine behavior of one man might reasonably be conscious and purposeful for another.

12. Copy 5b, "What did you do to learn?"

   b) Rewrite—using original or a new example?—in light of present knowledge of meaning of *learn*.

   c) Look at example of fluke and using the vocabulary of this course express what the difficulty is in learning how to perform a fluke.

13. Rewrite any paper you like.

14. a) Describe a technique that has become a routine.

   b) Briefly describe a situation where this routine performance would be unsatisfactory.

   c) Tell exactly what you would do and how you would do it to make your performance satisfactory.

15. Describe exactly the situation (circumstances, time, place, persons) when you learned something from another person, a coach or teacher, at the moment when you became aware that you had learned it.

   b) What had the coach or teacher done to teach you?

   c) What did you do to learn?

16. Make a list of the verbs which you used in paragraph "c" [above].
    b) Write a new paragraph using these words [and] showing how you learned this action.

17. Rewrite or [write] a completely new version of a technique and the process of learning it.

18. List three standards or scales of successful performance, omitting those used as examples in class, such as a batting average.
    b) Select one and translate the figures standing for very good and very bad performance. By translate we mean, express in English.

ON SATURDAY, NOVEMBER 16, 1940, Cornell defeated Dartmouth 7–3. With less than three seconds to play, the score Dartmouth 3—Cornell 0, Bill Murphy caught a pass in the end zone, sealing the doom of one of the fightingest Dartmouth teams in history.

Cornell had advanced to the Dartmouth 6 yard line. There followed three line plays which netted 5 yards. Cornell was then penalized 5 yards for an extra time out period. Cornell passed and Hall of Dartmouth knocked it down instead of catching it as he might well have done. An official started to put the ball down on the 20 yard line, meaning it was Dartmouth's ball on downs, but he changed his mind and replaced it on the Dartmouth 6 yard line and gave it to Cornell. With 3 seconds to play Scholl passed to Murphy in the end zone and the game was over, Cornell 7—Dartmouth 3. Coach Snavely supposed, it was said, that on the pass which was knocked down both teams had been offside.

After the game coaches and officials admitted that Cornell had five plays in the scoring series. Referee Friesell refused to make a statement.

ON MONDAY, NOVEMBER 18, Asa Bushnell, head of the Eastern Intercollegiate Football Association declared his association has no authority to change the 7–3 score. Nor, he said, do the officials have any authority to change their decision after it has been made. The Dartmouth–Cornell game was, he said, "a rather unique case."

Compiling records of football games is done by an organization that has no power to make any changes in the scores of games.

The whole point seems to revolve about the question whether there was a double offside on the pass thrown just before the final pass. Films of the game are being developed feverishly.

The Dartmouth Indians were hailed on the Dartmouth campus as "victorious heroes." The Dartmouth coach told a rally that Friesell was a "great referee" and that Dartmouth will abide by the decision of the Eastern Intercollegiate Football Association.

ON TUESDAY, NOVEMBER 19, Referee Friesell publicly admitted he had been in error when he gave the Big Red a fifth down. Cornell relinquished all claim to victory. Dartmouth accepted the triumph. Only by this combination of circumstances could the score be reversed, for there is no authority beyond the colleges themselves for correcting the error. Cornell in doing this removed itself from the list of undefeated teams, and it has had 18 straight victories.

ON WEDNESDAY, NOVEMBER 20, President Day of Cornell in speaking at a rally likened Cornell's tribulations to the ill fortunes of Job, and he said he has been "deeply resentful of some of the things the season has brought to the university and the team." The Captain of [the] football team is reported in the hospital with a stomach ailment.

ON NOVEMBER 21, Commissioner Bushnell of the Eastern Intercollegiate Football Association said that revising the score of the Dartmouth–Cornell football game should not establish a precedent. Only when an official reverses his decision on the last play of the game is it possible to accept a change in score.

ON NOVEMBER 23, the "fifth down" sundae is reported as setting the ice cream style at Hanover.

19. Make a narrative of events in chronological order and within the limits of a page.

20. Write a definition of a game.

21. What went wrong with the famous Dartmouth–Cornell game? Wrong from the point of view of a) Scholl and Murphy, b) Referee Friesell, c) the Dartmouth Captain, d) Asa Bushnell, e) the Dartmouth Coach, f) the Cornell Coach, g) the President of Cornell, h) the Captain of the Cornell team.

22. Rewrite [your] definition of a Game.

23. a) Make a list of keywords in this course.
    b) Do you want to add some? You don't have to do this.
    c) Arrange these keywords in a diagram to indicate relations.

24. a) Describe exactly a situation (place, time, circumstances) in which you taught some one something he needed to know.
    b) What did you do to teach him?
    c) What did he do?
    d) How did you know he finally succeeded in learning?
    e) Point out those things which are unteachable (those things which no one on earth can supply for another person).
    f) What kind of experience can be taught?

25. Make a list of five orders you know how to make.

26. a) Select a particular order you know how to make.
    b) Make it in particular terms—and in manageable form.
    c) Explain briefly your reasons for establishing each position in this order.
    d) How else could this order be made?
    e) How would you prove that one [(b) or (d)] is "right"?

27. Describe a mess of physical objects and tell how you straightened it out, how you put it in order.

28. Go to the Library. Note the number of any card in the catalog. Find the book which the number designates. (If it is not in its place, you may assume that it has been loaned. Return to the catalog and begin afresh with another number.) In writing, report a) the number, b) how you got from a number on a card to the book, c) the author and title of the book.
    d) What, specifically, is signified when you say of this book that it is *in its place?*
    e) What is demanded of anyone wishing to find the book?

29. Go to the library and follow the directions in the above assignment, taking another book number to start with. On finding the book examine the other volumes on the same shelf.
    a) What subject do they appear to have in common?
    b) What elements of their numbers do they have in common?
    c) What inference can you draw as to the relation between the number and the subject?

d) With respect to other elements these numbers will all differ. By examining the backs of books as they sit on the shelf ascertain what relation these elements of the numbers bear to the books.

e) You have established two relationships between the numbers and the physical objects. How, then, would you describe the order employed in arranging books in the Library?

30. a) Assume that you have a newly purchased book and have the task of assigning it to its appropriate number. What decision would you first have to reach?

b) What means would you have for reaching it?

c) Your next operation would be to determine the proper number (which, you have observed, consists of two elements). What sort of information would you require in order to do this?

d) Which is the more complex, finding the book after it has been assigned to its place in the order, or placing the book where it may be found?

e) What does the phrase *in its place* signify to the Library? To the user?

31. a) Make a complete vocabulary with definitions for this course.

b) Express the argument or order of this course in a paragraph.

ASSIGNMENT FOR LONG PAPER

1. Make a complete list of assignments.

2. Make a vocabulary for this course, i.e., make a list of words and define them in the context of this classroom.

3. Write an essay of not over five pages expressing the sequence of ideas you have perceived in this term's work.

GENERAL DIRECTIONS: Do not merely repeat your list in No. 1 in sentence and paragraph form. Do not make the sequence of ideas the sequence of time in which you did the assignments. What you should do is translate the list in No. 1 into terms of your own conclusions, as if you were telling someone who is interested what you have learned.

PARTICULAR DIRECTIONS: Your list in No. 1 should refresh your memory of what you have done. You should read over the papers you have written. Your list in No. 2 will lead to the "subject" of your essay if you decide which one of these words in your vocabulary is the keyword of the course. By keyword is meant the word most important for you to use and understand to get on in this course. Make a statement about this word, a statement of what you have done, and this ought to give you the "subject" of your essay in No. 3. Now write this essay, expressing the argument as it has been built up in your mind, the sequence of ideas, telling what you think and how step by step you came to think it.

FINAL EXAMINATION

The purpose of this examination is to test your ability to reflect and to write under pressure of time and with no resources but your own. Connect your answers to the questions in part II to form a coherent essay. You must finish this examination.

PART I. The two following passages are excerpts from term papers written in this course. Read them carefully.

A

The keyword of this course is thus "order." This is so because we have been learning to eliminate confusion from our thoughts and our writing, and this we must do if we are to succeed as college students. By our trips to the library, as I have shown, and by the other examples I have given, it will be seen that our instructors have been exposing us to the principle of orderly thought, the principle that underlies all the basic forms of knowledge. This principle, now that I see it, is as simple as it is obvious. I have found that just as I eliminated confusion from my workshop by putting each tool in its proper place, so I eliminate confusion from my writing by putting each word and thought in its proper place. In this course I have thus learned first to consider the principle of order in my subject and then to write. In this way I am sure to write clearly and with the correct order of my subject in mind.

B

The keyword of this course, to sum up, seems to me to be "order." This word suggests the kind of answer we have agreed to give to the key question of the course: "What are you doing?" When some one asks me this question, I cannot tell him *all* I am doing, even if he had time enough and I had words enough. I must select *from* my action, I must talk *about* it. Now the answer to this question that communicates knowledge, we have seen, is the answer that enables the questioner to follow us in doing the action. We must therefore answer him in words that communicate some of the possible steps he can follow to perform the action himself. For it is a sequence of steps that really makes the difference between doing and not doing the action. A good football coach is one who can size up a prospect and give him a few, often a very few, instructions that turn the prospect into a valuable player. The coach knows, as my coach knew in the example I described earlier, that if a prospective guard can move his body so as to do this, then that, he can control the rest of the actions involved in "pulling out." A bad coach is one who fusses about little acts that don't help you to do anything else.

It would seem from all this that the "order" of any action is a varying thing. It varies from situation to situation and from person to person. It changes constantly and is constantly modified to meet new conditions. But that is only natural. It is still true that if I communicate the order of an action to some one, then he will know just what he *can* change and adapt. Order then means a describable relationship between individual movements I can direct and a successful result. And to describe this relationship has meant good writing in this course.

PART II

1. What meaning is given to "order" in passage A? Work it out and state it in your own words.
2. What meaning is given to "order" in passage B? Work it out and state it in your own words.
3. Which passage, A or B, do you find the more useful for your guidance in writing? Or do you find them equally useful? Or do you find neither useful? Why?
4. Illustrate your answer to 3 by showing how you would select and define a subject to write about from your own experience. This subject, preferably, should not be one you have used in a course assignment. Do not write the paper: merely show how you would go about writing it and why.

Appendix C

An Exchange of Letters between
T. Baird and R. Varnum

Regarding a visit to the Emily Dickinson house
in Amherst, Massachusetts

Transcript of handwritten letter from T. Baird to R. Varnum, December 6, 1990:

Dear Mrs. Varnum,

While this is fresh in my mind let me add to your admirable summary of my incoherent remarks. As you describe it, was this different from other freshman courses in composition? Of course I think it was and there is evidence others thought so in the way it caused hostile criticism or notice at least and as it lives in the minds of students years after it is all over. This is the problem: how to express what—if anything—was this uniqueness?

As you state it and as I certainly described it it was an attempt at making teachers and students aware of a common enterprise, what one would expect of a college (and no longer exists). As you also say, it was an attempt "to stimulate intellectual exchange" isn't this where your "subject" (if Eng 1 is a subject?)lies? What was intellectual abt it?

That man at Wesleyan what is his name? wrote a book abt composition teaching. He called Eng 1 a course contemptuously in problem solving. There is something to be said for this if you add how language works in setting and solving a problem. I think the course over the years at least for me developed the capacity to stand outside a problem, to see it as a matter of how language is used, of what language can do in solving it. How much of experience anyway, can be expressed in language? 5%? What abt in music? in other symbols? What then was the 95% unexpressed? Can you be aware of that while talking and writing? What does the awareness of the inexpressible do to your own conviction in what you are saying? Will you, say, die for these words? No? Then what?————Here we fade off in each one's belief. And will. I used to try to say, finally, *I exert my WILL.* I'm, say, patriotic, finally. Not reasonable I know. Lots of faults.

I wonder if I am saying somethg abt the unsayable? This was for me the heart of my teaching. I say this in so many ways.

So we had assignments—as I tried to make them—that faced this. How do you find the car keys when they are "lost"? What does "lost" mean? (We had some nice ones on this).★ How do you "see" a Historic Object? Say E. Dickinson's House. I used to take visitors over there, stand. What did they "see"? Someone who taught the course when on a sabbatical in Rome (Italy) wrote me that indeed he had just discovered that you have to "know" what you are looking for to "see" it. He was surprised that an assignment he had taught told him something he hadn't known. And so on. Here is what made the course different (if it was). The kind of assignments we (or I) made. Not true of all of them. Incredibly simple some of them. But extremely difficult really. Better minds than ours have been occupied. What is order? What is chaos?

So I say it was not only a social event, an attempt at collegiality, but an intellectual search or exercise.

As for "moral" purpose, which you mention, well I always cd spot a Xian Scientist. Their use of language was different. Also a strictly brought up Catholic, whose use of language was different. I am aware of how delicate this distinction is, I mean how hard it wd be to try to explain myself. "Moral" in an awareness of how words are used, how listening to, say, a president of the US you feel he is deceiving or self deceived etc etc etc. This goes on endlessly, once you move out of the classroom.

Oh yes, I said nothing abt the attempt we made to interest teachers in other departments, classics, economics, etc to teach the course. Only partly successful, I wanted it not to be an English Department course, but a college course. It was this not being an Eng Dept course that aroused feelings among teachers who wanted it to be an Eng Dept course, read *I H IV* [Shakespeare's *Henry IV, Part 1*] say.

★*Where are all the lost objects in the world? A chapter in Gulliver?*

As for the inexpressible as I call it, look at (say)
Neither Out Far nor In Deep?

What is that abt? Frost is full of poems where you are using language abt the final mysteries. In that sense then we were a literary course.

Ah well, it is all in the past and I never cd say what was going on.

Yours etc

Theodore Baird

PS. I think you would learn more by simply doing an assignment than by listening to me run on.

E.G.

Go to the E. Dickinson House
Look at it
What do you see?
Define "Looking at a poet's residence"

or

I lost my car keys
I found them
Where were they?

Endless examples.

Transcript of letter from R. Varnum to T. Baird, December 13, 1990:

Dear Professor Baird,

I went to the Dickinson house yesterday. I had made an appointment with my friend, Ruth Jones,[1] to go through the house and had let her know it was for your sake that I was coming. I was intrigued that in giving me an assignment, you were setting yourself up as my teacher. In submitting the following to you, of course, I am indicating my willingness to be your student.

The assignment you gave me, in case you have forgotten its exact wording, was this: Go to the E. Dickinson house. Look at it. What do you see? Define "Looking at a poet's residence."

I arrived a little early for my 1:30 appointment with Ruth. As it was a pleasant afternoon, I took a few moments to stroll around the grounds before ringing the doorbell. What I saw from the outside was a two-story brick house in the federal style, crowned by a third story, white-clapboarded attic and, ultimately, a cupola. The main entrance is on the south side, facing Main Street. The door is framed by white pillars and surmounted by a small balcony. All the windows, of which there are two in each quadrant of the front facade, are framed by green shutters. The main section of the house is quite square, but a secondary wing extends to the east and back. There is a screened porch at the back of this wing and a colonnaded verandah off the main section of the house on the west. The house stands on the western side of a double or perhaps a triple lot. A huge oak tree is immediately to the east of the house, and a small herb garden is laid out to the east and back of the tree. A double garage, adorned with a weathervane, is behind the house on the west.

I rang the doorbell at 1:30 sharp. Ruth welcomed me and informed me that as no one else had signed up, I was to have a private tour. She told me a number of things about the house I could not have known just by looking at it. She said the house was built in 1813 by Emily's grandfather. Emily was born in the house in 1830 and died there in 1886. She lived within its walls all her life except for the fifteen years between approximately her tenth and twenty-fifth birthdays. It was Emily's father, Edward Dickinson, who in 1855, added the wing at the back of the house, the verandah on the west, and the cupola. Ruth also told me that the house next door to the west had belonged to Emily's brother, Austin. There had been a trolley line up Main Street during Emily's lifetime, and the railroad tracks crossed Main Street two blocks to the east, as they still do today.

The floor plan of the main section of the house is arranged neatly in quadrants around the central entry way and stairwell. On the first floor, only the front and back parlors on the west side of the house are open to the public. Upstairs, only Emily's bedroom in the southwest corner is open.

Ruth invited me to sit with her in the front parlor while she told me a little about the history of the house and showed me some historic photographs. We sat on either side of the Italianate, marble fireplace, just as if we were Emily's guests for tea, and I admired the dainty tea service which was arranged carefully on a table to my right. Ruth told me the tea service had actually belonged to the Dickinson family. She added, however, that Emily had not been comfortable in the role of hostess. Once, when she was in her thirties, she had been expected to help entertain her father's guests, who were all dignitaries from Amherst College. Emily had merely swept downstairs in her dramatic white dress, stridden quickly through the back and front parlors, and disappeared upstairs again.

Ruth said that the now austerely furnished parlors must have looked very different in Emily's day. The woodwork, which is now painted white, was covered in dark varnish then. As can be seen in old pictures, there used to be heavy drapes at the windows and French doors, flowered rugs on the floor, and as was usual in Victorian homes, quantities of bric-a-brac. Much of the present furniture never belonged to the Dickinsons. The square piano in the back parlor, however, resembles the one Emily used to play.

Upstairs, before we entered the poet's bedroom, Ruth showed me the old Dickinson family cradle in which Emily herself may have been rocked, and portraits of the four men who are thought to have been, along with her father and brother, the important men in Emily's life. In the bedroom, she pointed first to the narrow, sleigh bed which had actually been Emily's own. She then directed my attention to the basket, set on the windowsill, in which the poet is said to have lowered gingerbread to her nephew. She showed me a facsimile of the small, cherry writing table, its writing surface not two feet square, at which Emily penned thousands of letters and many of her 775 poems. Together, Ruth and I admired the poet's white damask dress, with its hand-crocheted lace and fine vertical tucks, which is displayed on a dressmaker's dummy inside a glass case. Ruth pointed out the deep pocket in the right side seam of the skirt in which she likes to imagine Emily always carried the stub of a pencil and a scrap of paper. From the smallness of her dress and the shortness of her bed, we could infer that Emily was a short-statured woman. Ruth pointed out a silhouette that was made of Emily when she was fifteen and shows her to have had a receding chin. She also showed me a photograph of a painting done for Emily of Indian pipes, her favorite forest plant. I asked about the Japanese tatami matting on the floor of the bedroom, and Ruth said similar matting had covered the floor in Emily's day.

I asked Ruth if she ever imagines Emily to be present in the house. Ruth said she has felt Emily most strongly in the cupola and in the basement, both of which areas are closed to the public. The basement is still much as it was when Emily lived in the house, with an earthen floor, cavernous shelves for storing canned goods and preserves, and a large granite table, with a trough down the center, at which Emily and her sister used to slaughter chickens. Emily is known to have spent many private hours in the cupola and from there, Ruth attests, she could have seen the whole of the Pioneer Valley, including Amherst College and the Holyoke Range to the south, Mt. Sugarloaf and Mt. Toby to the north, and on a clear day, Mt. Greylock far to the west.

A sense of place infuses her poetry, I mused, or as Dickinson herself said, she saw "New Englandly." Without the harshness of her native winters, I do not believe she would have found life adequate to the measure of her Calvinistic soul. Clearly, she was much acquainted with grief.

I asked Ruth if she didn't find a kind of arrogance in Dickinson's poetry.

"She knew she was brilliant," Ruth said. "That may partly explain her reclusiveness. She couldn't afford to waste time on those less brilliant than she."

"I find it remarkable in a woman of that period," I said, "to have believed in herself so strongly as to have resisted the allures of marriage and society. She must have felt herself elected to the poet's calling."

"Many women in those days chose not to marry," Ruth said. "Also, Dickinson had some sort of eye ailment. It may simply have hurt her eyes to go out in the direct sun."

"I may be misinterpreting her," I conceded. "A historian has always to be aware of her limitations."

Ruth asked me how I intended to handle my assignment for you. I said I wanted to write it up as if it were actually an English 1 assignment, and thus not to allow it to exceed three pages.[2] I wanted it to include some kind of discussion of how I knew what I knew, so I would organize it in at least three sections: first what I had seen with my own eyes, then what I had learned from her, and finally what I had inferred with the help of my experience and my knowledge of Dickinson's poetry. I said I wanted also to give you some idea of my operating principles as a historian.

"I need to say something about empathy," I concluded.

Ruth told me pointedly that she had occasionally taken actresses through the house who had performed or were performing in *The Belle of Amherst* and who wanted to imbibe the spirit of the place. Recently, she had shown the house to an actress from Czechoslovakia who couldn't speak a word of English.

Ruth and I know something about one another's writing. In 1987/88 we were classmates in Stephen Oates's[3] biography seminar. Oates, as I knew Ruth remembered, had taught us that empathy was the most important quality a biographer could bring to her enterprise. Ruth and I have continued to meet every six weeks with five other former participants in Oates's seminar to discuss and critique what one of us will have written and circulated in advance. I am the rhetorician in our group. Two others have backgrounds in literature. Ruth and the remaining three are historians. Their function, as it has evolved, has been constantly to remind the rest of us of the importance of evidence. My function has been to focus the group's attention on the issues of audience and purpose.

"You must find it intimidating to be writing this for Baird," Ruth remarked. "Do you think it is because you have recently been to his house that he chose this assignment for you?"

I told her that the thought had occurred to me. I also told her that I was in the process of reading your "A Dry and Thirsty Land," and that I knew from the evidence of that essay of your own historical bent and of your deep identification with the town in which you have lived for 63 years. She told me she thought you had been pleased when she succeeded in having your house listed in the National Historic Register. She said it is an example of Wright's Usonian House and that the floor functions as a solar collector.

I thanked Ruth for her time, then drove south on Route 116, past Shays Street,[4] over the Notch, to the late Victorian, Eastlake style house in Springfield where I have lived for thirteen years. A house, I felt sure, can be read much as one reads a poem—as holding secrets of a human heart. Our houses, moreover, both shape and reflect our personalities.

I shall expect some response from you, but I will not presume to say what form that response should take. I shall leave the next move in this game up to you.

Respectfully,
Robin Varnum

Transcript of handwritten letter from T. Baird to R. Varnum, December 17, 1990:

Dear Mrs.Varnum,

I did not presume to be your teacher when I proposed you try doing an assignment, suggesting that you wd then learn something abt Eng 1. The assignment, looking at a house, and seeing it as a poet's residence, then defining how this seeing was done, was not well phrased. I had no chance to talk abt "seeing," as I wd have done to a class.

Your paper is excellent, A+, very nicely written, perceptive, well-organized. No one can teach you anything abt this kind of writing.

If, speaking as an Eng 1 teacher I say to you, it is entirely unsatisfactory you will understand why students felt frustrated, disgusted, angry with me. So that is something to learn.

Let me see if I can explain myself. My brother-in-law owned and operated a factory that made X-ray tubes. When we visited we wd always make a tour of the factory. I cd, I suppose, have written a paper on going to see a factory that made X-ray tubes. I cd begin on the ground floor, having reached the building down Stamford Avenue, & then moved from floor to floor, from department to department, making relations in time and space: then . . . there . . . Finally I wd look at the balance sheet. If you read this you wd say quite fairly, yes, yes, you have located operations and things, you have made a sequence of sentences that move smoothly one after another, it is good English. Certainly but what is this being made, what is an X-ray tube, how does it go together, how does it work? Then I should have to say to you, I haven't the faintest idea. I know a few words electron, anode, cathode, but not what they mean. I can write and write well about something I know nothing about. In other words the person who saw this building and the things in it on one floor after another did not know what he was looking at or did not know how to see what was there to be seen.

Do you accept what I have been saying? As a writer I was undefined, just a brother-in-law, ignorant. I wd say to him, A temple of marvels, as far as I cd go in imagining and expressing that imagining.

This is my third attempt to respond and I do not want to raise too many issues but stay with what you say you saw. Sentence by sentence makes me ask who is this person saying this? What position is she taking in using these words? As a teacher I wd ask this of every sentence.

You have no trouble with what I have just said, do you? You are as undefined as I was looking at the manufacture of a delicate instrument.

The Emily Dickinson house as you write abt it is a museum. Define museum. Here is a cradle, E.D. may have slept in it. Here is a table. E D may have written poems on it. Poems? Was she a poet? Where as you look at these objects do you see poetry? How do you get from the doorway, a certain style, to a poem? What do you SEE? You use the word *empathy,* as if that could, that word, possibly lead you to the poet. What do you suppose the woman from Czechoslovakia who knew no English made of looking? Mrs. Jones must have wondered many times, what do people think they are seeing. You say top of p.3, you want to do something abt D.'s poetry. You don't do it, do you?

Why not? One answer might be, nobody knows how to. Of course English professors we know go on abt Social History, the very latest way of talking, and place furniture and an unpaved cellar floor in some context "to explain" a poem, as if houses weren't much alike at any one time, as if the house somehow made the poetry. But not for other members of the family. How I run on.

The plain fact is the person who looks at a poet's residence is really not able to express much of what he feels.★ That was (as I see it) the point of the assignment. And the point of many assignments we made, to bring the writer to an awareness of the inexpressible.

Frost once made a sentence, the endg of which I cannot recall, but it began, "it has always been a matter of wonder to me that Emily Dickinson"—what? lived and wrote poems in Amh? It is this wonder, the marvel of it, that she did I see when I look if I think at all abt it in passing the house. Just as I called that factory a temple of wonders. This is my response to what I do not understand. One response I mean. There are others.

Have I by concentrating as I hope on *seeing* made myself clear? I think maybe something can be learned abt what went on from this exchange.

Yours etc
T.B.

★*I do not deny the feelings.*

APPENDIX D

Selected Student Papers
Written for or about English 1–2

1. ROBERT BAGG, ARMSTRONG PRIZE-WINNING PAPER, SPRING 1954

THE ARMSTRONG PRIZE, in the form of books to the value of $55 to members of the freshman class who excel in composition, will be awarded this year for the best paper on the following exercise.

English 2: Reading Period Exercise.   due May 21–22

The world's contents are *given* to each of us in an order so foreign to our subjective interests that we can hardly by an effort of the imagination picture to ourselves what it is like. We have to break that order altogether,—and by picking from it the items which concern us, and connecting them with others far away, which we say "belong" with them, we are able to make out definite threads of sequence and tendency; to foresee particular liabilities and get ready for them; and to enjoy simplicity and harmony in place of what was chaos. . . . As I said, we break it: we break it into histories, and we break it into arts, and we break it into sciences: and then we begin to feel at home. We make ten thousand separate serial orders of it, and on any one of these we react as though the others did not exist. We discover among its various parts relations that were never given to sense at all, and out of an infinite number of these we call certain ones essential and lawgiving, and ignore the rest. . . . . The miracle of miracles, a miracle not yet exhaustively cleared up by any philosophy, is that the given order lends itself to the remodeling. It shows itself plastic to many of our scientific, to many of our aesthetic, to many of our practical purposes and ends.

William James, *The Will to Believe,* 1897, p. 118–120

Your project is to document this passage—and qualify it if you wish—in the light of your own experience as a student at Amherst. You should write a connected and graceful essay. What follows is a suggested order of steps, but you should feel free to organize your argument in any way that seems appropriate to your own particular situation.

1) Reflect on your courses during freshman year, and choose a particular experience from one of them that seems relevant to what James is talking about.

2) Describe the situation: where were you; what were you doing?

3) Describe—"by an effort of the imagination"—how the world's contents were given to you in an order foreign to your subjective interests. Just what subjective interest was this order foreign to?

4) How did you come to break that order? What items did you select and connect?

5) What sequence and tendency thereupon emerged; what liabilities were you then ready for?

6) What simplicity and harmony could you then enjoy? Did you feel at home, or not? How did you feel?

7) Conclude with a paragraph on "the miracle of miracles": in the light of your own student experience, can you suggest why the world is plastic to our purposes and ends?

While re-examining the year's notebooks and hour tests, trying to remember a "given order" I had broken, I noticed that all the relationships I was making were being made right now, in the present, for the purpose of writing this reading period paper. I decided that when I found an order "foreign to my subjective interest," which I had broken, I would be answering this larger interest. I would be breaking the given order of my student experience for the purpose of documenting James's passage and writing this paper. Answering this paper, then, is my present subjective interest.

The "given order" was the welter of history lectures, calculus equations, translated Greek classics, and old English One papers on

Goldie the Lioness. I *gave* myself this "order," though it was fashioned from a set of circumstances I was *subjected* to. But viewing the note-books and quizzes in the light of my interest in finding a broken order I had nothing with which to work but chaos.

When I had been studying my courses during the year I hadn't felt they were chaotic. "The Renaissance" seemed a perfectly logical way of talking about an outgrowth of the Commercial Revolution. The equation, force equals mass times acceleration, was a spectacularly useful tool in physics. What made these once comfortable ideas "for-eign" was my attempt to rearrange them into a broken order.

A recent physics paper demanded that I derive a given equation for the charge/mass ratio of an electron. What I was interested in was the derivation, and my world at that time was my previous knowledge of physics. The quantities in the Arons-given equation were related in a way I had never seen before. But I had seen them related in my pre-vious world of physics. By eliminating the language of quantities not contained in the equation I was able to manipulate the remaining concepts dexterously enough to write a paper deriving the right expression.

A history question asked me to explain why monarchies arose in Northern Europe and city states arose in Italy at the time of the Com-mercial Revolution. My reading about the rise of monarchies and the Commercial Revolution must be connected. I break the order of the reading to answer the question. When reading a French passage I often lose track of the meaning, and am confronted with a garbled mess of unlooked-up vocabulary words. I look up the words and the passage is no longer foreign to me.

Every sentence I read is an automatic application of my subjective interest to an order. Years ago, as a child, I must have constantly strug-gled to comprehend. Now I break the order of words and letters so fluently I am not aware of chaos.

A child lives in a chaotic world of relations "not given to sense" which are impressed on him by grown-ups. He must wash behind his ears, pick up his toys, put everything in order. It is conceivable that a two year old might frolic with a lion, if he had not made our adult relation between "lion" and "danger." What does a young boy think of when we tell him that the Moon causes the ebb and flow of the tides? He won't perceive for years the mathematical paraphernalia necessary to make this relation. As a child acquires more and more feeling for subjective interests, and more and more skill at solving complicated chaoses, he grows up.

The things I do in the electron derivation, in answering test questions, in taking notes, and in writing this paper follow the same sequence. I always begin with a purpose, like finding out what Socrates meant by Virtue. I think this "interest" is essential, even if it is the *determination* of an interest.

Once I am interested, a chaos is revealed to me out of a world I had formerly thought orderly. Each purpose has its own type of chaos. If I perform a difficult integration I am bewildered by a mathematical and algebraic chaos which is different from the fuzziness I encounter as I translate Balzac. James says it is my imagination which reveals this "order-chaos" to me. But I think his "miracle" is already in action. I have, as soon as I begin to think in a mathematical language, already eliminated most of the world's contents from consideration. And I keep eliminating and relating until I feel satisfied and comfortable. This "at-homeness" is arrived at when I make a phone call after looking up a number or pass a physics test. When I have broken an old order to new order I may have rendered one type of order-breaking automatic, like learning to read French. But still better I have created an order which may be turned to chaos at some future date by a new interest, like learning to write French.

In thinking about my student experience I have discarded everything I cannot explain in terms of "chaos" and subjective interest. I probably haven't discarded very much, but the order is so simple and everything fits together so nicely I feel like I have tossed out a lot of worthless ideas. Another sensation I get is one of layers of chaos being solved by interest, and in turn being rendered chaos by new interests. I feel like I am looking at a magazine cover with a picture of a girl sitting on the beach looking at the magazine she is appearing in. I see covers inside covers *ad infinitum*.

I can use this language of "chaos" determined by "interest" to build up a concept of time. I can define the future as "chaos", the present as using the subjective interest to make a comfortable order, and the past as an order already made, or rendered automatic.

If an anthropologist is intensely interested in deciphering some cryptics found in a Grecian temple, these three thousand year old figures become the future to him. His present is devoted to deciphering the secret language. Only when he succeeds does the stone language become a part of the past. When I say, "The Yankees will win in '54" the outcome of the pennant race is in the past according to my new language. Star calendars too are antique things, even if they extend to the year four thousand.

When I become interested in the "miracle of miracles" James talks about, I feel useless, speechless, and uncomfortable. The harmony I have built up to talk about what I did in my courses becomes chaos when I try to *explain* what I did to make the derivation, or write this paper. All I can do is tell *what* I did. All I can do is copy down the algebra, which is chaos when I try to explain the "miracle."

The last things I can say about the "miracle" before I am cut off by the barrier of silence is that the "miracle" distills to my power to say one thing is like another. And what gives this paper its punch is our corresponding ability to discover the differences in things that are "alike." For instance, in the course of retracing Thomson's derivation of the electron charge/mass ratio I say that the magnetic force acting to deflect the electron beam is the "same" as the centripetal force acting on the electrons. But then I say that each of these forces has "different" equivalents, and I can equate these differences in the language of physics to yield a useful expression. It is this same power over likeness and difference which allows me to say that what I do in the electron derivations is like what I do in this paper, and like what I do every time I use my subjective interest. But still I know that all these examples are different.

The "miracle" is the something that makes sentences, metaphors, and models. It is the wonderful "I" that plies our chaos into comfortable shapes. Words like "relate," "connect," "associate," and even "like" are euphemisms to disguise the fact that we have no way of talking about what we do to "relate." We can use this miracle I to talk about anything but itself. When I try to get closer to the "I" than this, everything is chaos, and, to kind of rephrase Dylan Thomas, "after this chaos there is no other."

—Bob Bagg

2. W. Geoffrey Shepherd, "Creativity and Apathy"

Shepherd's editorial appeared in the Amherst Student, *November 10, 1955, page 2.*

In some respects, the outlook for creative thinking on this campus is appalling. By and large, students here have a good measure of mental prowess. By and large, they learn their lessons well. But after this, by and large, they put their higher powers into cold storage.

Our case in point is the Amherst Literary Magazine. Its first two issues have been quite good. Co-editor Velton comments, "With respect to former years and to other college magazines, we are in a strong position." For the next, post-Thanksgiving issue, perhaps 40 men will submit copy, much of it of sub-par quality. Some 15 or 20 will make print during the year. About one-half of the magazine's content will be penned by the several members of the Board of the Magazine. The effective fraction of creative writers roughs out to two percent of the student body.

A Young Magazine . . .

The year-old Magazine has the handicap of youth, insofar as acquiring prestige as an undergraduate activity is a long process. Willy-nilly the Magazine leans on the creative writing course for a portion of its material. This course is limited to 15 men. The Board, which supplies the real motive force of the Magazine, is small and needs replenishing with several talented and interested men from each new class. In this sense, it is in a vulnerable position.

Yet prestige will come as the Magazine further strengthens its position, and the lower classes are showing some interest and talent. In all likelihood, the Magazine will continue its good job.

But this two percent fraction nettles us. We choose to think that creative thinking and writing, involving as they do "the integration of imagination," are on an intellectual level equal to, if not above, the learning of lessons. We hold also that there does exist, dispersed among the student body, a far greater ability to create in this fashion than the Magazine turnout indicates.

Capable Students . . .

It is easy enough to analyze why, given these assumptions, the creative output is so puny. It is a truism that the fabled rise in student capability has been matched by revised and augmented demands on time and effort. Also, most secondary schools neglect to offer training in creative thinking and writing.

A more obscure factor is the literary hyper-criticism ingrained into each of us. Who of us, armed with the tools of analysis of English 1–2 and 21–22, can but be discouraged by our own first efforts to write a short story or poem?

Furthermore, this campus, perhaps more than most, breeds a non-creative air. Do your lessons well, relax on weekends, mix in some activities and get to know the frosh. Athletic participation compares to creative writing by 15 to 1. The Amherst graduate, it is said, is admirably suited to become a personnel director for a large business. This is essentially a non-creative occupation.

If it does nothing else, English 1–2 teaches us that writing is a strenuous job, especially at first. This is perhaps the greatest deterrent to would-be spare time writers. The prospect of mental struggle, together with a host of easy distractions, can easily dissolve a creative urge.

. . . And Untried Abilities

We are not trying to deify creative writing. It is not inherently superior to other activities and the conditions which discourage it are not "bad."

Rather we suggest that the situation is worth some thought, even a little introspection. We have a hunch that some of the many who tell themselves, "I could write if I really wanted to," really couldn't. We guess too that there are a good many potential creative writers who have not as yet sounded out their own abilities.

For them the Literary Magazine provides a valuable opportunity and outlet for a skill which should not be allowed to atrophy. The contribution deadline is November 18.

—W.G.S.

3. DOUGLAS WILSON, ARMSTRONG PRIZE-WINNING PAPER, SPRING 1959

The Armstrong Prize, from the income of a fund of $2500, established in part by Collin Armstrong of the class of 1877 in memory of his mother, Miriam Collin Armstrong, consisting of $60 awarded to a member of the freshman class who excels in composition, is awarded in 1958–59 to

DOUGLAS C. WILSON

MARCH 28. On returning to London after an absence I find the people of my acquaintance abraded, their hair disappearing, also their flesh, by degrees.

People who to one's-self are transient singularities are to themselves the permanent condition, the inevitable, the normal, the rest of mankind being to them the singularity. Think, that those (to us) strange transitory phenomena, *their* personalities, are with them always, at their going to bed, at their up-rising!

Footsteps, cabs, etc., are continually passing our lodgings. And every echo, pit-pat, and rumble that makes up the general noise has behind it a motive, a prepossession, a hope, a fear, a fixed thought forward; perhaps more—a joy, a sorrow, a love, a revenge.

London appears not to *see itself.* Each individual is conscious of *himself,* but nobody conscious of themselves collectively, except perhaps some poor gaper who stares round with a half-idiotic aspect.

There is no consciousness here of where anything comes from or goes to—only that it is present.

—Thomas Hardy, 1888

*   *   *   *   *

In April it happened: the days ran together, and his mind grew passive with the weather. His books had grown heavy, and friends, in full friendship, lost that mystery of strangers by which they were acquainted. There were only the old things to repeat, or the new silence.

Aware of the dying spirit, he felt a slight frustration. It was ugly then, the failure; more days than moments, and weeks than days, were his schedule. Only something of habit kept him up; and then, in the spring, he found the remedy.

At night he retreated from college and sought a domestic scene. When the life was trite he slipped out along the streetlamps and the telephone poles, under the sky where pines were pointed. He came to a wooden footbridge, and clapped across, leaving the rush at the head-lights' traffic center.

Then he was there, and he slowed. Freshness was in the air from the courtyard hedges, and the scent of mowing. He passed the dusky houses with the dark chimneys, and a place where the doorlights slanted through gaping porches. Curtains hung bright in orange win-dows, and there were the clapboard patterns in the street light. He knew the silence by the rattle of a passing car; then the crickets were ticking. People were sitting on a terrace; he saw their cigarettes glow-ing, and the shadows. Once there was a house with children, and he stopped where another had a piano playing.

He was cleared with a fresh spirit. It was not just the people, but the trees. There were groves and the white smudge of fruit trees light-ing the landscape. He passed under the new-hanging branches and the age of the trees with their slender, skyward rising.

He could return to the college, then, when the sidewalk ended. And again, when he suffocated, he knew where to come. It would always be there; they would play the piano.

His fortune lay in this perspective. The place refreshed him because it was novel, yet suburbia to itself is rarely so diverting—not only because the people have been there since before last night and last year, but because it is a part of their existence, and every continuity is a whole without parts. A writer, on the other hand, is like a visitor, and can record only parts. Writing is a kind of important-events diary which cuts away the largest portion of an existence and can only roughly forge the rest together. This selection and joining is inevitable in writing essentially because the use of language itself involves choice. A sentence is one word at a time, and consequently there is the elimination of some total dimension.

The true-life continuity of an existence, which contributes the vital dimension to every moment, cannot be written into the moment. And although the writer must deal in moments, he cannot force the whole experience into its parts, making pools of conscious-ness. He cannot deal with life as it is to the self, but only as it might be observed. A moment of laughter is a shallow sound to any person who misses the joke, and the jokers in turn are surprised at a solemn response. In an instant they may realize the outsider's situation, but with this they lose little of their own merriment and hardly sense the other's experience.

The passing student, the outsider, hears only the sounds of some piano. He is not there relaxing after dinner, with a day's work behind him (but with him, too), and waiting for some member of the family to finish reading the evening newspaper. Nor is he seated there in the bright interior. The scene, like the time, and the touch, is a part of every moment; yet the writer must see these elements sorted and placed apart—phrased and paragraphed over a page. Experience is inexpressible because language dismantles it.

Experience is also inexpressible because language views it from without. Language, and therefore literature, is objective; words are only labels, and the writer is at best an interior decorator who paints a tear, and the word "frustration," on walls which the reader must provide for himself. He comes with half-realities.

The writer is perplexed, therefore, when he gropes for the total dimension. He would like to give his readers the whole fare, and sets about to devise some "stream of consciousness." He creates a flash-work of images and thought sequences. But the problem cannot be solved by adding more links to the chain.

It seems, then, that the author must remain the student passing. Though he may draw close to his subject, he remains an outsider. Consigned to language, he must ever be dealing in parts. And more than to a full reality, which appears to be unattainable, his readers perhaps subscribe to this distortion.

What is the writer obligated to do? It would indeed be severe to demand full reality. Good writing can only be skillful prompting which creates an intended response in the reader. If the writer cannot create an individual existence, he can suggest one. Basically, this involves the proper choosing of singularities to record; the gentle person will not commonly be found beating his wife, and trees will be green in the spring. Observed singularities are easy to reproduce. There is a word for every singularity.

A writer can observe the singularities of many lives, which surround every existence, and he can link these into some fresh confederation—like suburbia—which is rarely seen uncentrally by any insider.

And here he somewhat becomes Hardy's "poor gaper," for though he is wholly unsuited to know and reflect the sum experience, he has easily cast aside his personal preoccupation.

If a writer could catch the total dimension of a single experience, he would achieve a common position. Instead, by standing apart, he maintains his originality. Perhaps this shortcoming is his chief distinction. With half-achievement, the "poor-gaper"—the student passing, the writer—is better off than he thinks.

—Douglas C. Wilson

4. JOHN STIFLER, "LONG PAPER" ASSIGNMENT, DECEMBER 1964

Long Paper **Wed.–Thurs., Dec. 2–3**

Consider the following quotation from
W.B. Yeats's *Autobiographies:*

Some one at the Young Ireland Society gave me a newspaper that I might read some article or letter. I began idly reading verses describing the shore of Ireland as seen by a returning, dying emigrant. My eyes filled with tears and yet I knew the verses were badly written—vague, abstract words such as one finds in a newspaper. I looked at the end and saw the name of some political exile who had died but a few days after his return to Ireland. They moved me because they contained the actual thoughts of a man at a passionate moment of his life, and when I met my father I was full of the discovery. We should write our own thoughts in as nearly as possible the language we thought them in, as though in a letter to an intimate friend. We should not disguise them in any way; for our lives give them force as the lives of people in plays give force to their words. Personal utterance, which had almost ceased in English literature, could be as fine an escape from rhetoric and abstraction as drama itself. But my father would hear of nothing but drama; personal utterance was only egotism. I knew it was not, but as yet did not know how to explain the difference. I tried from then on to write out my emotions exactly as they came to me in life, not changing them to make them more beautiful. "If I can be sincere and make my language natural, and without becoming discursive, like a novelist, and so indiscreet and prosaic," I said to myself, "I shall, if good luck or bad luck make my life interesting, be a great poet; for it will be no longer a matter of literature at all."

Yeats recalls for us many of the problems concerning Masks that we have been discussing and writing about this term. He raises especially the question of his relationship to his own language, and in dealing with it, suggests an interesting paradox: in writing out his own thoughts and emotions exactly as they came to him, in writing "sincerely" or "naturally" about himself, he feels he will escape egotism. He also feels that he has been moved by what is only conventional newspaper verse.

Address yourself to this paradox in a graceful and coherent essay of five pages, using examples from your own experience and from your own or the writing of others wherever you see fit.

When the sample papers for discussion were handed out one day last September in English class, I discovered that mine was one of the two essays that Prof. Craig had selected for the class to read that day. I was a bit nervous, wondering what the general reaction would be and how my classmates would compare my work with that of the other student whose paper accompanied mine. My paper was read, and then the second one was read. As I looked at the other paper, I was impressed by its creativity in dealing with the assignment (#3); the author had developed a sort of metaphysical concept of himself in respect to the question of being true to oneself, and the whole paper seemed very imaginative. Then I looked back at my paper. It was plain and simple; it used straightforward language, with no embellishments or colorful frills. All I had done was briefly to describe three situations in which I felt that I had not been true to myself, hoping that I might thereby satisfy the question asked in the assignment. It seemed so dull and flat compared to the other paper; I said to myself, "How come I can't write something like *that*—something imaginative, something *different* from the ordinary?!"

A few minutes later, however, I was compelled to reconsider my feelings about the matter. As I listened to the class discuss the two papers, I was surprised to discover that *mine* was the one the class in general preferred. Someone said, "You know, this first paper is much easier to understand than the second one. You can tell what the first author is saying." Another student said, "The thing about this first paper is that it's *real*. I mean, he talks about the same sort of things that have happened to everybody else, and because of this you can really feel what the writer is saying."

I looked once more at my paper and realized that, in using a style that was completely straightforward and *natural,* I had succeeded pretty well in writing an essay that conveyed a response—an expression of feeling—which was clear and understandable for the reader. The other student had wrapped himself up in a contrivance which, although clever, did not clearly tell the reader what the author was saying. There was no *common ground of understanding* between reader and writer in the second paper, as there was (I venture to say) in mine.

Now that I look back at it, this experience seems to me to be an illustration of what W.B. Yeats is talking about in his *Autobiographies,* concerning writing that is "sincere" and "natural." What I did in my paper on Assignment 3 was to write down my thoughts and emotions just as they had come to me in life, not changing them to make them more beautiful. The result was—on a relative scale—similar to Yeats's experience with the poem by the dying Irish political exile. Yeats was reading a fellow Irishman's thoughts concerning his native land at a deeply passionate time of his life. The verses were not written like a creditable work of creative literature; the words were "vague and abstract." Yeats was moved by these verses, however, for he shared with the political exile a *common experience*—common feelings about his native land. Yeats knew what it was like to gaze upon the shores of Ireland and feel the spirit of patriotism in himself, and this sensation was evoked for him when he read another man's thoughts on the same scene and the same emotion. Just so, what I had written was not really what one would call a distinctly creative work of literature; it was simply an account of my emotions and thoughts from a particular experience in life. My writing had a solid effect on my fellow students, however; they quickly grasped a feeling for the experience I was recounting, because they had in all probability been through similar ones. It was not a question of *literature*—of what sort of interesting twists and turns, inventions and devices, that I could put in my writing—it was a question of *life*—of what common experiences could become the basis on which I might communicate my feelings to the reader.

I feel that this has been the general pattern of almost all the writing we have done this year in English 1. Anyone who looks at the papers we have written can see that most of them involve describing situations from our experience. I have found that what is inevitably the easiest, the clearest, and perhaps the *only* way to describe some situation is simply to *write down what happened*—what I said and thought—without any added devices, contrivances, etc. In this way, I think that I am following Yeats's directions for good self-expression, for it appears that if I can "be sincere and make my language natural, and without becoming discursive, like a novelist, and so indiscreet and prosaic," then my writing will be effective and possibly even good.

At the same time, I feel that I am not being *egotistic* in writing so much about myself in this matter. As I interpret it, egotism means biased self-representation; i.e., if I am being egotistical, I am trying to show "what a good boy am I;" I am implying that I am a "good guy," the fellow on the "right side" of the situation; I am not being at all objective about the matter. The egotistical writing that I have done has invariably been returned with comments *other* than "good." On Assignment 5, I was writing about a situation in which one of my friends had asked me if I wanted to go dump garbage on someone's front yard for a joke, and I had said no, thereby being true to the Golden Rule and asserted other ideals by which I, the great and noble White Knight, lived. The comment on the paper when it was handed back was: "A little *contrived?*" Another time, I described a water fight as a situation in which I gained knowledge. I started out by cutely saying that I wasn't trying to evade the question in the assignment by writing a comic parody or by otherwise being funny. I talked about the fight and came to the conclusion that it had taught me a lesson about the necessity of spending my time carefully, not wasting it as I had just been doing. I must have really been egotistical to think that I was good enough to write on such a frivolous experience (—it was a *classroom* experience that the assignment called for in the first place—) and come up with a good paper. When the paper was read in class three days later, my work received from Professor Craig a comment something like this: "Well, look at this student! He goes out in the hall to participate in a 'class' he calls 'water-fighting 1–2,' and, lo and behold, just like that, he learns to be a *good boy*! How amazing!" In assignment 28, I was asked to describe a situation in which I went from not being myself to being myself. In the paper I turned in, I declared in effect that I had been given an impossible task—that there had never been a situation in which I had not been myself. I defended myself as the poor frustrated freshman who is asked to do the impossible. When I got the paper back, the comments on it began, "O dear! O dear! All these complaints and self-lacerations!" Once again I had been egotistical in my presentation of myself, and my writing had not turned out very well.

The problem in my writing is to avoid this egotism, and I think that I have finally begun to learn something about how not to be egotistical in my work. When I don't try to contrive something in my writing, when I don't try to "clown around" in my paper, when I don't try to make all-encompassing defenses for "poor little me," but when instead I simply set myself to the task of describing a situation and relating my thoughts from that situation, I come up with an essay that is a relatively objective piece, not slanted through the eyes of prejudice or egotism on my part. It is probably in this way that Yeats resolves the seeming paradox that personal utterance about himself does not have to be egotism.

A question still remains in my mind, however; I understand this matter of expressing oneself sincerely and naturally, and I see what sort of writing Yeats intends to do, but in the midst of all this, I am reminded of Assignment 8 and the words of T.E. Hulme, who calls language the lowest common denominator of the emotions and says that when we write, we leave out all individuality of emotion and substitute for it a sort of stock or type emotion. Now, a talented writer like W.B. Yeats may be able to make the best of such a situation; the stock or type emotion that he expresses may be very powerful and clear, even if it has to be a *type*. Not everyone is W.B. Yeats, however, and what I ask myself is, how could this political exile, with poorly written lines and vague, abstract words, evoke in his reader such deep *personal* emotion? Certainly the poem Yeats was reading, written with words such as one finds in a newspaper, must have been an *extremely* low common denominator of emotion, yet it moved Yeats to tears. I think that the answer lies in the factor of common experience, of which I have spoken before in this paper. Yeats had shared a similar experience with this dying emigrant; therefore, it was not necessary for the writer of these lines to try to search the depths of his resources and hope to come up with verses that would be powerful enough to convey his tremendously passionate love for Ireland. All he had to do was to mention the experience of gazing upon the shores of his native land and to describe his feelings as well as he could; the reader could do the rest. In this sort of writing, the emotion is conveyed from writer to reader in the same way that electric current is conveyed from a generator to the place where the current is to be used. A current of very high voltage is generated by the generator; then this high voltage current goes through a transformer, so that the voltage is greatly reduced, say, to one hundredth the number of volts that were originally generated. This current passes through a wire, and then, when it reaches the other end of the line, its voltage can be multiplied many times by another transformer, so that the current could be made to have the same voltage which it had when it was generated. Just in the same way, the political exile transformed his deep emotion into common, newspaper-style words with no great quality; when Yeats read these same words, however, they became transformed back into deep emotion for him, because he had experienced similar feelings.

—John Stifler

NOTES

Chapter 1: A Maverick Course

1. Baird's comments are from his "Memo to the instructors, July 19, 1960," in Box 1, English 1–2 Collection, Amherst College Archives.

2. The version of the description of English 1–2 from which I have quoted is an undated, four-page document entitled "Excerpts from description of English 1–2, usually read aloud on second day of class," in Box 1, English 1–2 Collection, Amherst College Archives. I have printed this course description in Appendix A.

3. In *The Making of Knowledge in Composition*, Stephen North dates the birth of composition as a distinct academic field to the 1963 publication of Richard Braddock, Richard Lloyd Jones, and Lowell Schoer's *Research in Written Composition* (North 1987, 15).

4. Butler's assignments may be found in "Eng. 1 1954/55 Assignments as used," in Box 2, English 1–2 Collection, Amherst College Archives. These assignments have been published, and may be more easily accessible, in John Carpenter Louis, *English 1–2 at Amherst College: Composition and the Unity of Knowledge* (1971, 199–211).

5. This may be found in "'Statement for Publicizing the New Curriculum' by T. Baird—1946/47," in Box 1, English 1–2 Collection, Amherst College Archives.

6. These interviews were tape-recorded and were, for the most part, conducted in 1991. Interview sessions generally lasted ninety minutes, and I interviewed some men once, some twice, and some three times. When I had completed transcribing each of the tapes, I offered the transcript to the appropriate interviewee for his review and emendation. When he was satisfied with its wording, I used it as though it were a text.

7. It was Theodore Baird who placed much of this material in the Amherst
   College Archives. For most of the semesters during the twenty-eight years
   English 1–2 was offered, Archives now has a file folder of materials Baird
   saved from staff meetings and from his sections of the course. For each
   semester between 1946 and 1957, Archives also has a folder of materials
   from Walker Gibson's sections. Gibson told me that when he left Amherst,
   he gave these materials to Baird, who then turned them over to Archives.

Chapter 2: Running Orders through Chaos

1. Babbitt was the author of *Literature and the American College* (1908). Gerald
   Graff has described him as an "Arnoldian humanist" and as a leading critic
   of research professionalism (1987, 6, 83).

2. This series may be found in "Eng 1 1959/60 'Assignments as Used,'" Box
   3, English 1–2 Collection, Amherst College Archives.

3. On September 4, 1956, Baird sent a memorandum to his English 1–2 staff
   in which he expressed much this same principle. In 1956, he told his staff
   that "the only approach I have ever known to the difficulty of making
   teaching stick, of saying something so that another person will know and
   henceforth act differently, is in engaging the other person's interest at
   some point in what he is doing. Once his interest is engaged in trying to
   say something, of feeling the drive for expression, then, it seems to me, he
   will clean up his writing for himself. Hence we aim at his interest, using
   our utmost ingenuity in reaching him there." A copy of this memorandum is in "Eng 1 1956/57 [sec 4?] [Baird?]," in Box 2, English 1–2 Collection, Amherst College Archives.

4. Baird regularly taught the Shakespeare course right up until his retirement in 1969.

5. *The Amherst Student* is the Amherst College student newspaper.

6. This series may be found in "Eng 1 1960/61 'Assignments as Used,'" Box
   3, English 1–2 Collection, Amherst College Archives.

7. A copy of the mimeographed list which Baird circulated on May 24,
   1947, is headed: "English 1–2, Suggested Reading, May 24, 1947," and
   may be found in "Eng 2 1946/47 Sec E [Gibson]," Box 1, English 1–2
   Collection, Amherst College Archives. A copy of the list he circulated in
   April 1946 may be found in "Eng 1 1945/46 Assignments 'Brower and
   Castle,'" in Box 1, English 1–2 Collection, Amherst College Archives.

8. Baird's fall 1948 assignments are in "Eng 1-2 'Assignments as actually
   used'—1948/49," in Box 1, English 1–2 Collection, Amherst College
   Archives.

9. The fall 1956 assignments are in "Eng 1 1956/57 'Assignments as Used,'" in Box 2, English 1–2 Collection, Amherst College Archives.

10. John Butler's assignments for the fall of 1958 are in "Eng 1 1958/59 'Assignments as Used,'" Box 3, English 1–2 Collection, Amherst College Archives.

11. These excerpts are from the *Constitution* of the Charitable Fund established for Amherst College in 1818 and are quoted in Le Duc (1946, 2) and in Greene (1992, 5). Greene adds that although the Charitable Fund was created in order to provide for the expenses of "indigent" students, the college never discriminated against those who could pay for their tuition, room, and board (6).

12. My statement simplifies the actual situation. Strictly speaking, Genung and one colleague staffed the English department while another colleague, with whom they worked closely, headed his own Department of Logic and Oratory.

13. This reference to Genung is on page 5 of a 24-page memorandum entitled "English 1–2, History and Content," a copy of which is in "Eng 1 1946/47 Sec E [Gibson]," Box 1, English 1–2 Collection, Amherst College Archives.

14. A copy of this final examination is in "Eng 1 1960/61 'Assignments as Used,'" Box 3, English 1–2 Collection, Amherst College Archives.

15. Amherst College underwrote the construction of the house by advancing a mortgage loan of $7,000 to the Bairds. My information on the financing of the house is from a typescript dated November 20, 1989, written by Theodore Baird, and entitled "On Building in Amherst a House Designed by Frank Lloyd Wright," which is held in the "Baird House" file, Special Collections Dept., Jones Library, Amherst, Massachusetts.

Chapter 3: Charting the Course

1. Among other "old boys" from Amherst College on the Hum 6 staff were Thomas R. Edwards, Neil Hertz, Piers Lewis, Floyd Merritt, Thomas Whitbread, and William Youngren (Pritchard 1985, 243).

2. For his part, Craig remembers the day, shortly after the conclusion of World War II, when Poirier walked into his classroom. Craig told me, "It was a bitter cold, winter morning, and he was wearing his G.I. infantryman's winter coat, which was very long. He sat down and said, 'Teach me!' He was a very tough guy, and well, we got his attention."

3. The typescript of Craig's review is in his personal possession. The sentence I have quoted appears on page 9.

4. While English 1 was generally offered in the fall and English 2 in the spring, during the war years, both English 1 and English 2 were frequently offered during a single semester or during the summer. Whereas the course was officially an elective, it was required during the war for students who had been sent to Amherst by the Navy and recommended for those who had been sent by the Army (*Amherst College Bulletin: 1942–43*, 61).

5. According to a twenty-four-page memorandum of Baird's entitled "English 1–2: History and Content" and dated August 5, 1946, "Baird, Brower, and Craig were responsible, singly and in collaboration, for planning and administering the following army programs: the 'C' Pre-Meteorology Training Program, 48 weeks, Feb. 1942–Feb. 1943, 244 students; the Enlisted Reserve Corps Program, 4 terms of 12 weeks, Nov. 1943–Oct. 1944, 242 students; the Paraprofessional Program, 3 terms of 12 weeks, Feb. 1944–Oct. 1944, 49 students; the 2nd USMA Program, Sept. 1944–March 1945, 329 students; the 3rd USMA Program, Sept. 1945–June 1946, 802 students" (3n). A copy of this memorandum is in "Eng 1 1946/47 Sec E [Gibson]," in Box 1, English 1–2 Collection, Amherst College Archives.

6. This statement appears on page 7 of "English 1–2: History and Content," the unpublished memorandum cited in note 5 above.

7. Both the memo and drafts of the assignments themselves are in "Boundaries: working paper for developing an assignment on—n.d.," in Box 1, English 1–2 Collection, Amherst College Archives.

8. This description of English 1–2 is in "'Statement for Publicizing the New Curriculum' by T. Baird—1946/47," in Box 1, English 1–2 Collection, Amherst College Archives.

9. "English 1–2: History and Content" is in "Eng 1 1946/47 Sec E [Gibson]," in Box 1, English 1–2 Collection, Amherst College Archives.

10. A copy of "Some Practical Matters" is in "Eng 1 1946/47 Sec E [Gibson]," in Box 1, English 1–2 Collection, Amherst College Archives.

11. Assignment #25, to take the extreme example, appears in four different versions on five separate memoranda. These memoranda and other materials generated in the fall of 1946 are in two separate folders in Box 1 of the English 1–2 Collection in the Amherst College Archives. One of these folders, labeled "Eng 1–2 1946/47 Sec 1g [Baird] Assignments," contains materials saved by Theodore Baird. The other, labeled "Eng 1 1946/47 Sec E [Gibson]," contains materials saved by Walker Gibson. I worked from the materials in these two folders in order to assemble the complete list of fall 1946 assignments that I present both in the present chapter and in Appendix B. My editorial practice was to use the last mod-

ified version of each assignment. Some of the assignments appearing on Baird's typed memoranda were further emended in his hand, and these emendations probably reflect last-minute decisions reached at staff meetings. In the few cases where I could not make sense of a handwritten emendation, I consulted the somewhat abbreviated "List of Assignments," which an English department secretary typed for Baird's records at the end of the semester.

12. Baird's three-page memorandum of September 15, 1946, is in "Eng 1–2 1946/47 Sec 1g [Baird] Assignments," in Box 1, English 1–2 Collection, Amherst College Archives.

13. A Tuesday-Thursday-Saturday schedule was the alternative.

14. I have quoted this assignment and #2 to #6 below from Baird's memorandum of September 15 (see note 12).

15. Baird's three-page memorandum on "Hobbies" is in "Eng 1 1946/47 Sec E [Gibson]," in Box 1, English 1–2 Collection, Amherst College Archives.

16. This selection of student paragraphs appears on a one-page document which Walker Gibson prepared, mimeographed for his students, and discussed with them in class. The document, entitled "English 1, Section E, Assignments 2 & 3," is in "Eng 1 1946/47 Sec E [Gibson]," in Box 1, English 1–2 Collection, Amherst College Archives.

17. I have taken this assignment and #8 to #10 below from a mimeographed typescript emended in Baird's hand and entitled "Assignments for English 1–2 to be rephrased or rewritten entirely, weeks 3–4." A copy of the typescript is in "Eng 1–2 1946/47 Sec 1g [Baird] Assignments," in Box 1, English 1–2 Collection, Amherst College Archives.

18. These student responses to assignment #9 appear on "English 1: Section E, Assignment 9" in "Eng 1 1946/47 Sec E [Gibson]," in Box 1, English 1–2 Collection, Amherst College Archives.

19. I have taken this assignment and #12 to #21 below from Baird's memorandum of October 25, 1946, entitled "Assignments for English 1–2: A revised revised list and some suggestions for the future, weeks 4–7," which is in "Eng 1–2 1946/47 Sec 1g [Baird] Assignments," in Box 1, English 1–2 Collection, Amherst College Archives.

20. A copy of this document, entitled "The Famous Dartmouth–Cornell Fifth Down," is in "Eng 1 1946/47 Sec E [Gibson]," in Box 1, English 1–2 Collection, Amherst College Archives.

21. These student responses to assignment #20 appear on "English 1: Section E, Assignment #20" and are in "Eng 1 1946/47 Sec E [Gibson]," in Box 1, English 1–2 Collection, Amherst College Archives.

22. Gibson's letter of November 13, 1946, to Louis Young is in "Eng 1 1946/47 Sec E [Gibson]," in Box 1, English 1–2 Collection, Amherst College Archives.

23. These student responses to assignment #21 appear on "English 1: Section E, Assignment #21" in "Eng 1 1946/47 Sec E [Gibson]," in Box 1, English 1–2 Collection, Amherst College Archives.

24. This assignment and #23 and #24 below are from "Assignments for English 1–2: Revised list, Nov. 18–26" in "Eng 1–2 1946/47 Sec 1g [Baird] Assignments," in Box 1, English 1–2 Collection, Amherst College Archives.

25. This student response to assignment #24 appears on "English 1: Section E, Assignment #24" in "Eng 1 1946/47 Sec E [Gibson]," in Box 1, English 1–2 Collection, Amherst College Archives.

26. This assignment and #26 and #27 below are from Baird's memorandum of November 22, 1946, entitled "Assignments for English 1–2: A revised revised list," a copy of which is in "Eng 1–2 1946/47 Sec 1g [Baird] Assignments," in Box 1, English 1–2 Collection, Amherst College Archives.

27. This assignment and #29 to #31 are from Baird's memorandum of November 5, 1946, in "Eng 1–2 1946/47 Sec 1g [Baird] Assignments," in Box 1, English 1–2 Collection, Amherst College Archives.

28. The long paper assignment is outlined on a document dated January 3–4, 1947, and entitled "English 1–2: Assignment for Long Paper," which is in "Eng 1–2 1946/47 Sec 1g [Baird] Assignments," in Box 1, English 1–2 Collection, Amherst College Archives.

29. I have quoted the entire exam from "English 1: Final Examination, 27 January 1947" in "Eng 1–2 1946/47 Sec 1g [Baird] Assignments," in Box 1, English 1–2 Collection, Amherst College Archives.

30. The English 2 assignments for the spring of 1947 are in "Eng 1–2 1946/47 Sec 1g [Baird] Assignments" and in "Eng 2 1946/47 Sec E [Gibson]," in Box 1, English 1–2 Collection, Amherst College Archives.

Chapter 4: No One Knows the Answers

1. Although since leaving Amherst College, William Walker Gibson Jr. has styled himself professionally as "Walker Gibson," his Amherst colleagues knew him as "Bill."

2. Gibson's letter of November 2, 1946, to T. Baird is held in "Eng 1 1946/47 Sec E [Gibson]," in Box 1, English 1–2 Collection, Amherst College Archives.

3. Baird's letter of June 18, 1948, to W. W. Gibson is held in "Eng 2 1947/48 Sec 9 [Gibson]," in Box 1, English 1–2 Collection, Amherst College Archives.

4. Gibson's assignment appears in a memorandum circulated by Baird on March 28, 1947, which is in "Eng 1–2 1946/47 Sec 1g [Baird] Assignments," in Box 1, English 1–2 Collection, Amherst College Archives.

5. Gibson's assignments on the use of a wind anemometer are in "Eng 2 1953/54 Sec 10 [Gibson]," in Box 2, English 1–2 Collection, Amherst College Archives.

6. There is an abbreviated version of this series of assignments in Gibson's 1959 textbook, *Seeing and Writing* (121–129). As recently as 1978, Gibson was reporting that "each year I have my students in a writing class construct a homemade anemometer, and measure the wind. They build these gadgets out of Ping-Pong balls and Dixie cups" (1978, 48).

7. Baird asks this question in assignment #17 of the series which may be found in "English 11 1968–69 Assignments," in the English 11 Collection, Amherst College Archives.

8. I have printed this entire exchange, including Baird's letter of December 6, 1990, in which he gave me the assignment, my response of December 13, and his reply of December 17, in Appendix C.

9. A copy of Baird's memorandum is now in "Memo to the Instructors—July 19, 1960," in Box 1, English 1–2 Collection, Amherst College Archives.

10. Versions of this course description exist from at least 1956 on. One version of it can be found in William E. Coles Jr.'s *The Plural I* (1988a, 10–14). The version I have used, although not dated, can be found in "Excerpts from description of English 1–2, usually read aloud on second day of class," in Box 1, English 1–2 Collection, Amherst College Archives.

11. Frost's couplet, originally published in *A Witness Tree* (1942), was included in an assignment series written by Craig and used in the fall of 1962. It appears in assignment #30 of that series: "Here is a short poem by Robert Frost. What do you take this to mean? Could the 'Secret' be a lie? Could the 'Secret' be the truth? How, then, do you read this poem? Is it a joke? Is it profound?" (in "Eng 1 1962/63 'Assignments as Used,'" Box 3, English 1–2 Collection, Amherst College Archives).

12. John Cameron's explanation of the origin of "the seven dwarfs" is that "it was a historian named Richard Douglas (now at M.I.T.) who coined the phrase, but we picked it up and used it about ourselves ironically."

13. Although Pritchard says publication was not a factor either when he was hired or when he was granted tenure at Amherst College, he has in fact published extensively, perhaps most notably a 1984 biography of Robert Frost.

14. Pritchard not only told me, as Sale and Gibson also did, that Baird had come through the window, he took me to the very window in South College and showed me how Baird had done it. Later when I asked Baird about the incident, he said, "That's all junk! I would hate to think that I was to be remembered at Amherst for coming in through the window. I am a serious man. That is the kind of story people tell about the good old days at Old Siwash."

15. Sale's assignments are in "Eng 1 1961/62 Sec 4 or 7? [Sale?]," in Box 3, English 1–2 Collection, Amherst College Archives. Like Sale, Cameron and Pritchard also each wrote a series of assignments. Cameron's was used in the spring of 1963 and Pritchard's in the spring of 1965. Cameron's assignments were published in Louis's dissertation (1971, 259–269) and may also be found in "Eng 2 1962/63 'Assignments as Used,'" in Box 3, English 1–2 Collection, Amherst College Archives. Pritchard's assignments are in "Eng 2 1964/65 Assignments," in Box 4, English 1–2 Collection, Amherst College Archives.

16. I summarize *Occupational Hazard* with Robert Cornish's permission. His seven-page play script may be found in "Eng 2 1947/48 Sec 9 [Gibson]," in Box 1, English 1–2 Collection, Amherst College Archives.

17. Gibson and Taylor's assignment is headed "Assignment No. 9, Due 12–13 May," and it may be found in "Eng 1–2 1947/48 Sec 101–5, Sec 102–5 [Baird]," in Box 1, English 1–2 Collection, Amherst College Archives.

Chapter 5: Boot Camp

1. The assignments for the fall of 1953 may be found in "Eng 1 1953/54 Sec 10 [Gibson]," in Box 2, English 1–2 Collection, Amherst College Archives. Incidentally, this set of assignments is parodied in Alison Lurie's *Love and Friendship* (1962).

2. With Robert Bagg's permission, I have reproduced his Armstrong Prize-winning paper in Appendix D.

3. With Geoffrey Shepherd's permission and the permission of the *Amherst Student,* I have reprinted Shepherd's 1955 editorial on "Creativity and Apathy" in Appendix D.

4. John Butler did write the assignments for the fall of 1958. John Cameron has told me that the identity of the principal author of a series of assignments was not generally revealed to students and that so far as students were concerned, assignments seemed to issue from the staff as a whole. The fall of 1958 was Cameron's, as well as Wilson's, first semester at Amherst College, and Cameron said that Butler "was here when I arrived.

He was here for at least another year after that. He did the assignments on paying attention." Cameron added that "John Butler's assignments were at the time much admired. He was thought to have a knack for them and for a certain kind of playful humor—an intellectual, playful approach to the whole concept." Butler had written at least two earlier series of assignments, including the series for the fall of 1954 to which historian Albert Kitzhaber alluded in 1963 when he described the "maverick" writing course that "at least until recently, required each student to buy a box of colored crayons to use in preparing some of the assignments" (1963a, 13).

5. With Douglas Wilson's permission, I have printed his 1959 Armstrong Prize-winning paper in Appendix D.

6. Townsend's assignments for the fall of 1964 may be found in "Eng 1 1964/65 'Assignments as Used,'" in Box 4, English 1–2 Collection, Amherst College Archives. While I have considered only Stifler's and Looker's responses to these assignments, another complete set of student responses to them is held in the Amherst College Archives. This set was written by Jere Mead, who was a student in Baird's section in the fall of 1964. It is available in "Eng 1 1964/65 Jere Mead student papers written for the assignments in Professor Baird's class," in Box 4 of the English 1–2 Collection.

7. Stifler's 1964 essay in response to assignment #3 is in his personal possession. I quote from it here with his permission.

8. John Bookwalter, who took English 1–2 eight years before Looker did, told me he had never heard the term "shit sheet."

9. Stifler's 1964 essay in response to assignment #28 is in his personal possession.

10. With John Stifler's permission, I have printed his 1964 response to this Long Paper assignment in Appendix D.

11. The class of 1962, which Sale and Pritchard addressed in 1987, is the same class which invited Sale in 1962 to deliver "The Senior Chapel Address."

12. The typescript of Bagg's three-page "Talk" is in his personal possession. I quote from it here with his permission.

Chapter 6: Be Your Own Man

1. Baird retired officially in 1970, but because he was on leave in 1969–70, his effective retirement date is 1969.

2. The typescript of the "Report on the Curriculum of Amherst College," which was issued by the Committee on Educational Policy in April 1964

and which resulted in Amherst's 1966 curriculum, is now available in Folder 6, Box 1, Curriculum Reports Collection, Amherst College Archives.

3. This passage is quoted from page 5 of Baird's letter of June 6, 1966, to Calvin H. Plimpton. The copy of this letter which I have seen is in Professor Baird's personal possession. Walker Gibson quotes from this letter also in his article on "Theodore Baird" (1985, 149).

4. Baird's assignments for the fall of 1968 are available in "English 11 1968–69 Assignments," in Box 1, English 11 Collection, Amherst College Archives.

5. Baird's memorandum of October 1, 1968, is in "English 11 1968–69 Assignments," in Box 1, English 11 Collection, Amherst College Archives.

6. This and other anonymous student responses to the fall 1968 assignments are in "English 11 1968–69 Assignments," in Box 1, English 11 Collection, Amherst College Archives.

7. Figures for the fall of 1993 given to me by the registrar of Amherst College confirmed Dizard's rough observation. Of 1,593 full-time students, 995 identified themselves as "white/non-Hispanic," 112 as "black/non-Hispanic," 129 as "Hispanic," and 180 as "Asian/Pacific islander." The remaining 177 students either identified themselves with other, smaller groups, or indicated they were of mixed heritage, or chose not to declare a racial or ethnic identity. Incidentally, of the same 1,593 students, 705 were women.

8. In his 1991 article on social stratification, Dizard noted that a little over 50 percent of the students in Amherst's class of 1991 reported that their parents earned $75,000 or more (153n).

9. Bartholomae concludes "Against the Grain" by quoting a Walt Whitman passage which he believes skillfully represents "the paradox of teaching and learning" (1985, 28). The passage reminds me of Theodore Baird, engaging his students in hand-to-hand combat, and is as follows:

I am the teacher of athletes.
He that by me spreads a wider breast than my own proves the width of my own.
He most honors my style who learns under it to destroy the teacher.

10. Coles relates this publishing history on pages 273–274 of *The Plural I— And After,* which is the title of the expanded 1988 edition of his book. This 1988 edition, consisting of the original text plus two new supplementary essays, is the one I have used.

11. *Composing* and *Teaching Composing* were first published in 1974 by Hay-
    den. *Composing* was republished in 1983 by Boynton/Cook. *Teaching
    Composing* is not currently in print.

12. A copy of the reading list which Baird circulated on May 24, 1947, may
    be found in "Eng 2 1946/47 Sec E [Gibson]," in Box 1, English 1–2 Col-
    lection, Amherst College Archives. A copy of the list he circulated in April
    1946 may be found in "Eng 1 1945/46 Assignments 'Brower and Castle,'"
    in Box 1, English 1–2 Collection, Amherst College Archives.

Appendix C: An Exchange of Letters

1. Ruth Jones is a docent at the Dickinson house. She is a mutual acquaintance of Professor Baird's and mine, and it was she who did the research
   and paper work that resulted in the listing of Baird's house on the National Historic Register.

2. In my original formatting, it did not.

3. Stephen Oates is a professor of history at the University of Massachusetts.

4. Professor Baird's house is on Shays Street.

WORKS CITED

The English 1–2 Collection consists of documents filed in manilla folders in five storage boxes located in the Amherst College Archives. Although I used an informal numbering system for my convenience while working with the documents, the archivist's official system that I cite in the "Notes" section should be adequate for anyone wishing to examine the collection.

Abramson, Doris E., and Robert C. Townsend. 1978. "Versions of Community." In *Essays on Amherst's History,* ed. Theodore P. Greene, 191–241. Amherst, Mass.: Vista Trust.

Adams, Henry. 1973. *The Education of Henry Adams,* ed. Ernest Samuels. Boston: Houghton Mifflin. Originally printed privately in Washington, D.C., 1907.

Amherst College Bulletin. Selected volumes for the following years: 1938–39 through 1944–45, 1955–56, 1960–61, 1964–65 through 1971–72. Amherst, Mass.: Amherst College.

Amherst College Student Handbook. Selected volumes for the following years: 1953–54, 1963–64, 1964–65, 1967–68, 1968–69. Amherst, Mass.: Amherst College.

Applebee, Arthur N. 1974. *Tradition and Reform in the Teaching of English: A History.* Urbana, Ill.: National Council of Teachers of English.

Arons, Arnold B. 1955. "The Amherst Program." *The Journal of Higher Education* 26: 75–81, 112–113.

———. 1987. Letter to the Editor: "On the Influence of Theodore Baird." *Amherst* (Spring): 26–28.

Babb, Lawrence A., Elizabeth W. Bruss, Hugh Hawkins, William M. Hexter (committee chairman), Mark A. Peterson, and Joel M. Upton. 1978. *Education at Amherst Reconsidered: The Liberal Studies Program.* Amherst, Mass.: Amherst College Press.

Baird, Theodore. 1931. *The First Years: Selections from Autobiography.* New York: Richard R. Smith.

———. 1939. "English 1 C." *Amherst Graduates' Quarterly* (August): 326–334.

———. 1946. "Darwin and the Tangled Bank." *American Scholar* 15: 477–486.

———. 1952. "The Freshman English Course." *Amherst Alumni News* (May): 194–196.

———. 1978a. "A Dry and Thirsty Land." In *Essays on Amherst's History,* ed. Theodore P. Greene, 78–138. Amherst, Mass.: Vista Trust.

———. 1978b. "Reflections on Amherst and English 1." Unpublished transcript of a tape recording made in March 1978. Amherst College Oral History Project. Horace Hewlett, project director. Amherst College Archives.

Bartholomae, David. 1985. "Against the Grain." In *Writers on Writing,* ed. Tom Waldrep, 19–29. New York: Random House.

Bartholomae, David, and Anthony Petrosky. 1986. *Facts, Artifacts, and Counterfacts: Theory and Method for a Reading and Writing Course.* Upper Montclair, N.J.: Boynton/Cook.

Berlin, James A. 1984. *Writing Instruction in Nineteenth-Century American Colleges.* Carbondale: Southern Illinois University Press.

———. 1987. *Rhetoric and Reality: Writing Instruction in American Colleges, 1900–1985.* Carbondale: Southern Illinois University Press.

Berlin, James A., and Robert P. Inkster. 1980. "Current-Traditional Rhetoric: Paradigm and Practice." *Freshman English News* 8(3): 1–14.

Berthoff, Ann E. 1985. "I. A. Richards." In *Traditions of Inquiry,* ed. John Brereton, 50–80. New York: Oxford University Press.

Bishop, Jonathan. 1972. *Something Else.* New York: Braziller.

Boe, John. 1992. "From the Editor: Puritan English." *Writing on the Edge* 4(1): 5–7.

Brereton, John. 1985. "Sterling Andrus Leonard." In *Traditions of Inquiry,* ed. John Brereton, 81–104. New York: Oxford University Press.

———. 1993 (April 2). "Harvard's Hum 6 and the Interdependence of Composition and Literature." Conference on College Composition and Communication, San Diego.

Bridgman, P. W. 1959. "Philosophical Implications of Physics." In Walker Gibson, *Seeing and Writing,* 148–157. New York: McKay. Originally published in *American Academy of Arts and Sciences Bulletin* 3(5), 1950.

Broderick, James H. 1958. "A Study of the Freshman Composition Course at Amherst: Action, Order, and Language." *Harvard Educational Review* 28(1): 44–57.

Brower, Reuben A. 1951. *The Fields of Light: An Experiment in Critical Reading.* New York: Oxford.

————. 1962. "Reading in Slow Motion." In *In Defense of Reading: A Reader's Approach to Literary Criticism,* eds. Reuben A. Brower and Richard Poirier, 3–21. New York: Dutton.

Burke, Kenneth. 1969. *A Rhetoric of Motives.* Berkeley: University of California Press. Original edition, Prentice-Hall, 1950.

Cary, Harold Whiting. 1962. *The University of Massachusetts: A History of One Hundred Years.* Amherst, Mass.: University of Massachusetts Press.

Coles, William E., Jr. 1974. *Teaching Composing: A Guide to Teaching Writing as a Self-Creating Process.* Rochelle Park, N.J.: Hayden.

————. 1978. *The Plural I: The Teaching of Writing.* New York: Holt.

————. 1981a. *Composing II.* Rochelle Park, N.J.: Hayden.

————. 1981b. "Teaching Writing, Teaching Literature: The Plague on Both Houses." *Freshman English News* 9(3): 3–4, 13–16.

————. 1983. *Composing: Writing as a Self-Creating Process.* Upper Montclair, N.J.: Boynton/Cook. Original edition, Hayden, 1974.

————. 1988a. *The Plural I—and After.* Portsmouth, N.H.: Boynton/Cook.

————. 1988b. *Seeing through Writing.* New York: Harper.

Connors, Robert J. 1983. "Composition Studies and Science." *College English* 45(1): 1–20.

————. 1984. "Historical Inquiry in Composition Studies." *The Writing Instructor* 3(4): 157–167.

————. 1985. "Mechanical Correctness as a Focus in Composition Instruction." *College Composition and Communication* 36(1): 61–72.

————. 1986. "Textbooks and the Evolution of the Discipline." *College Composition and Communication* 37(2): 178–194.

Crowley, Sharon. 1988. "Review of *Rhetoric and Reality: Writing Instruction in American Colleges, 1900–1985* by James Berlin." *College Composition and Communication* 39: 245–247.

Dizard, Jan E. 1991. "Achieving Place: Teaching Social Stratification to Tomorrow's Elite." In *Teaching What We Do: Essays by Amherst College Faculty,* 145–162. Amherst, Mass.: Amherst College Press.

Fogarty, Daniel, S.J. 1959. *Roots for a New Rhetoric.* New York: Columbia.

Ford, Julienne. 1975. *Paradigms and Fairy Tales: An Introduction to the Science of Meaning.* 2 vols. London: Routledge & Kegan Paul.

Frost, Robert. 1949. *Selected Prose of Robert Frost,* eds. Hyde Cox and Edward Connery Lathem. New York: Holt.

Genung, John Franklin. 1887. *The Study of Rhetoric in the College Course.* Boston: D.C. Heath.

————. 1894. "English at Amherst College." The Teaching of English at American Colleges and Universities. *The Dial* 17 (August 1): 54–56.

Gere, Anne Ruggles. 1987. *Writing Groups: History, Theory, and Implications.* Carbondale: Southern Illinois University Press.

Gibson, Walker. 1950. "Authors, Speakers, Readers, and Mock Readers." *College English* 11: 265–269.

———. 1959. *Seeing and Writing: Fifteen Exercises in Composing Experience.* New York: McKay.

———, ed. 1962. "Introduction." In *The Limits of Language.* New York: Hill and Wang.

———. 1966. *Tough, Sweet and Stuffy: An Essay on Modern American Prose Styles.* Bloomington: Indiana University Press.

———. 1969. *Persona: A Style Study for Readers and Writers.* New York: Random House.

———. 1970. "Composing the World: The Writer as Map-Maker." *College Composition and Communication* 21: 255–260.

———. 1978 (April 17). "The Knowledge of Human Minds." *The Chronicle of Higher Education* 16(8): 48.

———. 1985. "Theodore Baird." In *Traditions of Inquiry,* ed. John Brereton, 136–152. New York: Oxford University Press.

Graff, Gerald. 1987. *Professing Literature: An Institutional History.* Chicago: University of Chicago Press.

Greene, Theodore P. 1978. "The Gown Overwhelms the Town." In *Essays on Amherst's History,* ed. Theodore P. Greene, 283–332. Amherst, Mass.: Vista Trust.

———. 1992. "Piety and Play in Amherst's History." In *Five Colleges, Five Histories,* ed. Ronald Story, 3–26. Amherst, Mass.: University of Massachusetts Press.

Hairston, Maxine. 1982. "The Winds of Change: Thomas Kuhn and the Revolution in the Teaching of Writing." *College Composition and Communication* 33: 76–88.

Kantor, Kenneth J. 1975. "Creative Expression in the English Curriculum: An Historical Perspective." *Research in the Teaching of English* 9: 5–29.

Kennedy, Gail, ed. 1955. *Education at Amherst: The New Program.* New York: Harper.

Kim, Richard. 1992. "New Plan Urges End to English 11." *Amherst Student* (January 29): 1, 3.

Kitzhaber, Albert R. 1953. "Rhetoric in American Colleges, 1850–1900." Ph.D. diss., University of Washington. Ann Arbor: University Microfilms International, 1953.

———. 1963a. *Themes, Theories, and Therapy: The Teaching of Writing in College.* New York: McGraw-Hill.

————. 1963b. "4C, Freshman English, and the Future." *College Composition and Communication* 14: 129–138.

Korzybski, Alfred. 1948. *Science and Sanity: An Introduction to Non-Aristotelian Systems and General Semantics.* 3rd ed. Lakeville, Conn.: International Non-Aristotelian Library. Original edition, 1933.

Kuhn, Thomas S. 1970. *The Structure of Scientific Revolutions.* 2nd ed. Chicago: University of Chicago Press. Original edition, 1962.

Le Duc, Thomas. 1946. *Piety and Intellect at Amherst College 1865–1912.* New York: Columbia University Press.

Longsworth, Polly. 1978. "The Growth of Civic Consciousness." In *Essays on Amherst's History,* ed. Theodore P. Greene, 139–161. Amherst, Mass.: Vista Trust.

Louis, John Carpenter. 1971. "English 1–2 at Amherst College: Composition and the Unity of Knowledge." Ed.D. diss., Harvard University. Ann Arbor: University Microfilms International, 1971.

Lurie, Alison. 1962. *Love and Friendship.* New York: Macmillan.

Miller, Susan. 1982. "Is There a Text in this Class?" *Freshman English News* 11: 20–24.

————. 1991. *Textual Carnivals: The Politics of Composition.* Carbondale: Southern Illinois University Press.

North, Stephen M. 1987. *The Making of Knowledge in Composition: Portrait of an Emerging Field.* Upper Montclair, N.J.: Boynton/Cook.

Ogden, C. K., and I. A. Richards. 1923. *The Meaning of Meaning: A Study of the Influence of Language upon Thought and of the Science of Symbolism.* New York: Harcourt.

Peterson, George E. 1964. *The New England College in the Age of the University.* Amherst, Mass.: Amherst College Press.

Poirier, Richard. 1990. "Hum 6, or Reading before Theory." *Raritan* 9(4): 14–31.

Pritchard, William H. 1984. *Frost: A Literary Life Considered.* New York: Oxford.

————. 1985. "Reuben A. Brower." *The American Scholar* 54: 239–247.

————. 1991. "Ear Training." In *Teaching What We Do: Essays by Amherst College Faculty,* 127–143. Amherst, Mass.: Amherst College Press.

Resnick, Daniel P., and Lauren B. Resnick. 1977. "The Nature of Literacy: An Historical Explanation." *Harvard Educational Review* 47: 370–385.

"Review of English 11: Writing." 1969. In *Scrutiny: A Review of Courses Given First Semester 1968–69,* 17. Amherst, Mass.: Amherst College.

"Review of English 31: Shakespeare." 1969. In *Scrutiny: A Review of Courses Given First Semester 1968–69,* 18. Amherst, Mass.: Amherst College.

Richards, I. A. 1929. *Practical Criticism: A Study of Literary Judgment*. New York: Harcourt.

Rockas, Leo. 1981. "The Quintillian of Amherst: John Franklin Genung." *New England Quarterly* 54(1): 54–73.

Rose, Mike. 1981. "Sophisticated, Ineffective Books—The Dismantling of Process in Composition Texts." *College Composition and Communication* 32: 65–74.

Rudolph, Frederick. 1977. *Curriculum: A History of the American Undergraduate Course of Study Since 1636*. San Francisco: Jossey-Bass.

Russell, David R. 1990. "Writing Across the Curriculum in Historical Perspective: Toward a Social Interpretation." *College English* 52(1): 52–73.

Sale, Roger. 1962. "The Senior Chapel Address 1962." *The Amherst Student*, special supplement for May 21, 1962. Folder 79, Box 9, Commencement Collection, Amherst College Archives.

———. 1970. *On Writing*. New York: Random House.

Shepherd, W. Geoffrey. 1955. "Creativity and Apathy." *The Amherst Student* (November 10): 2.

Smith, Charles Kay. 1974. *Styles and Structures: Alternative Approaches to College Writing*. New York: Norton.

Stewart, Donald C. 1988. "Some History Lessons for Composition Teachers." *Rhetoric Review* 3 (1985): 134–144. Reprinted in *The Writing Teacher's Sourcebook*, eds. Gary Tate and Edward P. J. Corbett, 16–23. 2nd ed. New York: Oxford.

Theta Xi Fraternity, 1954–55. 1955. *A Student Evaluation of the Amherst Curriculum*. Amherst, Mass.: Amherst College.

Varnum, Robin. 1992. "A Maverick Writing Course: English 1–2 at Amherst College, 1938–1968." Ed.D. diss., University of Massachusetts at Amherst. Ann Arbor: University Microfilms International, 1992.

Whicher, George F. 1931. "Genung, John Franklin." In *Dictionary of American Biography*, eds. Allen Johnson and Dumas Malone. Vol. 7, 210–211. New York: Scribner's.

Wittgenstein, Ludwig. 1958. *Philosophical Investigations*, trans. G. E. M. Anscombe. 3rd ed. New York: Macmillan. Original edition, Macmillan, 1953.

Wozniak, John Michael. 1978. *English Composition in Eastern Colleges, 1850–1940*. Washington, D.C.: University Press of America.

Young, Richard E. 1978. "Paradigms and Problems: Needed Research in Rhetorical Invention." In *Research on Composing: Points of Departure*, eds. Charles R. Cooper and Lee Odell, 29–47. Urbana, Ill.: National Council of Teachers of English.

INDEX